AF441702

German Soldiers in the Great War

German Soldiers in the Great War

Letters and Eyewitness Accounts

Edited by Bernd Ulrich and
Benjamin Ziemann

Translated by Christine Brocks

Foreword by Jay Winter

Pen & Sword
MILITARY

First published in Great Britain in 2010 by
Pen & Sword Military
an imprint of
Pen & Sword Books Ltd
47 Church Street
Barnsley
South Yorkshire
S70 2AS

ISBN 978-1-84884-141-3

Typeset in 11pt Ehrhardt by
Mac Style, Beverley, E. Yorkshire

Printed and bound in the UK by CPI Books

Pen & Sword Books Ltd incorporates the imprints of Pen & Sword
Aviation, Pen & Sword Maritime, Pen & Sword Military, Wharncliffe
Local History, Pen and Sword Select, Pen and Sword Military
Classics and Leo Cooper.

For a complete list of Pen & Sword titles please contact
PEN & SWORD BOOKS LIMITED
47 Church Street, Barnsley, South Yorkshire, S70 2AS, England
E-mail: enquiries@pen-and-sword.co.uk
Website: www.pen-and-sword.co.uk

Contents

Foreword

This book provides us with a unique collection of documents on the outlook and language of the on average 4 million men who served in the German field armies during the First World War. What their years of service meant to them and did to them is the subject of a substantial literature dominated hitherto by what may be termed the 'brutalization hypothesis'. This argument, most fully developed by the late George L. Mosse, drew a direct line between 1914 and 1933. In other words, military service in the Great War exposed millions of men to violence on a scale the world had never seen before. Not only were individuals inured to butchery, but there was as well a change for the worse in the norms governing the use of violence in domestic political and social conflict. Thus the bitterness of the war bled into the bitterness of the immediate postwar period, including the brutal suppression of the Sparticist revolt in early 1919. Here was fertile ground for the hard men of the extreme right who took widespread popular dismay over the terms of the peace treaty Germany was forced to sign and turned it into a call to arms against the 'November criminals', the Jews and communists at home they said were responsible for Germany's defeat and humiliation. Out of this sense of outrage, the Nazi party was born and came of age.

The problem with this interpretation of the effects of military service on German soldiers is that it rests on a very narrow documentary base. Privileging the published writings of educated middle-class soldiers and veterans, Mosse and others generalized from one perspective to that of the entire German army and nation. Drawing on the research of a younger generation of scholars, Ulrich and Ziemann enable us to do better. They restore the full range of thinking on the meaning of the war and the hardships it brought about, both to soldiers and to their families.

This is all the more important in that the body of material presented here reflects the social composition of the German army and nation much more fully than anything we have had before. Attending to their language and grammar enables us to bring out of obscurity the voices drowned by those of the educated urban middle classes, which had their own point of view, certainly, but theirs was not the voice of the army as a whole. In this collection of documents, a Franconian farmer asks his wife how the calves are doing, before meditating on when will this murdering ever stop, and why don't we hear more about peace? Miners in uniform report how widespread was soldiers' disgust about the war and the privileges of the officer caste. Soldiers muttering about their officers is hardly news, but taking it into account does make it harder to stick to the view that military service in and of itself turned Germans into stern, obedient patriots or into Nazis-in-the-making.

The value of this multi-vocal presentation of the soldiers' point of view is that it enables us to avoid stereotyping soldiers as stoical idealists to a man. Yes, there were those whose eyes shone when they got the order to go over the top; there were also those who preferred the company of men in uniform to that of civilians; and who liked a good dust-up. They joined the paramilitary Freikorps and kept fighting after the war. But these men were a small minority of the men in uniform, and their voices must not be used to portray the masses of men who went to war wearing the field grey of the German army as Nazis *avant la lettre*.

Read this book and you will take away from it a sense both of the complexity of war experience and of the continuity of older languages soldiers used to make sense of it. They did not leave their earlier religious practices or political beliefs or material concerns behind when they put on their uniforms. We can see all of these sentiments at play here. Soldiers also did not write everything they knew or felt to family members already anxious enough about their well-being. There are epistolary codes in evidence, shaping the form and content of letter writing and reading, both among senders and receivers alike. And these conventions mattered, considering, as the editors note, that something in the order of 28 billion letters circulated during the war. We are indebted to the editors for capturing these voices, and for showing us the ways soldiers told their own stories in their own words to their own families.

There is a taste here of both the very local and the transnational. Imagine relatively quiet mornings during the war. After the stand to, front-line infantrymen on both sides of the line concluded that no attack was coming that day. Then imagine the same men putting pencil to paper in a corner of the trench system, writing home that day. Doing so will enable you to see how similar were the men who waged war in Turkey or Galicia or in the Austrian Alps or in France and Flanders. Most of them had the same concerns and used the same or roughly similar language to express them. Some of these men were brutal; most were not. Some were turned into killers and remained killers; most were not and did not, either in Germany or in any other combatant nation. Most wanted the killing to stop, and if it had to go on, then they wanted to know that the hardships they endured were for some purpose.

The specifically German predicament this book illustrates is that of the end-game in 1918. After the failure of the March 1918 offensive, and its sequels in June and July 1918, few men in the ranks retained their belief in outright victory. What was the point in going on and on? The outcome was what Wilhelm Deist called a hidden soldiers' strike against continuing the war, hidden not from the soldiers, but through censorship, from the public at large. Such a strike was so unpalatable to the army leadership and to their right-wing political supporters that they launched one of the biggest cover-up exercises in history – the 'stab in the back' legend. Ulrich and Ziemann expose it for what it was, and furthermore show through soldiers' letters when, why and how the soldiers' strike of 1918 came about. This is a major contribution, confirming the argument Deist made twenty years ago, and deepening significantly our understanding of why Germany was defeated in 1918.

The editors also make the important point that the language soldiers used at the end of the war was not the same as that used in the later 1920s or 1930s. And while they clearly recognize the need to take account of the human and political damage done by the Great War in plotting the history of the interwar years, their book reinforces the argument that there was nothing inevitable about any one political outcome in the turbulent decade after the war.

Contingency mattered. Men of many nations shared the ugliness of industrialized warfare, and grumbled about their officers and conditions. Most left the army and suffered from the economic instability and inflation the war had brought about. But on the whole, in Germany as elsewhere, soldiers were not brutalized men and did not demand the kind of brutality the Nazis represented. Reading these letters and eyewitness accounts reminds us of how many of them endured appalling conditions, in and out of combat, suffered fear and ill-treatment and other hardships, and still retained their dignity, their decency, their humanity. That, to my mind, after forty years of engagement with this subject, is the true mystery of the Great War.

Jay Winter
Yale University
January 2010

List of Plates

Introduction

Benjamin Ziemann

In early 1917, the artist Fritz Erler created one of the most iconic representations of German front-line soldiers during the First World War. His poster, published to advertise the sixth war loan, does not gloss over the hardship of battle. It shows a soldier leaning against a wire entanglement, in field-grey uniform and full combat gear, including two potato-masher grenades and a gas mask. His face under the steel helmet (which the German army had only introduced in 1916) is black from soot. His eyes, exhausted but determined, are gazing into the distance, to the enemies on the other side of no-man's-land.[1] This image not only gathers crucial elements of what was to become the classic iconography of the German soldier of the Great War, barbed wire, steel helmet and gas mask. It also vividly represents the determination that allegedly characterized German soldiers during the Great War, their eagerness to overcome obstacles and to hold out by any means. This is the iconography of the 'New Man' who was born in the trenches of Flanders and Northern France during the battles of materiel after 1916, with their systematic and intensive artillery fire and the use of shock-troops who were specially trained to overcome the stalemate of trench warfare. As a powerful set of symbols and connotations, it captured the imagination of right-wing artists and allowed them to promote their militaristic ideas. During the interwar period, Ernst Jünger and other prominent authors who promoted an aggressive 'soldierly nationalism' translated this iconography into literary texts.[2]

The primary sources printed in this volume offer, in contrast, a wider ranging set of perceptions and observations from the men who served in the German army from August 1914 to November 1918. While some of these voices and opinions were not raised and discussed in public during and after the war, others were in fact already present in the heated debates about the legacy of the war experience that divided German society after the armistice. For an understanding of this collection of documents, a brief tour d'horizon through the conflicting interpretations of the front-line experience since 1918 is thus necessary (I). Secondly, some basic institutional characteristics of the German army before and during the war are outlined, as they provide the context for many of the observations and grievances that are reflected in the sources (II). The final section of this introduction explains the range and provenance of the materials we have included in our collection and the principles that have informed our selection (III).

I. Interpretations of the Front-line Experience

Germany during the 1920s was in many respects a postwar society. The social and economic consequences of the war, such as the need to pay pensions and benefits to an estimated 2.7 million disabled war veterans and to the many war widows and orphans, exerted tremendous pressure on the public finances and triggered a wave of political mobilization. Among the war victims there was growing resentment against the bureaucratic nature of the welfare-state provision and against pension cuts.[3] Another crucial aspect of the 'internal denial of peace' was of course the widespread rejection of the terms of the Versailles treaty and hence the inability of many Germans to come to terms with the fact that Germany had been defeated.[4] The infamous 'stab in the back' legend, or *Dolchstoß*-myth, invented immediately after the armistice and propagated by right-wing circles in an attempt to blame Jews and Socialists for the collapse of the army, is another case in point. It was the most blatant but not the only example of the coordinated efforts by the nationalist camp in Weimar to undermine the Republic with their interpretation of the legacy of the Great War.[5]

Since 1918/19, the battle experiences of front-line soldiers provided another crucial arena for the Weimar debate on the consequences of the First World War. Subsequently, the immediate experiences of soldiers at the front were transformed into memories and public remembrances which gave meaning to the ongoing symbolic presence of death and destruction and the absence of those who had been killed. In a complex cultural development that relied on a variety of communications media and public rituals, the *Kriegserlebnis* (war experience) of soldiers at the front fed into and gave way to symbolic representations of the front generation. This was, of course, a highly selective process, as there are no clearly delineated or even authoritative memories. Already during the war and immediately after battles, the surviving soldiers as eyewitness had started to doctor their short-term recollections. The novelist Carl

Zuckmayer, a war volunteer of 1914 who later served as a lieutenant on the Western Front, described this tendency in his autobiography:

> In those days, in the short periods of rest which followed the most terrible weeks of the battle at the Somme, I learned how quickly man is able to forget. Among the troops who had just left, the mood was like one would find in a veteran's association, although they would lie in the same mud the day after tomorrow. They had already forgotten that it was in fact mud. It was a dreadful thing. Mate, what have we gone through! Not a single word that they used to discuss or narrate what they had experienced was correct.[6]

This transformation of the reality of the war experience into selective recollections and affirmative narratives not only continued, but intensified after the armistice. In effect, it led to a syndrome of public representations and symbols that the historian George L. Mosse has called the 'Myth of the War Experience, which looked back upon the war as a meaningful and even sacred event'. This myth 'was designed to mask war and to legitimize the war experience'.[7] While such mythological representations of the front-line experiences emerged in all belligerent nations, they were certainly most 'urgently needed' and most widely appreciated 'in the defeated nations'.[8] It is, however, incorrect to assume, as Mosse does, that the nationalist memories of the war experience 'informed most postwar politics' in Germany, 'which proved most hospitable to the myth'.[9] Although it is correct that heroic and affirmative representations of the front-line experience were hegemonic in the early 1930s, towards the end of the Weimar Republic they had successfully permeated the German public only by way of a contested and protracted process. In the immediate postwar years, it was anything but a foregone conclusion that it would be possible to cover up the large number of grievances that had been voiced by the troops. Since 1916, these grievances had substantially undermined the morale of the troops and had prepared them for their widespread support of the revolutionary events in November 1918.

Amidst this wave of discontent with the injustice in the army, which spilled over in postwar critiques of the vanished Imperial state and also affected the national camp, we have, for instance, to consider a book on the 'Causes of the Collapse', published in 1919.[10] The author, Walther Lambach, was a leading official in the German National Union of

Commercial Employees (*Deutschnationaler Handlungsgehilfen-Verband*, DHV), whose 123,000 members (according to the figure for 1913) had been staunch supporters of the monarchical system and followed a right-wing agenda.[11] Lambach's book presented a cross-section of the many war letters he had received from DHV members serving in the field army. The prevalent tone was highly critical of the Jews – following the anti-Semitic ideology of the DHV, but also of the junior officers, who were keen to exploit the system for their personal advantage but not at all interested in the welfare of their subordinates. Other points that attracted the ire of the white-collar employees were: the lack of a comradeship that transcended differences in class and status, a fact that undermined their hopes for national unity held in August 1914; and the hypocrisy of the Patriotic Instruction Programme (*Vaterländischer Unterricht*) that was rolled out in the summer of 1917 across the army in order to boost morale. But the reports filed in the context of this programme simply glossed over the prevalent mood and did not address any of the numerous grievances.[12] The gist of this critique of the national war effort from a nationalist perspective was summed up in the following letter from the Western Front in May 1917:

> I went to the front on the third day of mobilization as a member of the Landsturm, full with ideals, true to my affiliation with the German National Association. But what I have experienced in the course of time from our officers has already killed my idealism. I could tell you incidents which would amaze you. The war is only considered as a profitable business, from which everyone is trying to earn as much as possible.[13]

When Lambach published these and many other eyewitness accounts from the members of his association in 1919, he wanted to demonstrate that the DHV had tried to end the grievances and boost the morale of the troops by including these materials in petitions filed to the Prussian War Ministry. Another reason, however, was to be found in the wave of post-revolutionary critiques of the Imperial system, which also targeted the corruption and injustice in the field army. Lambach clearly hoped for a restoration of 'order and for a new German advancement'. But in 1919, far from being able to propagate a 'myth' of the war experience, he had to respond to the prospect that leftist currents could use the grievances 'to attract customers, in order to talk them into accepting also their other dubious products (anti-militarism, cosmopolitanism)'.[14] And Lambach was quite right to worry about the negative consequences of wartime testimony in any attempt to reaffirm a nationalist interpretation of the front-line experiences in the early years of the Republic. From 1919 to 1921, many pro-republican authors, pacifists and socialists published booklets and brochures that were meant to serve as an indictment against the corruption of the Wilhelmine army and the cruelty of war. During those years, the worm's eye perspective was predominantly used not to glorify, but to condemn the bitter reality of trench warfare.[15]

Competing interpretations of the front-line experience continued to make claims in public debate during the 1920s, and evidence given by ordinary soldiers, and war letters in particular, remained a crucial point for contention in these debates. Another important arena for the controversy about these issues had opened up in the autumn of 1919, when the fact-finding committee of the Reichstag, which dealt with a whole raft of judicial and political issues emanating from the Great War, including German offences against international law, established a subcommittee. This particular one, the fourth subcommittee, had to deal with the political and military reasons for the collapse of the German military in 1918. Like other subcommittees, its composition reflected the majority enjoyed by the liberal and conservative parties in the Reichstag. These currents used the committee as a forum to reiterate the legend, now based on an allegedly 'objective' historical record, that the army had been 'stabbed in the back' by socialist revolutionaries. Hermann von Kuhl, former chief of staff in the army group *Kronprinz Rupprecht*, and another officer, Colonel Bernhard Schwertfeger, provided the two main expert opinions on the military responsibilities for and the conduct of the German offensives in 1918. Kuhl in particular used this opportunity to lay blame on the Independent Social Democratic Party (USPD) for their demoralizing 'subversive activities' (*Wühlarbeit*).[16]

When the subcommittee, after almost eight years of deliberation, finally reached a verdict on the causes of the German collapse in 1918, it was a compromise that tried to evade a proper judgement on all crucial issues.[17] But while high-ranking officers and representatives of the right-wing German National People's Party (DNVP) had used the subcommittee to reiterate the *Dolchstoß*-myth, their propagandistic attempts had not gone uncontested. Two liberal-democratic historians in particular tried to counter this attack on the legitimacy of the Republic. One of them, Ludwig Bergsträsser (1883–1960), who served on the subcommittee as a Reichstag member for the left-liberal German Democratic Party (DDP), included a selection of war letters and diary entries by front-line soldiers mainly from 1918 in the published proceedings of the committee.[18] On the basis of these voices from the front, he tried to substantiate his claim that the disintegration of the army at the Western Front had already begun in the summer of 1918. Almost immediately after the troops understood that the spring offensive had come to a final halt, despite the repeated follow-up attacks that took place in May and June, they lost all hope that further fighting would serve their main aim, to secure peace and go home. Consequently, already in early August troop morale dropped to an all-time low, a fact that sealed the subsequent disintegration and ultimately the defeat of the German army.[19]

The other critic, Martin Hobohm (1883–1942), was like Bergsträsser a professionally trained historian. He also worked with him as one of the few civilian archivists in the Reichsarchiv in Potsdam. As an expert witness, Hobohm compiled a report on 'Social Grievances in the Army as a Partial Cause for the Collapse in 1918'. Although his report was not used in the final statement of the subcommittee and its publication was delayed – which prompted Hobohm to go public and launch a scathing attack on the bourgeois majority in the committee, it was finally published in 1929 in the proceedings of the committee.[20] More than eighty years after its publication, Hobohm's book-length report is still in many respects the most sophisticated and comprehensive account of the inner workings of the German army during the war, at least as far as it impacted on the lives and the morale of ordinary soldiers. Hobohm made ample use of the – then still existing – collections of the Reichsarchiv, analyzing both military despatches, high-level reports and orders by the Army Supreme Command (*Oberste Heeresleitung*, OHL), as well as war letters from private soldiers and censorship reports. He also reproduced a number of key documents. Thus, he was able to show how the privileges granted to the officer caste and the authoritarian nature of the Wilhelmine military effectively undermined the motivation of the troops and substantially contributed to the disintegration of the army. As an outspoken and devoted supporter of the Weimar Republic, Hobohm was surely driven by his political values when he vehemently denied the ruthless falsification of the *Dolchstoß*-myth.[21] But his historical scholarship was accurate and beyond any factual or methodological doubt. And, certainly, the gist of his argument has been confirmed by subsequent historians, notably by the late Wilhelm Deist, who described the collapse of the German army in 1918 as the result of a 'covert military strike' by the exhausted and war weary front-line soldiers.[22]

Both Bergsträsser and Hobohm used war letters and other private eyewitness accounts as crucial and legitimate sources for a proper assessment of the front-line experience. In their reading, they focused on the always vivid, sometimes heartening and often sobering observations and perceptions conveyed in these documents. On this basis, they tried to make meaningful assertions about the ways in which soldiers responded to the violence of war and the personal, social and political consequences it entailed. With such an approach, the two republican historians contributed to a social and cultural history of war experiences that anticipated, both in its content and in its methodology, more recent attempts to analyze the popular mentalities of German soldiers during the Great War.[23]

In the heated Weimar controversies about the 'myth' of the war experience, however, such an approach and the political challenge it posed received a hostile reception from the anti-republican, right-wing currents. Hermann von Kuhl was not the only military figure who rejected the source value of war letters out of hand. Eyewitness accounts by private soldiers, Kuhl opined, would need 'to be conceived with great care, in any case not as historical documents on which a history of the war and also of popular opinion could be based in exact detail'.[24] His criticism rested on the assumption that these documents would only reflect the subjective, psychological emotions of the soldiers and were hence not 'objective'. But von Kuhl also insisted that only the allegedly superior perspective of the commanders would allow for a proper assessment of the military situation: 'Someone who has no overall view, who is lying in the trench and not able to look further than 20, 30 steps to the left and right, such a person was after all not in a position to judge better whether the war should be continued or not.'[25] Such a restrictive view of the source value of war letters reflected the fears – during the middle years of the Republic still quite justified – of former Imperial officers and Reichswehr personnel that critical voices from the Great War could hinder their attempts to make the Germans *wehrhaft* (fit for fight) for another war. The Reichsarchiv responded to this challenge with the publication of regimental histories and other popular recollections that were geared towards a heroic interpretation of the front-line experience.[26] Only in specialist publications or internal reports would military employees of the Reichsarchiv admit that sources emanating from an allegedly 'superior' viewpoint, such as unit war diaries or official reports, were often highly unreliable or had been deliberately doctored in order to cover up mistakes or unwelcome news.[27] In his outright rejection of personal testimony from private soldiers, von Kuhl had also missed one crucial point. When the German government admitted defeat and signed the armistice on 11 November 1918, this was to a large degree due to the fact that hundreds of thousands of ordinary soldiers *had been* 'in a position to judge better whether the war should be continued or not' and had simply taken the decision in their own hands. Whether von Kuhl was ready to admit it or not, the end of the German war effort had been brought about by the collective agency of subordinate, but nonetheless insightful and determined men.

Our collection of eyewitness accounts by German front-line soldiers is thus at least to some extent an attempt to put evidence back into the public domain that had already been considered during the Weimar Republic, when debates about the reliability and content of war letters proved to be as divisive as any other aspect of the legacy of the Great War. The significance of these predominantly war weary and often bitter voices from the front has been – belatedly – confirmed by recent research.[28] It was, however, not only due to the concerted efforts of the political right that these voices were not properly represented during the Weimar Republic. Another reason is that the specific idiom of the German soldiers seemed to be much better represented through testimony written by members of the educated elite, the so-called *Bildungsbürgertum*. Already in 1916, Philipp Witkop, professor of German literature at the university in Freiburg, had edited a collection of war letters written by students. Reprinted in subsequent editions under the title 'War Letters by Fallen Students' (*Kriegsbriefe gefallener Studenten*), Witkop's collection seemed to epitomize the metaphysical interpretation of the sacrifices German soldiers had been ready to make for their fatherland. In particular, the 1928 edition was widely sold, not least through the help of state subsidies.[29] Reissued in 1933, after some critical letters had been removed, the collection sold 200,000 copies until 1942. From the beginning, Witkop had envisaged documenting the 'national uprising' of the Germans in his collection and to foster the 'unity of the people'. In the 1928 edition, though, he also emphasized the grief and distress of the individual soldier and the peculiar circumstances of his individual fate.[30]

Thus, the collection could do both: it served as a testimony to the personality of the individual soldiers who were represented. The letters do not only record the itinerary of their war service, they also chart the trajectory of their inner development under the impressions of military comradeship, and their struggle to cope with the strains of industrial warfare. Disillusionment and the hardening of the inner self are hence central themes in Witkop's collection, and in many ways it could be read as a latter-day form of the classical *Bildungsroman*, the novel of educational and inner development. But his collection was also meant to be a written memorial to the contribution of Germany's elite to the national war effort, and to be a powerful evocation of the larger collectives, Volk and fatherland, which were only able to give meaning to the ultimate sacrifice of death on the battlefield. The ambivalence and openness of these terms also characterized the reception of the collection already before 1933, which was unanimously positive on both sides of the political spectrum. Following the logic of Witkop's presentation, an emphasis on the disillusionment and despair of the students or on their heroic altruism were both legitimate readings of the letters.[31]

Endowed with a high level of literacy and introspection, students were able to express complex feelings and the contradictory experiences at the front in an elaborate manner. This is another reason, on top of the already well-established status of this collection, why historians have continued to turn to Witkop's book even after 1945 when they sought to analyze the war experiences of German soldiers. Forgetting or overlooking the efforts made by Bergsträsser, Hobohm and others, historians could – falsely – claim that industrial workers or peasant farmers had 'rarely kept diaries', and – also incorrectly – assert that 'no-one seems to have been interested, or at any rate successful, in collecting or assembling their letters after the war'.[32] And – only – on the basis of the selective evidence presented by Witkop the claim could be made that the inner resources that motivated German soldiers to continue their efforts were 'cloaked in mystical and romantic notions'.[33] This is, of course, a sweeping generalization. It cannot be sustained in the light of a broader cross-selection of evidence as presented in this edition. The student's letters are deeply steeped in the idiom of German idealism, and for this reason they display a peculiar linguistic code of expressing inner feelings and commitment to the collective. Thus, they seem to disclose a national register for the articulation of war experiences that was specific and unique to German soldiers.

But a closer inspection and interpretation of a wider sample of letters makes clear that a specific German register for the articulation of war experiences did not exist (or if it existed, then only in Witkop's collection). With their insistence on retaining primary emotional ties to their family, farm and village, for instance, the linguistic code of peasant farmers from Catholic regions was much closer to that of their French counterparts than to any other social group in the German army.[34] Similar observations can be made with regard to soldiers from the industrial working class, particularly those who were affiliated with the socialist trade-union movement. Both British and German trade unionists criticized certain aspects of the national war effort and of government politics. But both also hoped that their contribution to the war would prepare the ground for a better recognition of organized labour in the political fabric of postwar society. The written record of their 'war experience' was thus constructed according to the ambivalent terms of a working class citizenship.[35]

Ultimately, the documents in this collection could also serve to dispel the notion that the German front-line experiences and their cultural representations contributed to a *Sonderweg*, a special path that was characterized by the brutalization of politics in postwar Germany and that made the Nazi seizure of power almost inevitable.[36] In their published and unpublished written recollections of the Great War, members of the Nazi party were certainly keen to portray their commitment to a national revolution as a direct consequence of their wartime service. They stressed the significance of national enmity and of fight as an end in itself as key values for their fascist persona. Their narratives display crucial semantic elements of a brutalization, although it is difficult to determine whether these attitudes were directly shaped in the trenches or had been influenced by the militarized political climate during the late Weimar Republic.[37] And there are good reasons to assume that the latter was more important than the former, that the powerful symbolism of the 'New Man' owed its valency, and its significant impact on post-1945 historiography, more to the re-writing of rather diverse war experiences into a streamlined nationalist mythology after 1918, and especially since the late 1920s.[38] It was only since the late 1920s that even leftist veterans faced problems admitting in public that they had been anything but eager to excel as fighters during the war, but had rather hoped for a *Heimatschuss*, a lucky shot or blighty wound that would bring them to a hospital back in Germany, or had even participated in the covert military strike in autumn 1918.[39] Against the backdrop of these developments, our collection is an attempt to reestablish the richness and the full complexity of the popular archive for front-line experiences of ordinary soldiers during the Great War.

II. The German Army During the War

When German troops were mobilized on 1 August 1914, a conscript army made its way through neutral Belgium and Northern France and confronted Russian troops in the East. General conscription was one of the key defining principles of the German war effort, particularly in comparison with the United Kingdom. It not only allowed for the unprecedented scale of manpower mobilization –more details of which are given below, it also characterized the somewhat ambivalent position of private soldiers. As conscripts, they were technically speaking 'subjects' (*Untertanen*) of the emperor in an army that was designed to be a loyal instrument in the hands of its supreme commander. The position of private soldiers was strictly regulated by a tight disciplinary corset, and the repeated proclamation of the articles of war (*Kriegsartikel*), a catalogue of the punishment handed out for the most severe infringements of disciplinary rules, served constantly to remind them of their inferior position. Conscription, however, also opened up a space for a language of political entitlements and citizenship. It was not by chance that – building on an earlier Prussian tradition that dated back to the war of liberation against France in 1813 – universal conscription was introduced in 1871 in the newly founded German Empire, together with universal male suffrage for the Reichstag, the Imperial diet. To some extent, the latter was and could be seen as a corollary of the former. Certainly, personal accounts about peace-time military service, which was, apart from the cavalry and heavy artillery, reduced to a two-year period from 1893, provide ample evidence for the 'humiliations and personal abasement' meted out to the conscripts by authoritarian NCOs and arrogant officers.[40] But, as the former journeyman Michael Schwab noted in his unpublished memoirs, at the end of military service 'one felt a true citizen and a complete man'.[41] During the war, a growing number of soldiers tried to establish a connection between their sacrifices at the front and the entitlements they should have as a result of their conscript citizenship. Incrementally, a language of popular participation emerged, which focused on the perceived injustice both at the front and on the home front and ultimately paved the way for revolution in autumn 1918.

The emphasis placed here on conscription as the key underlying principle for the mobilization of the German army and the front-line experience seems to downplay the role of voluntary enlistment, at least for the early weeks and months of the conflict. According to a popular perception, Germans welcomed the war with a wave of patriotic enthusiasm, and hundreds of thousands of volunteers from all walks of life rushed to the colours in the process. In 1914, figures of up to 1.5 million volunteers circulated in the public. A closer examination of the historical record, however, has revealed the mythological elements of this perception. Enthusiastic crowds surely gathered upon the declaration of war, and the public spirit of belligerence did motivate many young people to volunteer. It did, however, also produce disappointment among those older men who were not yet called up during the early days of the war. But these public outpourings of enthusiasm were largely confined to the big cities, and to Berlin in particular. Most farmers and farmwomen in the countryside, Catholics in provincial towns and class-conscious Social Democratic workers reacted rather with despair, depression and political reservation to the declaration of war.[42] Even in Berlin, enthusiasm was largely confined to the (educated) middle classes. Consequently, high-school and university students, but also other strata of the urban middle classes were massively overrepresented among those who volunteered. And the actual numbers of volunteers were not massive, at least when measured against the public and private pressure to enlist that their peers exerted on young men from the patriotic middle classes, and against the subsequent mythological exaggerations of the *Augusterlebnis*, the 'spirit of August 1914'. In the first ten days of mobilization, 260,672 men volunteered in Prussia, of whom 143,922 were actually recruited for the army. For the whole of August, the number of recruited volunteers all over Germany can be estimated at 185,000.[43] These are still substantial figures. But they have to be interpreted against the backdrop of the overall strength of the German army, which shot up from the peace-time size of 0.8 million to 2.9 million men in August 1914. And this dramatic increase was largely achieved by the means of conscription.[44]

General conscription as the key organizing principle of the German military did, at least during peace time, have both a unifying and a levelling impact. Unifying, as an extended period of military service to the fatherland helped to generate 'an awareness of national belonging'. The military as the 'school of the nation': this popular slogan was to some extent an idealized notion based on a national-conservative ideology. But it also captured important side effects of conscription, as young men from diverse regional and also denominational backgrounds served together in one barrack and thus had a tangible experience of the wider national framework they lived in.[45] Conscription was a great leveller, as military service drew together men from different social backgrounds and forced them to live in rather modest material circumstances. There were, however, exceptions from the implicitly egalitarian arrangements for general conscription, and they proved to have a decisive impact on the perceptions and motivations of ordinary soldiers during the war. As had been the case in the Prussian army, young men with a high-school diploma in Imperial Germany could sign up for military service as a one-year volunteer (*Einjährig-Freiwilliger*). This would cut the period of service to half and allowed them to lodge privately instead of staying in overcrowded barracks with their tight discipline and mediocre diet. The 'one-yearers' had to pay for their own subsistence and also their equipment, though, indicating that this was a privilege not only based on formal education, but also on affluence. Consequently, only offspring from well-to-do middle-class families could afford to opt for this form of service.[46]

Service as a one-year volunteer was not only convenient but allowed an individual to bypass many of the hardships of conscription. For a sizable minority of the 'one-yearers', it also permitted them to qualify for and be accepted as a reserve officer. In this much sought-after position, they could extend the patriotic honour and prestige of military service into their civilian life. It was fairly common that reserve officers wore their uniform in public, and the military rank offered additional prestige when they participated in bourgeois forms of sociability.[47] The privileges granted to young men from the educated middle class, however, intensified the widespread perception of injustice and inequality among ordinary soldiers during the war. This was due to the continuing role of higher education certificates for the replenishing of the ranks of the officer corps. Already during the first year of the war, the active prewar officer corps had suffered major losses. Yet while the military authorities were well aware of how useful it could be to promote NCOs with front-line experience, it remained very difficult to rise to the rank of reserve lieutenant without a one-year-volunteer certificate. A mere 91 NCOs without this certificate were promoted to the rank of officer between 1914 and 1918 in the Bavarian army, mostly for acts of extreme bravery. Instead, NCOs who performed the duties of officers without the certificate were made *Feldwebelleutnant* (sergeant-lieutenant). Thus, they still ranked below the lowest rank of reserve officer and were only second-class officers, a fact that contributed to the widespread perception that the officer corps was a separate caste and endowed with unjustified privileges by the monarchical state.[48]

III. Principles of this Edition

During the four years of the First World War, on average 6.3 million men served in the German army. About 4.1 million of them were deployed in the *Feldheer* (field army), including the rear area or *Etappe* behind the front lines, and in the occupied foreign territories. The other 2.2 million served in the *Besatzungsheer* or replacement army, i.e. in barracks and garrisons on German territory where soldiers were trained and prepared for their spell of duty at the front. Altogether, 13.1 million men or around one-fifth of the entire population served in the German army during the First World War. From 1914 to 1918, the male age cohort born between 1869 and 1900 became eligible for military service. From this group of men, aged between 18 and 49 in the autumn of 1918, no less than 85 per cent were called up at some point during the war. About 2 million German soldiers were killed, and 4.8 million were reported as wounded during the war.[49]

These figures serve to demonstrate the enormous dimensions of the German military war effort. They also make clear that any pretence to cover comprehensively the front-line experiences of German soldiers and the inner workings of the military machine in this book would be fundamentally flawed. As every source collection must be, the present volume is inevitably selective. Nonetheless, the editors aim to present selected documents on the most important aspects and periods of the changing nature of war from 1914 to 1918. We have deliberately strived to combine different types of source. Diversity not only of the opinions expressed in the sources, but also of the types of source that are represented is a key organizing principle of this collection. Some of the sources documented here, such as war letters, extracts from diaries or complaints to the military authorities, represent the worm's eye perspective of soldiers who were directly in the line of fire and at the receiving end of the chain of command. Others, such as military despatches and orders, medical reports and correspondence or reports by officers, exemplify how the higher echelons of the military perceived the discipline within the army and the morale of the soldiers. Newspaper articles and excerpts from booklets and brochures demonstrate how the public discussed the nature of the front-line experiences.

Feldpostbriefe (letters that were despatched by the field post services) are a particularly important source for an understanding of the mentalities of ordinary soldiers, their perceptions of wartime society, their images of the enemy and their experiences of combat, and we have included many vivid examples and some longer excerpts in this collection. Any usage of war letters for a history of wartime mentalities must pay attention to the relevant source criticism. Censorship is the first key issue that needs to be addressed here. Censorship of war letters from the front was carried out by the military authorities. Until April 1916, officers in companies or regiments read selected letters from their units and withheld or censored them as they saw fit. From April 1916, military censorship was centralized. Postal surveillance units at the divisional or army level controlled a sample of letters on a regular basis. According to a more specified set of guidelines, the censors working in these units only took action when they noticed grave offences against the rules of military secrecy or discipline or severe criticism of the war effort. They were asked not to interrupt the private exchange of opinions or to prosecute general complaints about food or military service. Given that no less than 28 billion war letters were sent during the First World War, including those from and to the front, however, it was impossible to check everything anyway.[50] Military censorship of war letters was thus not able to hinder soldiers from expressing even highly critical or subversive views, as many examples in this collection demonstrate.

While military censorship is one problem affecting the source value of war letters, their representative nature is another one. To what extent can historians generalize from the available body of soldiers' letters? How reliable are these sources for an assessment of popular mentalities in the army, with regard to changes in troop morale and the growth of war weariness, and with regard to private perceptions of both the personal and political situation? These are important questions, and the answers will differ depending on the nature and scope of the enquiry for which war letters are used.[51] With regard to the latter, the possible range of studies extends from an investigation of the correspondence of a single soldier and his wife or other relatives to studies that focus on a particular group of soldiers in a specific social or regional context. For both categories, evidence gleaned from war letters must be carefully interpreted, if possible also in comparison with other source materials that shed light on subjective mentalities, such as diaries or reports by military chaplains.[52] Generalization with regard to the former aspect, troop morale, is a considerably less complex endeavour. Key changes in the morale of soldiers were, sometimes with a certain time-lag, reflected and assessed in reports by regimental, divisional or army commanders and can hence be determined with a high amount of accuracy. Here, war letters offer crucial additional evidence as they make it possible to chart the exact nature of grievances and of the expectations the soldiers held for the imminent future. They also offer insights into the semantics used to describe the war effort, i.e. the social and political vocabulary that was used to give meaning to the necessary sacrifices.[53]

Due to the work of the postal surveillance units from spring 1916 onwards, the representative nature of evidence on troop morale in war letters is relatively easy to establish for the latter half of the war.[54] The surveillance units at divisional level compiled monthly reports for their respective army command, and these reports were aggregated at army level and passed on to the *Oberste Heeresleitung*. These reports contained both an assessment of the situation and, from the viewpoint of the officers dealing with censorship, a representative sample of particularly telling excerpts. Their purpose was to inform top-level decision-making with regard to disciplinary matters and to provide an early warning system concerning rapid deterioration of morale. Since these reports were meant to provide reliable data, they provide extremely worthwhile and representative excerpts, as a comparison with other available war letters confirms.

However, difficulties for an only tentatively representative source collection on the front-line experience arise from the state of the archival record. In spring 1945, most of the holdings of the Heeresarchiv in Potsdam, which contained the files of the Prussian war ministry and army, were destroyed following an Allied air raid. The destruction of these files has produced substantial and characteristic gaps in the historical record, not least through the loss of the files of the Army Supreme Command. As a consequence of the federal nature of the German political system, however, a considerable part of the written record of the German army in the First World War has survived in other locations. Some aspects of top-level decision-making in the OHL can be reconstructed with the files of the *Kriegsgeschichtliche Forschungsanstalt des Heeres* (Army Research Unit on the History of War), a body that was set up by the Reichswehr in order to evaluate the lessons of the First World War, and, from 1933 onwards, to prepare the military for another one.[55] In the records of this institution, for instance, some of the postal censorship reports of the 5th army have survived. A wealth of relevant information can also be found in the files of the German navy, which are nowadays kept in Freiburg im Breisgau. The most crucial collections for this edition were, however, the military archives of the non-Prussian contingents of the German Imperial army, i.e. those provided by the Kingdoms of Saxony, Württemberg and Bavaria. Of these three, the files of the Bavarian contingent, situated in Munich, are by far the most extensive both in quantitative and qualitative terms. They not only contain documentation for numerous Bavarian field units, including a comprehensive set of court-martial records, but also the complete files of the Bavarian War Ministry, which was in constant exchange with the Prussian and Imperial authorities in Berlin and was *ex officio* obliged to cover most of the internal affairs of the field army. The prevalence of sources from the south of Germany in this collection is thus to a large extent a result of the gaps in the surviving archival record for the Imperial army.

As mentioned above, this source collection is inevitably selective. Two important aspects of the front-line experiences of German soldiers that are not covered in this volume have therefore to be mentioned. Both of them further accentuate the repressive and authoritarian tendencies of the treatment the Wilhelmine military handed out to the conscript soldiers, a treatment that in fact turned some minority groups into second-class citizens. The first minority to experience discrimination in the form of direct harassment and verbal abuse was the Jews. About 10,000 German Jews mainly from the middle classes, who were fully acculturated and imbued with patriotic fervour, had volunteered in August 1914. By 1915 at the latest, however, Jewish soldiers were confronted with widespread anti-Semitic sentiments both among their peers and their military superiors. Pressure groups of the anti-Semitic right-wing fringe bombarded the military authorities with accusations that Jewish soldiers would dodge front-line service and would mostly serve in the rear area or in the *Besatzungsheer*. Bowing to this pressure, but also following the wide-spread anti-Semitism in the Prussian officer corps, the Prussian war ministry ordered the infamous 'Jew count' of October 1916. Officially meant to dispel the rumours about Jewish dodgers by establishing the exact statistics of their front-line service, the decree opened up the gates for a wave of discriminatory practices in many field units. It also allowed for anti-Semitic resentment in the German army to flourish further, even more so as the results of the count were never officially published.[56] The front-line experiences of German-Jewish soldiers thus vacillated between their commitment to serve for their fatherland and their bitter disappointment about the fact that their sacrifice was not acknowledged by the military leadership and most of their 'comrades'.[57]

Another group whose experiences are not covered in this volume is the national minorities living in Imperial Germany, the Poles, Danes and people from Alsace-Lorraine. Alsace-Lorraine had been annexed by Germany following the defeat of France in the war in 1870/71. It had, however, not been granted the normal status of a state in the federal system, but was rather governed as a Reichsland with direct control exercised by an Imperial Governor (*Reichsstatthalter*) who was appointed by and had to report to the emperor in Berlin. The presumptuous attitude of the Prussian military in Alsace-Lorraine and their reckless treatment of the civilian population had become obvious in the Zabern affair in autumn 1913, when a lieutenant in the garrison town of Zabern had recommended to his recruits to make use of the bayonet in any brawl with the 'Wackes' (a derogatory term for the people from Alsace-Lorraine). In the ensuing storm of protest by local citizens, a colonel indiscriminately imprisoned a group of civilians, a procedure that was later backed up by the army despite heated debates and a vote of censure in the Imperial diet.[58] During the war, the army continued to disrespect people from Alsace-Lorraine. From the beginning, soldiers from this province were suspected of being fixed on deserting to the French lines. On 15 March 1915, the Prussian war ministry issued a secret decree that ordered that the army high commands should transfer all Alsatian soldiers who were deemed to be unreliable to the Eastern Front, in order to prevent further cases of desertion. Other discriminatory practices, such as a separate complete censorship of all letters from and to Alsatian soldiers, were added in 1917.[59] While the specific experiences of soldiers from Alsace-Lorraine are documented elsewhere, the perceptions of privates from the Polish and Danish minorities have yet to be studied.[60]

At the end of this introduction, a few technical remarks about the way in which we have arranged this volume. We have ordered the documents to form a mixture of a chronological and a thematic presentation. Several excerpts that illuminate the same topic are usually subsumed under one heading. Each document or group of documents is introduced by a few lines of commentary which aim to contextualize the source and also, where necessary, to explain details that are not straightforward for an

English-language readership. In addition, slightly longer introductory remarks to each of the chapters outline the historical background that is necessary for a proper understanding. We hope that the collection can be used even without previous knowledge as a historical reader of the front-line experiences in the German army from 1914 to 1918. We have thus also refrained from adding a scholarly apparatus. The exact bibliographical references and the location of archival sources are established in the Document Sources at the back of the book. Some abbreviations are explained in brackets within the documents, but we would also like to refer our readers to the general list of abbreviations and the glossary at the back. Upon the request of some private owners of primary sources, we have anonymized a couple of documents. Subject lines and distributor heads in official documents and decrees have not been included. Omissions in the documents are indicated by square brackets [...]. Finally, a note on the translation. Many of the excerpts from war letters and diaries, written by people without secondary school education such as workers, peasant farmers, artisans and their wives, are crafted in a peculiar style, very often without any punctuation and in blatant breach of the rules of grammar. For the convenience of the reader and because the specific flavour of the original is almost impossible to convey, these quotations have been translated into grammatically correct English.

The editors would like to thank a number of colleagues and friends for their support. Irina Renz of the Bibliothek für Zeitgeschichte in Stuttgart kindly granted permission to use the photograph printed on the front cover. She also effectively supported our archival research with her magnificent collection of eyewitness accounts. It was a pleasure to work with Rupert Harding, our editor at Pen & Sword. His support and attention to detail are much appreciated. Matthew Stibbe and Stuart Hallifax offered constructive feedback on a first draft of the introduction. For many stimulating discussions about the topics covered in this collection and about eyewitness accounts from the First World War, we would like to thank Richard Bessel, Michael Geyer, Christa Hämmerle, Wolfgang Kruse, Thomas Kühne and Jeffrey Verhey.

Prologue

'Just a small detail'[1]
From the book *The Plaster Boxes. A Novel on the Field Medical Services* (1929), written by Alexander Moritz Frey:

> Do not expect stories of extraordinary horridness, of spectacular coincidences, of unique events without any impact on the whole issue to be told here. Here you will merely find examples like meagre drops now and then. In its scope, it was all much worse, much more terrible, excessively immane. This here is just a very small detail.

A Question[2]
The paedagogue and writer Wilhelm Lamszus published his visionary book *The Human Slaughterhouse* in 1912. It was a vivid forecast of the horrors of an impending global war. In 1914, the second volume with the title *The Madhouse* was scheduled to appear, but the outbreak of the war made this impossible. When it was finally published in 1919, the journalist and pacifist Carl von Ossietzky wrote in his preface:

> 'Why this again, and why this now?' I can hear people asking. It is over and done. Just draw finally a line under the past. [...] In the meantime, we have witnessed everything ourselves, from the day of mobilisation to the days when the soil was flying through the air. We have also experienced the madhouse. Usually a realm in itself and thoroughly separated from the city of the reasonable people, the madhouse had become reality, horrible reality. We have all been obsessed. It was just by pure accident that one got wild, whereas the other one did not. We know that madness was calling up for physical examinations day by day, that young lads hale and hearty were tossing about on the ground in hysterical convulsions. We know the poor men sitting on the hospital trains, hollow-eyed and bent down with rattling jaws and trembling to such an extent that they were incapable to put a bite of bread to their

mouth. – 'Buried three times …' – Yes, we know all that and therefore: what is the point in opening this gruesome book over and over again – just give us nice pictures again, friends! Alas, we are not yet ready to talk like this. […] Fully soaked with red human blood, the dragon has retreated to his cave. But for how long?

Chapter 1

The War Begins

Already during the war, when domestic strife and popular protests seemed to undermine the German war effort, the beginning of the war was turned into the myth of the *Augusterlebnis*, the experience of enthusiasm and national unity in the days following the mobilization on 1 August 1914. But in reality, the overwhelming majority of the German population did not react with unanimous zeal and patriotic fervour to the declaration of war. Enthusiastic crowds gathered on the streets of the big cities, and the capital in particular. But even in Berlin the initial responses to the war were mixed and ambivalent. Curiosity was mixed with anxiety, and no cheerful crowds gathered in proletarian neighbourhoods. In the countryside, a rather depressive mood prevailed. The mostly youthful war volunteers epitomized already for contemporary observers the extent of popular enthusiasm. But their motives were as varied as the popular responses to war. Among these motives, voluntary enlistment as a rite of passage to fully fledged masculinity played a crucial role. The gendered perceptions and reactions to the war are more generally an important and often neglected facet of the *Augusterlebnis*. Whatever expectations conscript soldiers and war volunteers might have had in the early days of August, not only the realities of machine warfare they faced at the front, but the harsh treatment they had already received in the military barracks often led to a swift disillusionment.

Germany – A Madhouse[3]

Enthusiastic and patriotic crowds gathered on the streets of big cities in the days after the declaration of war. Their readiness to leap into action and to pursue suspicious persons endangered the public order. The chief constable in Stuttgart issued a decree to his force, cited in the *BZ am Mittag* on 9 August 1914:

Uniformed policemen! The townspeople are going mad! The streets are crowded with old women, both male and female, who take great pains to display disgraceful behaviour. Everyone mistakes the person next to him for a Russian or French spy and considers it his duty to give both the 'spy' and the policeman who is taking care of him a bloody nose. At the least, he draws a huge crowd when he delivers the person to the police. Clouds are taken to be aeroplanes, stars to be airships, the handlebar of a bicycle to be a bomb. There are rumours that telephone and telegraph lines in the city centre of Stuttgart have been cut, about spies who have been court-martialled and shot, about blasted bridges and poisoned waterpipes. It cannot be foreseen what will be happening when times get seriously difficult. It has been established that nothing has happened yet which gives even the slightest cause for concern. Nevertheless, it is like being in a madhouse, although everybody who is not a coward or a dangerous idler is supposed to be calm and do his duty since these times are serious enough. Policemen, just keep a cool head! Be men and not old women and do not let yourself be intimidated. Keep your eyes open as it is your duty! The chief constable.

Robert Gaupp, psychiatrist and vice-chancellor of the University of Tübingen, recalls the beginning of the war in a public lecture delivered in 1916:

And what was happening in August 1914 when the World War was descending on Europe? During those days of general tension and indignation we witnessed the most peculiar forms of mass suggestion, particularly in the large cities. [...] The spy fanatism did manifest itself in bizarre forms, false, deceptive memories and perceptions followed individual suggestions at a great and funny speed. Thermos flasks turned into bombs, the fear of famine caused a pointless propensity to hoard food, banks were stormed, salt was piled up without any sense, gold hidden in stockings. Enemy cars with the French gold treasures were seen speeding through cities and villages. I met a group of educated gentlemen and ladies on the Neckar bridge in Tübingen who were observing planets and fixed stars in the sky as enemy aeroplanes.

The *Rheinisch-Westfälische Zeitung* reports on 2 September 1914 in a rubric on 'war scenes in the capital city' on another facet of the excited mood:

> This is a brand new pastime in Berlin: 'cheering on.' [*Abschreien*] 'Do you have any plans for tonight?' 'We go cheering on.' A crowd is gathering on busy squares and crossroads and as soon as the people spot a field grey uniform in a car or a suitcase they sound a many-voiced 'Hurrah'! That's how they bid farewell to the leaving soldiers. And the officers stand up and wave their hats. The crowd is waiting deep into the night. They would not go to bed unless they have 'cheered on' at least 25 lieutenants.

The psychiatrist Heinrich Resch from the mental hospital in Bayreuth in Upper Franconia explains the following in a lecture delivered in 1915:

> Since the beginning of the war, a great number of articles about mental disorders during the war have been published, both in belletristic journals and in daily newspapers. In the latter case, all articles tend to inform and partly calm the readers down. And there is certainly a need for that. Let's just take the newspapers from the first days of mobilisation. There we read about many suicides and about mental breakdowns which have been supposedly caused by the fear for relatives sent to the front and for the enemy conquering German territory. [...] Does a war really have an impact on mental-health problems? This question is absolutely to be answered in the affirmative.

Walter Fuchs, a senior medical officer, coined the term 'mobilization psychosis' for various forms of 'excitement' among soldiers during the early days of the war:

> At the beginning of August 1914, they were filling up the hospitals at an alarming speed, even before the first battles had started. Since the roads in Alsace were closed for a longer period of time, the institutions in Baden had to provide neighbourly assistance and had to take over the care for the patients coming in with mass transports. Among them were cases of the most varying origins, from delirious alcoholics to detected paralytics; but for the overwhelming majority the mental excitement and the emotions of these times were unmistakably the trigger of their problems. [...] The prevailing mood during the days of mobilisation [...] was dominated by worry, fear and anxiety. [...] The old practitioner Colonel Pfülf says that in every unit there are some men who know no fear or danger, some others who are able to overcome the

impulse of their fear due to the inhibition caused by their military training and their well developed strength of nerves and will, whereas a huge number of men is helplessly fainthearted or only to be forced to withstand when they know they are observed. This correct classification is presumed to apply to the entire population.

A Protestant parish pastor from Berlin notes in his diary on 22 August 1914:

At night, we went to the 'Café Vaterland' (formerly 'Picadilly') at Potsdamer Platz where we happened to meet the Thimms. Just like us, they had come here because they had hoped to hear some possibly incoming dispatches. But our expectations were not fulfilled. The evening newspapers merely reported the pursuit of the French and the success of the Austrians at Lemberg. – The whole hustle and bustle in the Café Vaterland was remarkable. Huge German flags were hanging from the railing all around showing a golden 'W. II' [for Emperor Wilhelm II] in the centre, surrounded by a laurel wreath. In the middle, there was an Austrian flag attached right in front of the band. The most popular songs from the last operettas which used to dominate the concerts have almost vanished completely. Instead, the orchestra is playing some patriotic tunes and old folk songs, and the audience is singing along and clapping vividly. It is noticeable that public life has become more serious in character. But who knows how long this will last? – The hatred against England runs deeply in the blood of our people. Here is just a small example to demonstrate this which I observed this afternoon at the tram stop. Several ladies were standing there, and one of them was reading from a newspaper she had just bought that the English had difficulties mobilizing huge numbers of soldiers because the English workers did not want to join in. Instead of 50,000 as expected they had merely mobilized 2,000 men. How this information made the ladies' faces shine! Laughing happily they said: 'That's good, that's brilliant!' Hence, even our womankind is steeped in deep anger against the 'Christian Albion'.

Enthusiasm?[4]

A newspaper published in Munich reports on 4 August 1914:

We big-city dwellers have already lost our sense of proportion amidst the fanatic goings-on, since we have known the [Bavarian] capital only under the impact of alarming news for 14 days. One only notices the stark difference when coming from the quietness of the countryside. A deep peace prevails out there, for nobody notices anything of the precautions keeping thousands of people in the capital in suspense. Many of our peasant families are weighed down with great sorrow, though, for very often fathers of families with many children have to go, sons, horses and carriages are requisitioned by the military authorities, and out there in the fields is the crop to be harvested.

From the memoirs of a farmer from Lower Franconia:

We had the son of a local farmer as a stable boy who had just finished his military service the previous autumn. Around lunchtime, my sister suddenly came to us, crying. She was looking after the household since my mother had died. First we thought something terrible had happened. Agitated she said: 'Josef has to go home immediately and get on the 12 o'clock train. It's war!' Naturally, everyone working afield was confused and did not feel like going on with the work.

The journalist Siegfried Jacobsohn (1881–1926) was the founder and editor of the journal *Schaubühne*, entitled *Weltbühne* from 1918, one of the most important intellectual journals of the 1920s. During the summer of 1914, he was holidaying on one of the small islands in the North Sea. Hearing about the outbreak of war, he decided to travel back to Berlin:

Saturday, 1 August [Jacobsohn is still at the holiday resort] [...] If it is time, we will not only mobilize men but also higher feelings and we will bash everybody's hat who does not appear to have got plenty of those according to regulations.

Tuesday, 4 August. [...] But are those in the capital city really enthusiastic? I'm thinking of Fontane [a famous late nineteenth-century novelist]. He had a good heart like everyone else from the Mark Brandenburg [a rural region around Berlin], could smell gunpowder, had been prisoner of war, had composed Prussian ballads and – and he did not lose his skill to look behind the mere appearance of things and to listen. Therefore, he did not hesitate to interpret the cheers being shouted when soldiers stormed against batteries in unheroic terms, as 'exultation and angst'. Could this not also be the formula for the frenzy of the people in Berlin? [...]

Just bring the enthusiastic people from Berlin over here, among our fifteen farm houses, and they will fall silent. I walk around among the Sörensen, Sönksen, Hartwigsen, Christiansen, Bleiken, Callesen, Seiher and Jepsen families. In spite of their names, they are not less German, more stupid, more fainthearted, weaker than the majority of the 68 millions, to the contrary. But they do not feel the need to cheer in a situation when they might lose their life or fathers, sons, brothers, grandsons and their smaller or larger property. [...]

Wednesday, 5 August. [...] I cannot stop feeling ashamed about my behaviour this morning after I had heard the news about England's declaration of war. For half an hour, I acted like a bloodthirsty predator. Who knows how the raging city of Berlin would change me right now! [...]

Sunday, 9 August. [Jacobsohn is on the train to Berlin] [...] Families are bidding farewell to their dear ones. 'Good bye, Korl', cousin Michel shouts somewhere close to Wittenberge, 'See you again in the mass grave!' The man shouting is so droll that not even this harsh sentence sounds offensive. The humorous characters from Berlin are flourishing as well. Two lads, 17 years of age, equipped with an identification card as war volunteers describe how they have been crisscrossing from regiment to regiment and travelling through the whole Imperial Germany. On their way, they were lavished with gift parcels and sometimes even with cash. Their description is so graphic that it partly takes away the edge of the embarrassing character of the whole event.

From the war diary by Georg Schenk, a carpenter journeyman from Nuremberg, born in 1888:

It was 1 August. The whole German population was tense, as people were waiting for the mobilisation of the German army, after the state of siege had already been declared on 31 July. I went home from Nuremberg to say farewell to my parents. Finally, on 1 August at 6 p.m. it was announced that the general mobilisation was declared, and now everything was reaching a climax. Many a tear was flowing and many eyes that had been dry for ten years became wet. Particularly women and girls were crying, for many men and young lads had to leave the Heimat to fight for their fatherland that was threatened by Russia and France. Only few slept well during the first night, since the anxiety for the husband, the wife, the groom, and the bride was more severe than ever, as people knew that a very grave war was imminent.

Becoming a Man[5]

From the autobiography of the novelist Carl Zuckmayer (1896–1977), who volunteered in 1914:

> Becoming a soldier, serving my year, had always been a threatening and embarrassing idea during my days at the Gymnasium [grammar school]. [...] Now it meant the exact opposite: liberation! Liberation from middle-class narrowness and fussiness, from the necessity to go to school and to swot, from the doubts about choosing a profession and from all the things we perceived – consciously or unconsciously – as the saturation, closeness and rigidity of our world. We had already revolted against these things as members of the Wandervogel ['hiking bird', a middle-class youth organization]. Now this feeling was not any longer restricted to the weekends and the holiday sport activities. It had become serious, dead serious, holy serious, and at the same time a huge exhilarating adventure, for which we happily accepted a little discipline and armed forces stuff. We shouted out 'freedom' while we were jumping into the straight-jacket of the Prussian uniform. It sounds absurd. But we had become men with a single blow.

Attempts were made to facilitate the Abitur, or school leaving exam, for those secondary school students who had volunteered for the army. From an article with the title 'battle bravery and exam fear' published in early 1915:

> Carried unanimously, [...] the Prussian diet has expressed its sympathy towards those final year students who will leave school during the war. After all, it means quite something when all the university professors who are members of the diet signed a request suggesting that students from institutions of higher education who have left school during the penultimate year at school and have joined the army, [...] are not only supposed to achieve their leaving exam in a more simple manner, but should be able in certain cases to receive it from the provincial exam boards even without any exam. [...]
>
> The regular final examination is supposed to be resat after the war. Special courses, tailor-made to the situation of these young people, are planned to prepare them for the exams. All their equitable wishes can expect to receive a warm-hearted consideration. [...]
>
> May the final year students out there in the trenches get the comforting conviction in view of the proceedings of the Prussian diet

that the imminent exam distress at home is not as dangerous as it may seem to some of them during dark hours of brooding, at least not more dangerous than the shrapnells and the poisonous gas that is threatening them.

War Volunteers[6]

War memoirs by the high-school student Paul Wittenburg, who volunteered in August 1914:

We were then travelling home on a stopping train, via Ribnitz and Stralsund [harbour towns on the Baltic Sea]. At the calling points en-route many reservists entered the train. Very often a good-bye full of tears took place. One of them tried to console his wife or bride: 'Not every bullet is a hit'. In Neubrandenburg I heard from Putz Raspe [a friend from school] that his father was about to contact the headmaster of his school concerning an emergency graduation. The idea of getting easily through the exams without much effort by having an emergency graduation was exceedingly attractive to me. With regard to graduation, my chances were not yet very good. But in order to be admitted, we had to prove to be fit for field service. [...]

As a volunteer I was allowed to use the railway for free. We thus preferred to use second-class compartments. The trains used to have four classes then. Some of the volunteers might have abused this to travel across Germany. [...]

Anyway, it is hard to make generalizations when people speak of unrestrained enthusiasm. Such feelings were also fostered by the impression that now there might be ample opportunity to prove oneself and to excel. [...]

But when finally the time seemed to have come, I was happy, although the idea of getting to the front line at that very moment gave me a somewhat apprehensive feeling. It is not the purpose of these lines to picture myself as a hero. I never considered myself to be a hero at all and a hero's death with all its ingredients seemed to me extremely scary. [...] On the other hand, I quite liked the idea of a victorious return to the homeland as an officer, all decorated with crosses and medals. But therefore one had to survive, and with that it would under some circumstances not work out.

From the autobiographical novel *We are Captives* by the writer Oskar Maria Graf (1894–1967):

> I went to the police station in Wilmersdorf [a neighbourhood in Berlin] and volunteered for the 3rd Infantry Regiment, stationed in Augsburg. I was handed over a sheet of paper serving as a train ticket. I [...] went to the railway station Anhalter Bahnhof, entered a train and ended up in Munich after a four-day journey. It did not occur to me to report in Augsburg. It was a beautiful, almost idyllic trip similar to the journeys with the student fraternities through half of Germany. At every station, people from the Red Cross were waiting for us and fed us lavishly. All the train compartments were full of sandwich leftovers, sausage edges and cheese crumbs. Anyway, I thought how nice it was that there seemed to be always enough food in the war.

In the autobiographical novel *Ginster*, written by the journalist and sociologist Siegfried Kracauer (1889–1966), the protagonist muses about the reasons why he is going to volunteer:

> 'There is something else about it', Otto began again, 'see, I am a strong young man. If I stayed at home while the others are out there in the field – I could not bear it. How am I supposed to be special so that it is precisely me who is going to be spared. I am quite talented, all right, but it is not enough to become something really great, I am certain of that. In the end I'll become a teacher like many others, get married, have the usual children and my pension. No, I had to join in, otherwise I would have been ashamed of myself. I am sorry for my parents, but I do not regret my decision.'

On 11 August 1914 a newspaper in Berlin published the following poem, written by the Landsturm conscript Fischer from Berlin. Like many Germans, Fischer felt the need to express his patriotic feelings in verse form. The Landsturm comprised older reservists and those who had not been drafted for military service before the war. The second and third tier of the Landsturm in particular was not automatically drafted at the beginning of the war:

> I have not served, I am a Landsturm-man
> I have to wait until they might need me.

Have to wait – a hard and bitter word.
The Landsturm from Berlin may not go off.
Our brothers are now approaching the enemy
When will the Landsturm finally be called?

If only they called – and do not leave us at home
Otherwise our girls and women laugh at us.

Writing in 1931, the widow of a Landsturm soldier describes her feelings during August 1914. Her report conveys a sense of the social pressure that men were exposed to at the time:

We had just come back from a walk when we heard the news about the outbreak of the war. My husband was not supposed to be called up very soon, for he was Landsturm 2nd tier; and I was happy that I didn't have to give him away so soon. Who would blame me for that, he was my dearest, all I had got! One fine day, it was a week after the declaration of war, my husband asked me to allow him to volunteer for the army. I begged, pleaded and cried hysterically which was such a shock for him, for he had never seen me crying before, so that he promised not to volunteer. He went on with business as usual. But soon I noticed that he didn't like his food any more and that he could not sleep at night. When I realized one night that he was awake, I took his hand and said to him: L., I do allow you to volunteer, I want to be as strong as all the other wives. But you have to come back home. With a cheer, he embraced me and my heart sank.

A case example from a medical article on 'women psychoses in connection with the war', published in 1916:

The patient answered our questions calmly and quickly. (Name?) A.H. (How are you?) I have a bit of a headache and was sick a few moments ago, but otherwise I feel quite well. (Age?) 45 years. (Where are you here?) In the madhouse. (Why are you here?) Because my husband was killed in action.

At the beginning of the war, the Institute for Applied Psychology distributed questionnaires among soldiers who went to the front. The survey was quickly stopped by military censorship. In the answers that were gathered up to this point different motives of war volunteers are recorded:

> Upon careful consideration, I realized very well how utterly absurd and senseless this slaughtering of humans was. It was partly the love of adventure that motivated me. [...]
>
> Signed up as a volunteer out of a sense of duty. It was matter of course that I would sign up right on the first day. This is partly a result of my national views which were cultivated in my student fraternity. [...]
>
> Signed up as a volunteer on the first day of mobilisation. I realized right from the beginning that a modern war was a tragedy beyond all comparison and a crime against humanity. Therefore, I did not actually feel something like war enthusiasm. But the spirit of the first days was dictating my actions as a matter of course. My patriotism had not been unlimited until then; but now I considered myself as a good patriot. [...] There was certainly a good deal of love of adventure within this spirit of the first days as well. [...] And on top of it, a second motif: 'shame'. Should I, a young man, stay at home, while not only my contemporaries but also Landwehr and Landsturm were marching out into the field? I joined up as a volunteer on the first day to avoid at all costs wearing civil clothes any longer. [...]
>
> Never had any feeling of war enthusiasm. Joined up out of sense of duty.

'Shame'[7]

The physician and neurologist Otto Binswanger explains in his booklet 'The psychological consequences of war', which was published in the first months of the conflict:

> Every young lad and every man being fit for military service offers himself to the fatherland. And what a literally grief-stricken sorrow I have witnessed in many young men who were rejected from army service due to some physical disability and defect or due to some nervous disease. At the moment, I have to treat several cases of melancholia in my hospital which are without exception the results of these rejections. On the other hand, it has to be admitted that there might be deeper causes for these cases which had existed before.

Unfit For Service[8]

Many men who were classified as 'unfit for service' but nonetheless managed to be accepted as volunteers could not cope with the strains of the war of movement in the first weeks of the conflict. Some of them saw no other option but to kill themselves. Valentin Strohschnitter reports in his war diary, published in 1930:

> A man of my year group whose name was Schäfer and who, as a shoemaker, belonged to our skilled craftsmen, shot himself during the march. He had a weak constitution. The superiors did not accept his reasons for his complaints but considered him as being low-minded.

The Austrian neurologist Redlich describes the medical history of a patient whom he examined in 1917 in order to assess if he only simulated symptoms:

> A shoemaker of 43 years, married. Patient states that he used to be healthy. […] Already four or five years ago, it is believed, the patient's eyesight deteriorated. Therefore he was wearing glasses. He enlisted in early August 1914. On the day of his physical examination he is said to have been very upset. In the morning of this day, he had witnessed an enlisted reserve soldier's wife committing suicide by throwing herself under the wheels of the departing train, after she had said goodbye to her husband. On top of that was the difficult farewell from his family. Suddenly he felt a dizzy spell coming on, started to stagger and to falter; his eyesight and speech have become bad from this moment on.

First Disappointments[9]

On 22 August 1914, the Prussian War Ministry issued a decree that reprimanded the bad treatment of war volunteers by their superiors. On 2 September, the Bavarian War Ministry followed suit. Building on the Prussian decree, the officials in Munich sharpened both tone and content:

> The War Ministry has repeatedly received complaints suggesting that the treatment of war volunteers – who mostly belong to the educated estates – on the part of the NCOs is sometimes disgraceful and against the regulations. Even if these complaints might be exaggerated, it has to be assumed that not all of them are made up out of thin air. […] The superiors of all ranks, particularly those who have not been in service

for a long time and who therefore might not know how strongly I condemn every disgraceful treatment, are to be advised about the mean and reprehensible character of such courses of action, especially against those who have been rushing to the colours as volunteers. This evil can only be exterminated, if we are taking rigorous steps and if every superior is brought to justice who is guilty of abuse or improper treatment against an inferior. This is the only way to prevent damage to the martial spirit and the eagerness to make sacrifices that has shown up everywhere in these hard times.

The philosopher Karl Löwith, who volunteered in October 1914, notes in his autobiographical report 'My life in Germany before and after 1933':

The barrack drill in the Türkenkaserne of the Bavarian Infantry Leib-Regiment [in Munich] with its special brutality, particularly against the volunteers, had the effect that we all felt relieved on the day when we were transferred to the front lines.

While exercising in the Field Artillery Regiment 6 in Breslau, the miner and Social Democratic trade-union functionary Franz Tholl had similar feelings as Löwith. But his reaction to harsh treatment by superiors was more pronounced. At the end of his letter to the Social Democratic Reichstag deputy Hermann Sachse, written on 29 November 1914, he was spreading a threat that was mentioned time and again by disgruntled soldiers throughout the war, that they would try to kill brutal superiors:

Please believe me, I haven't been scowling when I was drafted. I just thought that it has to be like that. But one just completely loses all desire if one has to listen to nothing else than confinement and pack drill everyday. By the way, the entire battery is highly discontented. You have no idea how we curse our superiors sometimes. Fortunately, we are not sent into the field, for there a lot could happen in view of this discontent and revulsion.

Maltreatment and humiliation of volunteers continued at the front. An example of this is given in the brief diary entries of the war volunteer David Pfaff from Belgium and France, who died on 4 November 1914 at the age of 24. His entry from 23 August on 'civilians' refers to the shooting of so-called 'franc-tireurs', or irregular fighters, by German troops during their advance through Belgium. Due to perceptions that had been established already during the Franco-Prussian war of 1870/71, German troops expected attacks by civilians fighting as irregular combattants. In suspicious situations, often caused by their own confusion or by 'friendly fire', they responded with massive retaliation and the deliberate shooting of civilians. About 6,400 Belgian and French civilians were killed as a result of this franc-tireur scare:

11 August/digging out trenches and exercising. 12 August/drill exercises.

14 August/exercising and night drills. Lots of bullying by the superiors. Everybody wants to approach the enemy finally. In the morning, artillery was shooting at an aeroplane. Later on, it turned out that the plane was one of ours. 15 August/exercising. In the afternoon, swimming pool in the city of Luxembourg [Luxembourg had been occupied by German troops during the first days of the war]. Fantastic pool. Haven't seen a pool as terrific as that in all my life. […]

16 August/ […] In the afternoon, exercising. […] Grinding is getting so bad that one like-minded comrade explained that only the inborn patriotism of the Germans could bear a grinding as tedious as this without complaining. […]

23 August/civilians were shooting at us. They were all killed. 30 August/ in the morning field service in blistering heat. Singing: 'We meet God the Almighty praying.' We were very moved. Many who had turned away from God have found their saviour again, me too.

8 October/in the trenches, waiting. I have been very poorly. But the doctor didn't help me. –

2 November/the Battalion Lieutenant hit Jakob and Paul, because they were about to fetch firewood and entrenchment material without their rifles. Apparently, it is becoming a habit to act and behave as we were in Russia. It is disgraceful when an extremely young lieutenant hits an old soldier and reservist who is fighting for his fatherland. Naturally, the exasperation is huge. These sad incidents are as regrettable as those situations when young officers force the troops to advance with the pistol in their hands and then take cover and stay there. Unfortunately, I witnessed this again on 1 October.

3 November/we stay in the trenches. Artillery fire on both sides.

In late September 1914, an anonymous person passed on a war letter he had received from his brother, who served on the Western Front, to the Bavarian War Ministry:

> I have seen good and bad times. But it is not the enemy who causes the bad times but our own superiors. I wish you could see how my comrades are treated by the officers. Today (13 September), a reserve lieutenant ordered three innocent men to be tied up with their arms spread so that they turned blue. Meanwhile it was teeming down. One of them had just bought a piece of bread in the canteen, which was the reason for the ill-treatment. More of that later. [...] The newspapers only write about war successes and nice things, but there is not a word on how they squeeze all their strength and the last drop of blood out of the soldiers.

'If We Had an Armistice Now'[10]

The first weeks of the war are reflected in these excerpts from war letters sent by Stefan Schimmer, a Catholic peasant farmer and Landwehr soldier from a small village in Lower Franconia. He first served in Herxheim in the Bavarian Palatinate and was then sent to France on 1 October. Schimmer was 38 years old and a father of six children. Unless stated otherwise, all letters are to his wife Katharina:

11 August 1914, from Philippsburg, to his parents-in-law:

> I'd like to write you also a letter and like to know some news about Schorsch and how it is going out there at your place. I can't say much about us. Nobody knows if we ever face the enemy. You are allowed to seal the letter. I would like it best if we had had an armistice now.

24 August 1914, from Herxheim:

> Time has been hanging heavy on my hands as if I had been here for a quarter of a year. Sometimes I can't sleep at night. It's impossible to tell if we are leaving this place. You have to decide yourself what to do with the crop and when to sell it. Ask your father. Don't rush it with wheat and corn, under no circumstances before October. I'll write to you again. I know better.

25 August 1914, from Herxheim:

On 25 August, it was my birthday, I went to confession again early in the morning, because we were off duty. It is, after all, the last time for this year. Maybe even for my whole life, for nobody knows where we will be sent to. If I am not coming back, you will marry Michael. You will come out of the whole thing all right. As I have mentioned before, Germany will win the war, there is no doubt about it. The Belgian fortress Liège has been in German hands for two weeks and is besieged by German troops. But the war costs lives, and it can last until spring.

2 September 1914, from Herxheim:

Some people at home are complaining that we are not making good progress at the front lines. Well, they haven't got a clue, but we know. We are now getting news about the amount of losses. Nobody knows, if it's our turn still this year.

The weather here is fine again. […] Tell me when you've got the machine and when you've got the crop at home, but get it home right now.

I'm billeted with a poor family. But that doesn't matter. At least I'm safe. When we are sent to Lorraine, it will be different. Everybody has to have an armed rifle next to him while sleeping. The city of Luneville in France with more than 80,000 inhabitants was levelled to the ground. I could tell you a lot, but not in a letter. I have forgotten my rosary. We are geared up for war. We could go to battle immediately. We had to go to confession on 1 September, then we got our ensigns.

19 September 1914, from Herxheim:

My best wishes to all of you, mainly to Michel as well. He has been extremely lucky to lose his fingers. If he had to be in the army, he would appreciate that.

27 September 1914, from Herxheim:

Have two masses said about the Divine Providence once more. Today I went to confession again and heard two masses and one High Mass.

Please keep this letter safe and remember the following: When I am in France and write in my letters 'I am fine', it is the truth. When I write 'I am fine' and have underlined 'fine', then you may assume that it means the opposite.

2 October 1914, from Senones:

Letting you know that we have crossed the border on 2 October at 7am. Naturally, roaring cannon were the first thing to be heard. We could see bombed carriages there as well, a destroyed tollhouse. The air smells of gunpowder from the bombarded villages. We were just resting in a French village. It is basically deserted. One can only see the sky and the army.

13 October 1914, from Senones:

I'm really hungry. I've asked you for gloves. I don't know if you have received the card or not?

It is very cold during the night lying outside. Tell me how long the card took to arrive. I'm still healthy. I've had enough. Is there any news about peace talks?

14 October 1914, from Senones:

Have you heard anything about the end of the war? Please don't stop praying for me. And make the children pray for me as well, so that I can return home.

It doesn't look nice around here, for a battle has taken place here. Many soldiers' graves are to be seen.

17 October 1914, from Senones:

You can still seed wheat on two to three morgen [a traditional square measure, between 2,500 and 3,600 square metres depending on the region]. Please send me two letters every week. I don't need any bread. Here one can't feel safe at all even for one hour. [...] I had to cry because of the photograph!

18 October 1914, from Senones:

We are on duty almost around the clock, two days in the trenches, one or two days on guard. We have to hold the position firmly. When the Frenchmen want to break the lines, we have to repulse them, what we have done on Thursday, 15 October. We also had artillery fire, it was terrible. Two dead and three wounded men. Don't send me any newspaper, I haven't got the time to read. Two days and two nights we are lying in the trenches in the Vosges, the next two days we are on guard. Very often I can't sleep longer than two hours because I'm in fear of my life. If only I am not killed in action by a shot, just because of you and the children.

Seed wheat on three to four further morgen and don't stop praying. I pray in the trench and when I am on guard. Please send me two packets of sausages every week, nothing else.

The area where we are positioned has already been a battleground. It is a place of terrible devastation. There is shooting day and night. I can't even change my uniform clothes.

Chapter 2

The Realities of War

When they first arrived at the front, the soldiers were confronted with the new realities of machine warfare, including the intensive use of machine guns and heavy artillery, gas warfare, and, since the switch to a war of position in autumn 1914, the emptiness of the battlefield, which undermined traditional notions of combat. Where soldiers had held any romantic notions about the heroic nature of their wartime service, they had become radically disillusioned by the battles of materiel since 1916, which had entailed the destruction of both human beings and landscape on an unprecedented scale. The eyewitness accounts by German soldiers also reveal the relative lack of national enmity, with the one major exception of soldiers from a middle-class background. At least when their opinions were based on direct, personal encounters, many soldiers expressed empathy with the plight of the civilian population in occupied territories or with enemy soldiers on the Western Front. Amidst the backdrop of a wave of Anglophobia in German public opinion, particularly during the first months of the war, German soldiers had reasons to correct the public perception that British soldiers were cowards and came to appreciate their military professionalism. Perceptions of the enemy, however, differed at the Eastern Front. Even Social Democratic soldiers, who were ready to dismiss any aggressive nationalism and to criticize the Wilhelmine military, were at the same time able to justify a civilizing mission of the Germans in occupied Russian-Poland with the perceived backwardness of the Polish people and their inferior 'culture'. Together with a rejection of the authoritarian Tsarist regime, these perceptions fuelled a jingoist attitude vis-à-vis the Russian army.

After a Long Time of Peace[11]

A readiness to die in battle was, despite the stirring up of enthusiastic emotions in August 1914, not really widespread. Karl Bonhoeffer, psychiatrist and during the war a medical adviser to the Corps of Guards, sums up some of the reasons for this in an article written in 1922:

A long period of peace and the generously funded development of social, hygienic and humanitarian peaceful institutions caused an intensive concern and an extraordinary high appraisal of the individual human life as well as an increasing sensitivity against violent causes of death. Hygienic and humanitarian aims were to have a longer life and a natural end of life after a long time with as little sorrow as possible. Any deviation has been thoroughly noticed. The sinking of the *Titanic* [1912] or a brutal murder could fill the papers for weeks and attract the sympathy of the readers. Being used to this frame of mind, a huge number of people had suddenly to face situations for years and years which contained violent optic and accoustic perceptions as well as causes for depressive emotions such as fear, terror, intense expectation of death, sorrow, pain and grief to an utmost extent.

Newspapers and journals tried to play down the dangers and horrors of the beginning of war. An article in the weekly journal *Die Umschau* asks on 3 October 1914 'Have wars become more dangerous?':

During the last years we have been literally flooded with war literature, including also several books about the future war taking place in this very moment. Although very different in detail all these books resemble each other in one respect: They describe a war of enormous horrors, they create images of battles in our mind's eye which are a thousand times more terrible than those of previous wars, they increase suffering and sorrow to an immense extent. And all this, they say, are the natural consequences of progress in the technology of war in our times, which invented new means of destruction in restless work. Many people support the opinion and even take it as a dogma that the increasing technical perfection of the means of war will inevitably increase the horrors of war and the number of victims. But this opinion is without any foundation. [...] In general, it is fair to say that food provision for the troops in the field today is excellent. So there is no reason to fear an increasing number of losses in this respect. [...] The losses caused by the impact of weapons [...] are also decreasing. [...] Hence we have demonstrated how reality itself proves it to be a lie that the number of victims increases through ever more sophisticated weapons. On the contrary, it shows [...] that, if we may put it that way, wars are becoming more and more harmless.

In 1916, the sociologist Max Weber published an article on 'Stages and directions of religious rejection of the world', as part of his groundbreaking work on the sociology of religion. His reflections touch upon the issue of the meaning of death in wartime battle, in a passage that was surely written with regard to the current conflict:

> And moreover, the war offers something unique to the warrior himself with regard to the actual meaning of his life: It offers the sensation of a meaning and a blessing of death which is special to him. [...] Dying is the common fate of human beings and nothing else. It is a fate that overtakes everyone, and no one could ever say why death met just him or why just now. It is a fate that sets the end, although it seems that with the increasing development and sublimation of cultural assets in its immensity it seems that possibly only a beginning could make sense. The death in the field differs from this merely inevitable dying. Here, and in its massive appearance only here, the individual can believe to know that he dies 'for' something.

From the text on a postcard that the soldier Ernst Block threw out of a transport train near the railway station in Eggmühl in Bavaria. Block apparently hoped that the railway officials would expedite his card:

> To Miss Fany Schmalz/Kitchen Help, 'Schützenhof', Regensburg

> 17 September 1915. Dearest Fany. Unfortunately I haven't seen you before I left. Farewell and take care. Now we are off to Serbia. I am on the train already. Be good and truthful. Good bye, yours truthfully, Ernst. If I am well I will always write three ..., if I don't feel well – –.

New at the Front[12]
Johann Preisinger, a reserve NCO, writes to his previous employer, the bank director Müller in Munich, on 31 October 1914:

> Those who have freshly arrived and who are curious to see the emptiness of the battlefield, who are just not yet clever enough in many respects, are the cause of our foremost worries. On top of that there are the excitement and nervousness at the first hail of shells, the shell and shrapnel firing. It takes the newcomers 14–20 days on average to get used to the privations, exertions and the horror of war. [...] I'd also like

to mention briefly the dear and enormously discouraging manner of addressing us and the insults which our officers have been guilty of using until very recently. 'Bastards', 'son of a bitch' and tying to trees for the slightest misdemeanour etc. were the order of the day.

I was not afraid to object to this behaviour in a certain way and threatened with publishing and informing the relevant highest military authorities directly and indirectly. [...]

Life in the trenches is like the following: In the darkness of the night we go to unknown or known positions. At night being on guard, on patrol and on outpost duty. Unceasing constructing entrenchments – building trenches, communication trenches and cover trenches etc. During the day sleeping and sometimes on guard.

A war volunteer and typesetter outlines in retrospective some reasons for his disillusionment and his coping strategies:

The then often quoted 'baptism of fire' put a damper also on us war volunteers, as we had offered ourselves to the fatherland with great enthusiasm. The longer we were confronted with the bloody face of the war, the less we were convinced about its necessity, and one became a radical war opponent. 'Never again war!' was a widespread slogan after the First World War. But I like to mention something particularly despicable which helped a good deal to cure the German Landser of the First World War of their affection for the fatherland. I have been with many different units during that time and almost everywhere there was one type of officer who stood out because of their particularly harassing, even brutal behaviour against the front soldiers. They had no leadership qualities at all. However, in the trenches these 'heroes' failed just too often. More than once we had to fight without officers. Luckily, they were of course the minority.

I was like every other field-grey soldier in the World War: We did our 'duty', as they nicely put it during those days, at the front facing the opponent, our 'enemy', either due to the instinct of self-preservation, due to a sense of duty or due to other reasons. We did not contemplate throwing away our rifles and deserting to the enemy, even though we used to complain a lot and cursed the whole bloody war. But there were quite a few soldiers who did run away, i.e. who deserted. But the longer the war went on, the less severe became the sentences for desertion. My anti-militaristic opinion or attitude used to become visible behind the front, when we were at rest or in a garrison. I was sick to the teeth with the tedious duty and I got stubborn. The result was: The company commander who was always at the front with us liked me, whereas I used to fall out with the sergeant, who was called a 'topkick' [Spieß], and who was after all a 'base wallah'.

The carpenter journeyman Georg Schenk describes his 'baptism of fire' on 20 August 1914 in his diary:

We were all happy to have got away with our life, for it had been a hard day and we got our baptism of fire. Trust in God, he helps in the hour of need, that was my consolation. I wasn't that scared of the infantry fire, but when the shells exploded right behind us, some of us got really frightened and everyone jumped forward as fast as he could. When I was lying in the firing line, I was thinking of my Gretl and what she was doing and what she was thinking. And some thoughts occurred to me, what she might say in case I got wounded or would drop dead. I kept thinking that I had promised to come back and I had no doubt at all that I would get wounded. Well, thank God this battle is over. We have no idea how many will still follow.

The War of Position Begins[13]

The transition to a war of position during October and November 1914 increased the sense of disillusionment particularly among those soldiers who had gone to the front with images of a knightly, joyful war in mind. Excerpts from the war letter of a volunteer, written on 18 November close to Dixmuiden in Belgium:

Well-being is here nothing else than not being supposed to launch an attack across meadows that are completely flooded and poisoned by the odour of putrefaction, but rather to be able to stay quietly and peacefully in the trench with more or less straw that is not completely soaked yet. Or sheer heaven: To have one or two days rest which can be thoroughly enjoyed. Then the drenched clothes can dry, not at a fire though, but on our backs, or at least one can have a try. That way, however, one is prepared, to a certain extent, to be freezing for a long time when going back into the trenches.

Right now it is bad again. The enemy has apparently penetrated the dikes near Dixmuiden so that water is pouring cheerfully into the trenches. The flood is about half a metre high and might rise up to any possible level until the trench overflows and we can swim. [...] Now we are at the canal where we have been in combat for a couple of days. We also dared to make an assault attack at night again, but without any success, just losses, heavy losses. I have helped to lay several comrades to eternal rest. But one becomes hardened even with those things. – One is happy not to be hit yet – which is indeed a very good reason to be jolly glad. And what have the poor injured people often to suffer when they are lying for days without any help, without any food and drink, at risk of bleeding to death.

A soldier on the Western Front, in civilian life an employee of the state archive in Hamburg, wrote to his colleagues in December 1915. He aims to convey a sobering image of the realities of trench warfare:

Sometimes when the people who remained at home see some of the drawings and letters coming from the front, also my own letters, then they are bound to think of our life as a jolly one. Just to let you all know that there is a terrible hidden tragedy behind all these expressions of humour and of the joy of living. Our lines and those of the enemy are facing each other so closely that one can call this war of position also a drudgery. Once we return into our somehow safe accommodation and are out of life-threatening danger again, the healthy young person experiences a backlash: he just hovered between life and death, now his joy of living wins and becomes sometimes manifest as a rollicking jollity. [...]. If the people at home saw *only* this picture, they would be bound to think we had a peaceful and quiet life. It is just a pity that the warriors do not write home about the heavy rain making the trenches collapse and the mud rising over the top of the boots and up to the hips. It is a pity that they cannot send home the whining of even a very small shell for the ones who sit in the pubs and who like to deliver speeches in cafes.

Early Crises and Insights[14]

Shortly after the beginning of the war, war letters by young volunteers were printed in the German press in order to counterbalance the first signs of disillusionment by soldiers and their relatives. Almost all German newspapers printed the famous despatch from the German Army Headquarter about the 'heroic' sacrifice of many young volunteers in an attack near the Belgian town of Langemarck on 11 November 1914. It seems that many relatives of soldiers who were killed in this battle were worried about the reckless waste of the lives of hardly trained volunteers. As rumours about the incident spread rapidly, especially in Berlin, a newspaper printed on 14 November the letter of a 'young war volunteer' who had allegedly fought at Langemarck and was now being treated in a field hospital:

A young injured war volunteer in a military hospital writes to his father in Berlin: [...] The injury is not necessarily evidence for bravery. We were advancing like the fallen comrades, and all those who are still at the front have just done their duty, nothing more! [...] Nevertheless, I felt gratified today reading in the newspaper an excerpt from *The Times* about the fighting near the Yser canal. It says that they cannot speak highly enough of the newly set up German regiments, that their courage is above all praise and almost superhuman, and that we have inflicted heavy losses on them (the English). [...] And now some impertinent, mean liars go around in Berlin and elsewhere saying that we were being forced into battle combat by the revolvers of our officers. If it only were possible to shut these people up! I also heard that some parents were 'indignant' about their sons being sent to the front lines right away. But our motto was: 'Up and at them!' And in my opinion it was nothing but good for the character formation of those gentlemen who wanted to 'play' soldiers to get under fire immediately. Why did they volunteer in the first place? [...] On the other hand there is quite a serious aspect to this feeling of 'being indignant'. It does show that unfortunately there are still people among us who have not the slightest idea of military discipline and who on the other hand seem to believe that they have to give orders to the Army Supreme Command. These laymen! If his Excellency, the commanding general, gives the order: 'The regiment is swimming over to Dover' then it is a matter of course for the regiment to swim even if they cannot swim. And even if many drowned along the way, nobody in Berlin has got the right to get excited or even to get 'indignant'. First, this is a duty, and secondly it is for the fatherland.

Many volunteers from the educated middle class hoped to find a patriotic community at the front. The daily encounters with their 'comrades' from other social strata contributed to their disillusionment, particularly when those comrades realized that young volunteers with grammar school certificates could soon be, as 'one-year volunteers', their superiors. Christian Krull discusses these issues in a letter dated 28 June 1915 to Käthe Mancke, a friend in Berlin. Krull was a member of the Wandervogel (literally 'hiking birds'), a middle-class youth association that had been founded in Berlin-Steglitz in 1901. He served in an ammunition train unit behind the front lines:

> Well, in an acquiescent mood I had to reconcile myself to the thought of returning safely from this combat as a horseboy. But I had at least one advantage compared to my comrades. I groomed not only my horse but those of the sergeant as well. I could be proud! Then my further company. My so-called 'comrades' were all 30- to 35-year-old landwehr men from Schleswig-Holstein [a rural area in the far North of Germany], fat farmers, proper examples of selfishness. The term 'comradeship' has its own special meaning in the Prussian army, anyway. If it were just that they had stolen my things and that I had to clean up my NCO's boots, I would not have complained. Human beings are creatures of habit. But it was something different that I was always at risk of being beaten up by the guys and by my superior. The lieutenant does not care about absolutely anything and the sergeant feels called to make the life of the one-year volunteers a misery in every possible and impossible way.

Those soldiers who were members of the Social Democratic labour movement had a different set of experiences and expectations for the future. These expectations are illuminated by letters of miners who were members or functionaries of the Alter Verband, the Social Democratic miners' union, which had a regional stronghold in the Ruhr district. These soldiers all wrote to Hermann Sachse, who was the chairman of the Alter Verband and also a Reichstag deputy for the Social Democratic Party. Wilhelm Platta writes on 19 May 1915, from Galicia:

> If only the murderous World War came to an end soon. How the peoples are slaughtering each other. Whoever hasn't had enough, must be narrow-minded. [...] Sometimes I lecture my comrades about the consequences of the war, but you can't do much with these stable-boys who are used to caring for cattle. We easily get in each other's hair, because many of the men in my company are from the black area

around Münster [a region in the North-West of Germany with a mainly Catholic and rural population]. When I am reading my newspaper [*Bergarbeiterzeitung*, the journal of the Alter Verband], these guys start gibing at me, but I outdo the black blokes. So it goes, far away from the Heimat, far away from wife and children one is walking around in this wilderness.

Henrich Klöpfel writes on 29 June 1915. The party 'quarrels' he mentions refer to the inner party opposition from the left-wing group around Karl Liebknecht, who opposed the support of the majority party for the national war effort in the name of the 'fortress peace', the August 1914 decision to cease all domestic political strife:

After even in our division everyone could get furlough since the 28th of this month (according to a new order preferably with a special justification), one had a free ride home following a decision made by the Reichstag. But this was then again limited only to people on harvest-leave. These are mainly estate-owners and big landed proprietors: therefore people who are actually able to pay for the tickets. But the poor devils have to pay. We who are in the field and have been in the enemy country right from the beginning cannot understand that at all. When we asked the men in question who had already been on harvest-leave if they did work at home, they only laughed. The answer was: They didn't miss me during the first ten or eleven months of the war, so they won't miss me when I am away for a week. There is no rule without exception, this is probably true here as well. Could you not try to change that again? After all I love my family just as much as anybody else loves his land. This procedure is absolutely unbelievable. The quarrels in our party are most deplorable. None of our enemies wants peace and you need two parties to make peace. So it will go on like before. [...] After the war, there will again be a lot of conferences, meetings, party conferences and more of the like held to reinstate the complete unity of the party. All this will cost a lot of money and will take a lot of time which we could use better in my opinion. Such a time of weakness will have the effect that we cannot fight with vigour for what is absolutely necessary for the vast majority of our people. This row in our party at home gives several comrades a heavy heart. But these literates think they can just ignore it? They are going to hear many strong words later on.

Gustav Pröpper reflects upon the deteriorating shop-floor conditions of his comrades at home in a letter written on 15 July 1915:

> When will the miners eventually rouse themselves to shatter the so-called free labour contract, the most miserable of all systems, and put an end to the business of the modern slave-holders! The articles 'Controversial miners' issues' and 'Really sick or just skiving?' [in the *Bergarbeiterzeitung*] demonstrate that the pit-owners always find people who are masters in twisting the truth. They just deny all the harassment etc. On the contrary, with the help of misleading reports they make the miners appear as though they were all idlers and lazybones. This will never change, if, well, if the miners don't want to change it. My blood is really up when I just imagine the possibility of the re-installment of the old misery to an even greater extent instead of having better working conditions, better treatment, equal rights when concluding a labour contract etc. But for the time being, I have no hope that there will be a change for the better. You can hardly blame the uneducated worker when he refuses to join our organizations. Since the leading comrades present a picture of fragmentation and obstruction although they ought to gain as much as possible for the workers right now, for now is the time to do so. Even if this only means to influence the public or to destroy the weapons of agitation of the political opponent. At least the impartiality of the state within the struggle between the different political and economic parties and groups could well be achieved. [...] In my opinion, there is no doubt that the war will end with severe damage being done to our organizations which took a lot of effort to build up. And all that happens only because some highly educated people do not or do not want to understand that to reach a peace settlement right now is tantamount to Germany's defeat.

B. Meier writes on 5 November 1915 from the Eastern Front:

> As I see the circumstances, the whole workers' movement will find fertile ground after the war. And in this respect I just wish that we would strike while the iron is hot with all our joint strength. Self-laceration or the fragmentation of our strength would be a crime these days. The long period of wartime wears down several former hurrah-jingoists. As often as I can I stick the men's noses into these results of their own policy. But I should stop now. Let's hope for the best for our movement.

Nikolaus Osterroth, 29 December 1915, from Russia:

> Well, I do not understand the [party] minority, and that seems to be the case with all other conscripted comrades. Since whenever I have met other soldiers, they ask us very surprised (and in my view rightly so) 'Should all of our terrible sacrifices have been in vain?' Our propaganda suggesting the return to the old status quo would meet with no noteworthy response among the masses of German workers. Unfortunately, the minority seems to add fuel to the flames with their polemic attacks, so that we will have a rather anarchical situation until the next party conference.

Karl Otten writes on 27 August 1916:

> We are all trade-unionists, mostly construction workers and metal workers here at our Recruit Depot Landwehr Regiment No. 53. Although my last notes to you may have conveyed the impression that there were some sort of radicalism or some reckless people around here, there is on the contrary nothing of the kind. Almost nobody here agrees with the tone of the holding out policy [*Durchhaltepolitik*] which has been typical for the *Bergarbeiterzeitung* and the other union newspapers for the last two years. With this way of writing and this policy you help to prolong the war, and that's why one after another is getting weary. And later you are going to complain about the miners not getting themselves registered any more when they return. Is that a surprise? The grounds for this view are: Nobody here believes in any victory for Germany whatsoever. Even officers, we hear, don't believe in a victory. The longer it goes on the worse it becomes. Are you so struck with blindness that you don't understand this matter? Here at the front line everybody knows the soldier's mood. When the cripples who will remain are returning back home, then – and I am not exaggerating, it does not depend on me anyway – the politicians who are in favour of holding out won't have anything to laugh about. There is a wave of indignation and rage going from one man to another. Why these sacrifices which are in vain anyway? Of course, the people who want to make profit out of the murdering of the peoples wish that the World War would carry on for the next 20 years. But you should not let yourself be dazzled by these people. At every opportunity you do not only support these people with your paper, you would not even find

such empty phrases in the *Deutsche Tageszeitung* [the daily paper of the ultra-conservative 'League of Farmers', an agrarian pressure group]. Nothing else than empty talk. There is no conviction whatsoever to be found in these lines.

After Two and a Half Months of War[15]

In November 1914, a Bavarian Reichstag deputy received a war letter written on 17 October. The sender had written to his brother-in-law:

As you know, I am right in front of the enemy. In such a situation one doesn't know if one survives the next hour. Anyway, there is something wrong here, otherwise they would not have send these old soldiers of 36 years to the foremost front line. [...] I have no idea what we are still fighting for anyway, maybe because the newspapers portray everything about the war in a false light which has nothing to do with the reality. As we have heard, America initiated peace negotiations! Can this be true? Everyone who still supports the war is not any longer a human being. There could be no greater misery in the enemy country and at home. The people who still support the war haven't got a clue about anything. [...] Today we are sent again into the trenches of the foremost front line. One could freeze to death at night, since it is very cold in the North of France. But there is nobody who would come for help. The shooting goes on all night long. All men are exhausted. Very often we haven't had anything to eat for three days. The newspapers say that the provisions are excellent. That might be the case for the officers! Very often the horse does not get the oats it deserves. If I stay alive, I will make these things public. Dear brother-in-law, now you can imagine what the war is like. We all want peace. What is the point in conquering half of the world, when we have to sacrifice all our strength. [...] You out there, just champion peace! We don't want to get a mite out of the occupied areas, although we have paid a heavy price for them with our lives and our health. We give away all our worldly possessions and even our freedom. Our only goal is to be with our wife and children again.

Everyday Worries[16]

Since the beginning of the war, worries and concerns about their own situation, but even more about their relatives at home were dominant features of the correspondence of front-line soldiers.

Lance-corporal Jakob Eberhard, in civilian life a Bavarian peasant farmer, writes to his wife whom he addresses as 'mother':

26 May 1915. Dear Mother! Thanks a lot, I have received the butter and the eggs. I won't send you the empty box back, for that will cost me 10 Pfennig, add the 20 Pfennig for your postage that are 30 Pfennig. An egg costs 9 to 10 Pfennig here. If you get an egg for 9 Pfennig, we have to pay 5 Pfennig more, which adds up to 14 Pfennig for one egg. Many thanks to you and father for sending regards from Lieutenant Thaller. He said you should waive your benefits. How can the mayor be so stupid to make you do this? Lieutenant Thaller told father that you should not do that. I'm telling you the same. Go to the district authority. If they send you home, send a complaint to the ministry. I'm telling you, do not sign anything you do not understand, ask father, or just tell them that you don't understand and that your husband will deal with it when he is back. Do it, even if the mayor is coming. Tell him he should also go to the front, then he will know how things are, when the husband is away and the wife is just on her own people try to take advantage of her. Nobody is listening when it comes to all our costs and damages. Go to Hans Bader and talk to him. Tell him that I have sent you. He shall write everything down and send it to member of parliament B. If he meets Doctor Heim [Georg Heim, founder and leader of the Catholic Bavarian Christian Farmers' Association, a populist politician and powerful figure in Bavarian politics], he shall speak to him about these things. Dear Mother. Thank God I am still healthy and can go to church every day, I have received Holy Communion every Sunday which is my dearest. I hope that my letter will reach you in good health. Tell me in your next letter how much an egg is, how much the butter and how much beef. Tell me if the crop is doing all right, if there is plenty of hay, if the children are industrious and well behaved. Tell me how little Georg is and how Mrs Oggermüller and if she has recovered now. Tell me what Schorsch has said and what the fox is doing. You will be very frightened now, because of Italy's entry into the war. But that doesn't matter. Italy will get its share. Last night all bells were ringing between 9 and 10 o'clock because of the great victory in Austria at the fort Przemysl. God will bless us all and gives us victory, he will not abandon us for our cause is just, Mary Mother of God is with us.

A bricklayer writes to his wife in Heroldsbach (Upper Franconia):

Caleinkurt, 22 April 1915

Dear wife, I have received your letter and the tobacco for which I was desperately waiting. Please send a parcel every two weeks, for we don't know if we stay here and where we are going afterwards. Then the mail will take much longer. We have to gather the crop in the whole village now and thresh it. There is still plenty of crop here. Duty starts at five o'clock in the morning until six at night. We only get very little to eat. One doesn't even get what one deserves. And then there are the idle fellows who are rude to the people and who eat away their things and who get six to seven hundred Marks every month. I am boiling over with rage watching this swindle. It is about high time now to finish it. One gets rich and eats away everything, the other who doesn't get anything from home is starving or has to pay from the money received from home. There are quite a few people here who get money from home regularly, twenty Marks here and twenty Marks there. One litre of beer costs 30 Pfennig, a fried herring 20 Pfennig. With these prices the payment is spent in a blink. Dear wife, you write that you have to buy potatoes. How is this possible, when there are two people less to feed and you had more space for potatoes than in previous years? That is impossible! You told me to write to your godmother which I have done twice. But I didn't have a clue about her being godmother to our little girl which you just told me in your last letter. The other day I sent you three Marks in a letter, but I don't know if you have received the money. You always write empty letters, nothing about what I really want and have got to know. Every other soldier's wife tells her husband how much she gets in benefits [benefits paid to the wives of military personnel]. Well, I don't know if you are getting what you should or if I have to intervene. I would also like to know how they treat you back at home. Dear Lies, I think that the children ask for me every day. I think of you the whole day, too. And if you had told me in your last letter if you had received the money, I would have sent you some more. For I have no money to throw away, because I haven't got much. I'm sending you six Marks in this letter. Please tell me, if you receive the money. I am happy about our little Anna being so tall and strong and I am looking forward to the day when I can pick her up and hold her in my arms. But how long will that take and what will we have to undergo?

One hour away from our position a plane dropped some bombs on a railway station. Eight men from the Landsturm were killed and 80 men wounded. I am still healthy and hope the same is true of you.

Alois Wagner writes to his mother, a small-holder in Lower Bavaria, on 15 November 1915:

Dear Mother, just to let you know, I have received the two parcels. They contained cake which was excellent. Thanks a lot. Out here the weather is always bad, we have a lot of water now around here. I have also received the card with the stern verse at the top. We out here assume that the war will still go on for a rather long time. We are undergoing a hard time. Well, I have been here in the field for almost 10 months already, that is quite something in these critical times. We have had to endure a lot, so it is hard to write about what we come across sometimes. Well, I am surprised myself that I am still healthy and that something always saved my bacon. One needs to be lucky to get away like this. I have already told you what I need urgently. I am sorry myself that I need the same things again. Then again a lot of money is gone. And at home everything goes downhill and breaks down. If only the time would come again that I was garrisoned and that I could be together with you. Well, that would make a difference. Well, it can't go on forever. There must be an end sometime [...]. Furlough will commence again within the next few days. If I am lucky I might come next spring before the swallows are returning. How is it going at home, I suppose everything and food in particular is quite expensive, hopefully. Where will this all end when it goes on, further and further. How is the grain trade going? I suppose not very well, obviously. Have you got a lot of potatoes? How is it going with the sows. I reckon they are rather expensive. Please tell me about these things back at home. Well, it is a heavy cross to bear in this world. One always hopes that there will be another time. Well, I have to finish now. How is grandmother Katherina? Please stay healthy dear mother. I hope so much that it is God's will that I will be so lucky and see you all again, and if this is not going to be in 1915, then it will be in 1916. Send my love to Maxl and his wife, also to grandmother Hochhäusl and her mother. I send you all my love, also to Mother Mari and Father Hans and the four sisters. Please write again. When the weather stays like this, we will drown. The trenches are full of water, so that we have to walk across open fields. Although it is not nice, I am always in a good mood. I hope to see you again.

A farmer from Gollhofen (Central Franconia) writes to his wife:

France, 25 February 1917. Dear Rika! Today we celebrate Penance Day, but out here you wouldn't notice. Again, I am in position and everything is the same here, Sunday or workday. This time we are in a very bad position. We are at the same spot where the Frenchmen broke through on the 16th. The position is badly damaged by fire, which means a lot of work to do for us. The Frenchmen are just 30 metres, sometimes not even more than 10 to 15 metres away. There is fighting with hand grenades every day. It seems as if the war never comes to an end. When will this murdering finally stop? We don't like it at all to be out here around the clock in this hail of bullets and hardly have time to get some sleep. We don't hear anything about peace. How will this brutal struggle ever end? We hope from one day to the next, but it is always the same. We neither know where the attack will take place. But when it starts again, many thousands of people will die. Dear Rika, now your oxen are gone and Heinerle has pulled quite a bit. You can't have a lot of cattle left, after you have sold two of them. How are the twin calves doing, I reckon they can't be very big yet. Dear Rika, do you still have the old cow or what are you doing with it? The others will also calve very soon, then you will have some milk. The weather here is rather nice today. It was freezing quite a bit this morning. So you can already carry out the dung, there is time enough for seeding. Dear Rika, you told me you want to submit a request. But that won't make any difference, so save yourself the effort. If you haven't done it yet, just leave it. Dear Rika, you always say I should write more often, but we don't have much time. Besides, the light is very bad, sometimes it doesn't work at all. In our dugout we need light at day- and nighttime. What does Leonhard Keller write? I reckon he doesn't like it out here either. Dear Rika, I have received all your parcels, also No 14. I will write to Babett tomorrow. Please don't send me so much. Two parcels will be enough for a week, I haven't been in need yet. Thank God, I am still healthy and I hope the same is true of all of you as well. Now I finish this letter, will furthermore trust in God and hope for the best.

The miner and trade unionist Richard Schiller writes from Flanders on 13 October 1915:

> I can definitely assure you that the troops' mood out here is extremely bad. I simply cannot imagine them fighting successfully for another winter. I have heard too much in this respect. Some soldiers condemn the war in such a reckless manner that even I was surprised. Although it is the same over there, maybe it is even worse. If they still want to go on with the war, despite the increasing losses and the hatred against the war, they will gamble away any success in the long term. [...] And then it is the exorbitant prices at home which cause desperate complaints by the wives in their letters and worsen the mood fundamentally. On top of this, there is the unjust treatment against the hard-working troops compared to the military leaders. The contrast between payment and living conditions of soldiers and officers could hardly be starker.

Karl Matthias Schiffer, chairman of the Central Association of Christian Textile Workers, describes the mood of the population after two years of war in a letter addressed to Matthias Erzberger and to Arnold Wahnschaffe, secretary of state in the chancellery:

> 18 August 1916/[...] The mood at the front lines and also at home is worsening week after week, not only according to my own observations, but also according to the impressions of several earnest people with a good understanding of the mindset of our soldiers and of the people at home. For months one does not receive any war letters at all without moaning for peace. At home one can find the same alarming signs to an increasing degree, particularly among the working class and the lower middle class. [...] One cannot help but get the impression that the English and French soldiers know much better than our troops what they are fighting for. There is the widespread conviction among army members that the war is only going on for the benefit of the capitalists. For a long time there has been a sinister and silent agitation at work to spread ideas like this. It is frightening to see several politically quite educated people expressing this opinion more and more openly, verbally and in writing, although they once went to war with ardent zeal and patriotism.

Joseph Reininger was the son of a farmer from Upper Bavaria. His letters reveal futile hopes for peace.

18 February 1915:

Dear Parents and siblings, I received the large parcel and the card to Bertl today. The parcel was undamaged, but the smoked meat is all grey. It is still edible, though. Thank you very much for everything. I am still well and healthy and hope the same is true of you. I am still in the old quarters. We have an extremely tiny room and we have to sleep on straw. Food is sometimes not very good. Many horses coming back from the front have got lice. And now we have them, too. The horse lice are big ones and they bite. We burn them as soon as we get them and we beat our blankets properly, so now it is quiet again. Now I have got five heavy Belgian horses to look after, all beautiful animals. We are short on hay. Even the farmer hasn't got any hay left, just as much as he needs for his own livestock and we are not allowed to take everything from him. We have to feed the horses with field mangel [*runkel*], for there is a shortage of oats in Germany. There are lots of field mangels around here, many are buried in the fields. There are almost no cattle left. Some are still in the fields. Sometimes there are whole areas of several thousands of square metres completely frozen und rotten. They have to be ploughed up. It was read out that we have to save bread. Until now we used to get 750 grams every three days. Now they say 500 grams must be enough and they will pay us the difference. We are all right with that because we want to do everything to make Germany win the war. Apparently the Frenchmen over here are getting enough to survive, too, because they still believe that they can win the war, but that won't be easy. Over here they have already started to seed oats. The ammunition platoon drivers have to help on the fields, because many farmers haven't got any horses left. Much to my regret I learned about Ludwig Oberliner who was killed in action. Quite frequently I have heard stories about dead soldiers still lying far away in the field since early December. They can't be buried, because nobody can reach them and carry them away. On Sunday, I visited Zetl who was pleased. I wrote a card as well. Please tell me always when you have received some mail from me and tell me the date of the letters.

Postcard dated 14 July 1915:

Dear parents and siblings! I received the letter from 5 July, many thanks for that. The main thing is that I am still healthy and well and hope the same is true of you. As I could read in your letter it is all going very easy at home and when Bertl gets harvest furlough then you want for nothing. You asked my opinion about an end of the war. I don't know that either. It is a big question. I would be happy if it is in three months time, just let's hope for the best. It will all come to nothing with Hans' leave when Bertl is coming home. But it is all right, if just one is at home. My best wishes to all of you, good bye your son Joseph.

North of France, 19 November 1915:

Dear Parents and Siblings! Here I am sending again a short letter from the enemy country. I haven't received anything from you for a month. How are you all? Have you finished threshing by now? I read in the newspaper that everything at home is in short supply. Now almost nobody could be out there [i.e. at home]. A comrade from my quarters came back from leave three days ago and said that there is nothing outside any more. I am not longing for that any more. I am in an empty house with five others. It is not big, but we have enough space. Some days ago we set up the electricity which is good and cheap because we don't have to pay anything. Now we are sitting in the heated living room every night. There is just a lack of fuel, so we have to start stealing again. It is getting pretty cold here with some frost. I would appreciate it if you sent me the warm underwear. I always assumed we would get that sort of equipment, but nothing has happened yet. They haven't got anything left. Yesterday I got a card from Bertl. He is probably in the trenches already. He won't like it and he will need some time to get used to it. Hans is about 30 km away from my position, and Bertl is not much further away. So let's see if I can get furlough. Zetl is in Lille in a military hospital, but you will probably know that already. I couldn't visit him because we don't get any leave for trips to Lille. I received the newspaper only once in November. Please don't order it any longer. You can tell me all about the news from Wasserburg in your letters. I can read about the war news in the newspapers from Munich sent to my comrades. They are three or four days earlier than the Wasserburg newspaper. Anyway, I am losing my interest in reading any newspaper at all, for they are all lying to us. I don't believe in an end to the war anymore, unless they can definitely tell us that now we have peace. In an article it was said that the war is like a lawsuit: easy to start, but hard to get it over with. Hans hasn't got any furlough yet either, it is not easy for him, too.

Written 12 December 1916:

Dear Parents and Siblings! I received your letter from 8 December, many thanks. I read that you submitted a request for furlough for me. It is possible that I get furlough. It might be rather quick, for we are going into the trenches sometime. It would be all right. Sepp Simmer is with the 8th Company 16th Infantry Regiment. If I get back home I will sign up for the 8th company 16th Infantry Regiment. The weather here is dull and bad, nothing specific. How is it at home for smoking tobacco? I have more than enough here. I also sent a parcel with gaiters, a watch, old socks, vest and pants. You can mend and trim them. Some of them you can send back, but just trimmed, otherwise they will be ripped again easily. Maybe there will be an end soon. That is what we wish for the most. That is all news I can think of. Best wishes Yours Joseph.

Written 18 March 1917:

Dear Parents and Siblings! I received the two cardletters from 11 March and the parcels with butter, sausages, candles and smoked meat, many thanks for that. The main thing is that I thank God I am still healthy and well and hope the same is true of you. So far I have received all the parcels. If they confiscate them, they have to confiscate the gentlemen's ones as well. And I don't think they are prepared to do that. Bertl is lucky having some money and some quiet time, that is quite a lot these days. [...] We are on rest for five days. What a relief to sleep properly again. We don't have good quarters and no beds, but we are happy just to have a bit of peace and quiet at night. This time is was only five days that we were in position, but what a bad position it was! It was a shell hole. I was happy to save my bacon. They had laid in on us pretty badly. A comrade from Rott who also serves at the horse depot was lightly wounded by a mine splinter. One has to duck down nicely to get away. We are going back in position on the 21st, this time for ten days. The last time we were out there, a comrade of mine and I wanted to buy something in the canteen, but it was so expensive that we didn't want to waste the money. A pound of sausages for five Marks seven Pfennig and a pound of smoked meat and not even of good quality also for seven Marks. It is all a usurer's war. Why do they give us money out here in the first place and why don't they provide us properly with food? Now you see the great value of your parcels out here. That's why I don't want to buy anything here for the dear money when you at home get less than a third for your things. Within the next few days I will send you 20 Marks via postal order. Did you already get the two parcels? I think that we will see some change and that the long looked-for peace will come in two or three months. Best wishes to all of you Yours Joseph.

In the trenches, 7 June 1917:

Dear Parents and Siblings! I received your card from 28 May and the parcel with smoked meat and the parcels No. 2 and 3. Many thanks for that. I wish there could be a parcel every day, for we have really just very little bread. I'd rather have been with you on Whitsunday than in France, because here it was like every other day. I see that you still have plenty to eat. If only I could be at home once in a while then I could eat my fill again. Hopefully it is going to change soon. Today is the feast of Corpus Christi and I am sitting here in the trench. This morning there was a heavy drumfire, but a bit more to the right. We will soon have an offensive here. On our right, the Englishmen already launched a heavy attack. We had to move a bit to the right. The weather is nice and very hot. It is quite a tedious life in the trenches. Hopefully we won't stay here for too long. You think that I will get furlough soon, but it will all come to nothing, for there are so many comrades before me. If I hadn't been on leave at Christmas, I could go now. The request won't help and there is no point in asking at the General Command, for there are enough hands to work with you. What does Hans write? Does he not get any furlough, too? Have you been haymaking already? What about the machine? How are you doing with it? It doesn't really matter, if you cannot cut the hay. The machine will be fine even after the war. Maybe the war will come to an end soon and when we are back home everything will be easy again. The main thing is that I get through it all right. Best wishes to all of you. Yours, Joseph.

'Swindle' – that was the most popular expression for a seemingly endless war. Johann Friedrich, a shoemaker from Schweinfurt (Lower Franconia), writes a war letter to his wife on 23 September 1917:

I can't get used to the swindle any more since I have left you. I am always with you in my thoughts. I haven't got anything done since I am here. Yesterday I went to Colmar on an official journey. At least this way time goes by quicker than up there on our mountain. I am going to wait for another three or four more weeks, since people generally talk about an end of that swindle /: you know what I mean.:/ If not, then I'll quit, for I have been a prisoner of war in the German army long enough!

Perceptions and Images of the Enemies[17]

Otto Rümmler, a Social Democratic miner, informs his comrades at home in October 1914 of his impressions in Belgium. With the terms 'yellow' trade unions and Hintze-followers he refers to tame company unions:

Dear Comrades! Some experiences from organized and non-organized workers, respectively from some 'yellow' unionists or Hintze-followers. Before we marched out of the garrison, some of them stated: when we are eventually on enemy territory, then we will start to loot! But they could not wait and started to loot in their own country by stealing grapes and fruits from the trees although there was enough to eat. In the enemy country, they became even more mischievous. They did not ask if a family had enough to eat or not. I am not able to list all single cases, for it would take too much space and time, I would have to write an entire book. Therefore, I only want to highlight a few events. Unfortunately, I don't even know the wrongdoers' names. On 2 October, we have been in Ergunnites (Belgium). There, some Landsturm men took the bread of a family of seven (which is indeed quite a rare type of family) literally from their table. The husband or rather the family father wants to save the bread for his children and declares that it is the only thing they have got and that the family hasn't eaten for three days. But that doesn't touch our Hintze-followers. They hold the rifle on the father's chest, the man has to keep silent and stays hungry together with his family. Others did an even better job. They enter a family home and ask for everything they wish to have. Everything happens very calmly. Suddenly one of the men gets the spring feeling. The husband is in the way, however, but this obstacle can be overcome, one of the Landsturm men holds a rifle loaded with live ammunition on the man's chest, the other takes his anger out on the wife, then they swap and the man has to watch silently. However, these were private soldiers [*Wehrmänner*]. [...] When one is talking about the Germans in this respect, then it should be clear that the capitalists are to blame, as they have only created this brutal sect.

In January 1915, one of the members of the Social Democratic miner's union writes from Herseaux, a town in Belgium close to the French border, situated about 25km behind the front line:

Often, the roar of artillery guns is so intense that one can't even hear a single shot but only a ceaseless rumbling going on for hours. As much as we are terrified by this roar of guns and when we imagine the extent of the dreadful devastation it might have caused, we are as much puzzled about the few dry lines in the official war report by the Army Command the following day. The English and the French have done a pretty good job in getting entrenched in the soil. It was just recently that a cavalry constable and an artillery officer told me not to be fooled about the proficiency of the French and the English army. The latter in particular, they said, consists mostly of men who have been soldiers for 10 to 12 years and who are excellent shooters. When our formations come to us for rest after being at the front lines, they claim in unison: the French and the English are standing like a stone wall. Hopefully, our troops will be able to gain a victory soon on enemy territory. – Our first stop in Belgium was the city of Leuven. This city is well known due to the franc-tireur fighting which caused its destruction by our troops at the time [German troops destroyed about one-sixth of all buildings and killed 248 civilians in Leuven from 25 to 28 August 1914]. The German press then reported that only a fifth of the city was destroyed. But that is far from touching reality. At least 800 buildings have been destroyed. If there have indeed been franc-tireurs in every single building targeting our troops, then there can't be any doubt about a *well-prepared* franc-tireur war. From some houses, there was no shooting. These ones were marked with white posters given out by the back area headquarters with the inscription: '*This house is to be protected*'. Also, several people apparently wrote on their front doors: 'Please, protect this house, there are good people living here', or 'there are pro-German people living here'.

August Balke was a member and functionary of the Alter Verband, the Social Democratic miners' union. In a letter dated 8 August 1915 to Hermann Sachse, the chairman of the union, he describes his impressions of the occupied part of Russia and the conclusions he drew from his perceptions of Russian 'culture':

Dear Hermann!

Sitting here in Russia – I happen to be at rest – with a glass of Schultheiß [beer]. By chance I had the opportunity to see the havocked landscape of East Prussia. You have certainly heard and read about this, so it is unnecessary to write a lot about it. It looks bad. But a different story: It is well known that the first impression one gets about any matter is almost always right. And here I must say: The impression I've got here in Russian-Lithuania and Russian-Poland about the local 'culture' serves nothing more than to strengthen my view on the war of which you are already well aware. I have seen a lot of misery in my life, but what I have seen here beggars all description. If you judge the level of culture of a people by their housing – and I have found that this is nearly the best benchmark – , then you will come here to an almost horrifying result. Old wooden huts, not good enough to be cattle-sheds, poor furniture and vermin are the possessions of the lower classes. I claim: there is not one German worker who still lives in similar conditions. Only here one starts to realize what a blessing our unions are, and actually to appreciate the activities of the labour movement. These circumstances must have a terribly demoralizing impact on the Russian army. A people living in such conditions can only be driven to fight by force; compared to a people who loves its fatherland – although it is self-evident that there is a lot to improve – the first one is always at a disadvantage. Russia can harm us; but it will never be victorious. We would have to pull out the crosses from the soil and turn them into swords – in the words of Georg Herwegh [Balke cites a line from a poem by the radical-democratic writer Georg Herwegh, published in 1841] – to fight the introduction of such circumstances.

Could the great Hungarian Maurus Jorkeÿ [a novelist] and Henryk Sienkewicz [a popular Polish novelist who was awarded the Nobel Prize for literature in 1905] not at least mention *this* kind of culture in their glorifications of Poland once in a while? We German workers say thank you very much for a similar fate! If the separatists in the camp of the German workers are honest, then it is their duty to tell their people how it looked and looks like in National Poland. They have no reason at all to debase the virtue of the unions by their nationalist aspirations;

this should be told to the Polish workers among us [many industrial workers at the Ruhr and in Silesia were Poles].

There is just the one thing to be done: to ensure everything against a Russian invasion. And therefore, you have to grant whatever it takes to continue the war. The Russians have to be deterred from returning to Germany forever. Every German who has seen the situation here, however cursory, will and must support this wish. But those who like to give different, so-called 'good' advice to the German workers should go back to *their* own countries, for there is more, much more reason for improvement here. At the risk of insults being heaped upon us, we unionists have to stay away from elements like these. This applies first of all to the people at home. If we do come home, we will do what we ought to do. For the time being, all the best wishes to all colleagues.

Hermann Baur was a brother in the Pallotine order and served in the Reserve-Infantry-Regiment 87. In diary entries from December 1915 he notes:

11 December [1915]:
The position collapses partly, due to persistent rainfall. Our men have reached an agreement with the French to cease fire. They bring us bread, wine, sardines etc., we bring them Schnaps. When we clean up the trench, everybody is standing on the edges, as otherwise it is not any longer possible. The infantry does not shoot any more, just the crazy artillery. If an officer comes along, they are waving to us so that we can go back. It is just the same over here. The masters make war, they have a quarrel, and the workers, the little men, are [word missing] and have to stand there fighting against each other. Is that not a great stupidity. But God is allowing this divine punishment and it might end completely different than everybody is expecting today.

12 December:
Someone took a photograph of sergeant Wiesler standing on the edge of the trench together with a Frenchman! Afterwards we were relieved at midnight.

29 December:
Our lieutenant brought a note written by the French that they have to throw 15 mines (heavy ones) a day, but only 2 or 3 would explode. They

would only target dead spots. There they could explode. It seems as if they have grown tired, too. Well, if this were to be decided according to the number of votes, we would have been long home by now.

August Schmidt, a soldier serving in a replacement battalion in Cologne, comments in a letter from 28 October 1914 on his perception of British soldiers:

As I already let you know through a postcard, I have been with a convoy of POWs to Hameln near Hildesheim on 23 and 24 October. There were three convoys, largely Englishmen who had been captured near Lille. Some Frenchmen, Turkos [name for the Algerian regiments in the French army] and franc-tireurs were among them. For it is so common these days to bad-mouth the English, in particular the English soldier, it was very interesting for me to see for myself the quality of the English soldiers. And I have to say that I have experienced just the opposite of what is commonly said and written about this army these days. The English soldier may be a dangerous enemy and a good shooter in the field, and that is probably why there are so many resentments against him. On the other hand, the mood against English financial circles is transferred on to the soldiers. But as a prisoner of war, the Englishman acts very considerately and gentlemanly. At least, none of our men who accompanied the convoy has had any trouble at all.

In April 1917, Friedrich M., a lieutenant in the 240th Infantry Division, notes in his diary aspects of a conversation with a lieutenant from the 52nd Infantry Division. This officer had told him about his experiences during the battle of the Somme in 1916:

Anyway, according to these stories, the English are our bravest enemies. It was in particular the English aeroplanes that accomplished a big deal at the Somme. They were getting at the artillery with machine-gun fire. They attacked our captive balloons. At first, they shot the lookout dead who tried to get away with a parachute. Then, they set the balloon itself on fire. An English pilot who had crashed with his plane defended himself with a machine gun as long as he had enough ammunition. Only then, he surrendered. English pilots declared that our pilots do exactly the same thing over there. – He also said that the English over there had some prisoners in their trenches for services and that they treated them very badly. On the other hand, it apparently happened quite often that English prisoners 'died' during the convoys led by the uhlans [cavalry troops]. Here you can see that the Englishmen who are Teutons like us, are to a large extent as proficient as we are.

Franz B. had worked in the ready made clothing industry in Berlin before he was drafted in 1915. While on duty in the French village of Aussonce, he notes on 6 May 1917 in his diary:

The German army report is hung out in Aussonce every day and yesterday I could read that our aeroplanes have heavily bombed up military camps, ammunition depots, railway installations and suchlike behind the enemy lines with great success!!! But the army report did not mention that the Frenchmen took revenge in the following night, that they destroyed Chatelain almost completely and battered the village of Juniville terribly, that hundreds of our soldiers had to pay for the German 'bombing success' with their lives and hundreds with severe injuries or permanent crippledness, that enormous values of material and provisions, horses and cattle were destroyed!!!! Every pilot, no matter if he is German, French, English or from any other nation, who lets himself be drawn into this cowardly, excessively perfidious deed of throwing bombs, is a scoundrel, a criminal on an enormous scale. And whenever they can get hold of them, the infantry should crucify every one of them alive – irrespective of the nation – and let him hang there until ravens, crows and other scavengers have eaten the last bone of these pathetic 'heroes'.

Prussia and the Other German States[18]

The relations between troops from the different contingents of the German army, the Saxonian, Bavarian, Prussian contingents and those from Baden and Württemberg, were strained throughout the war. The Prussian troops were disliked, if not hated particularly among Bavarian units. Reports from police authorities, police informers or denunciations provide evidence for the resentment of Bavarian soldiers. Helene Wendtlandt, while on holiday, writes to the Prussian Secretary of War on 9 August 1918:

His Excellency the Secretary of War,

Being highly anxious about my fatherland I would like to inform you about some alarming and deplorable incidents I was able to observe during my journey from a spa across Bavaria.

I was sitting in a very crowded fourth-class train compartment from Buchloe to Munich. There was a soldier taking off his uniform coat and changing into a traditional Bavarian coat during the journey. He was talking filthily about the emperor suggesting that he, the emperor, had incited the entire world against us. Some others said that the King had sold us to the Prussians in 1870 and now we do not want to belong to Germany any longer. The French worker has a much better life than the German worker, so we'll be with the French who will welcome us with open arms. We are not playing this game any longer. Our enemies only complain about the Prussian militarism but not about a German one. Only the priests and the capitalists benefit from the long lasting war they are responsible for. If Germany would win the war it would be a divine punishment. I told him that he would be committing a criminal offence by talking like this, but he answered that he would talk the same way even if he sat next to a general for he had risked his life long enough. There were some more soldiers in the same compartment, but nobody stood up against him. They all agreed with him and poured scorn on me vindicating the emperor so that I had to fall silent. The mood was so hostile that it is not advisable to admit being from Berlin as long as one is in Bavaria.

When I was going from Munich to Tölz a Bavarian soldier told me that it would be a shame when the enemy would occupy German territory, but anyhow the Bavarians would not be participating [in the war] any longer.

Report of the Central Police Office in Bavaria to the Bavarian Ministry of War about railway surveillance on 10 August 1917:

During a further check I noticed several soldiers in an open third-class compartment, among them an NCO of the Bavarian train battalion, having a lively conversation with some civilians. I remained standing in the aisle and listened to this conversation for quite a while.

The soldiers mainly wished for an early end to the war and mentioned that Germany was partly also responsible for the prolonging of the war. Germany had devised a plan for itself and tried to implement it. As long as Bavaria was with Prussia there would be war, for the loudmouthed Prussians had been involved in every war yet. The NCO mentioned that most of the soldiers were prepared to do everything if only they were treated fairly. He had lost everything because of the war and his family was depending on the small family benefits, whereas the civil servants were getting cost of living bonuses and those civil servants who were active soldiers were even getting double salaries. Furthermore, a recent newspaper article had referred to the soldiers' wives as being lazy.

The liaison officer of the Replacement Battalion 20th Bavarian Infantry Regiment reports on 24 August 1918:

While accompanying a transport to the Western Front to which the liaison officer was admitted by the battalion on his own wish as an escort NCO, he noticed a specific dislike and even certain unjustified prejudices on the part of the Bavarian troops against the Prussian troops which quite often led to brawls.

In a letter sent to the Bavarian Ministry of War in August 1916 some of the rumours about the prevailing antipathy towards the Prussians are mentioned:

All kinds of tall tales that are considered hard facts whip up the mood. One of them that I heard not only in the Bavarian Forest, but also in Munich, in Upper Bavaria and even in Strasbourg, is particularly worth mentioning. It goes like this: At Verdun Bavarian troops had to recapture a position five times which the Prussians had lost to the enemy. In the end, the Bavarians felt so bitter about this that a Bavarian regiment turned against the Prussians, resulting in some dead and wounded men in the Prussian unit. The Bavarian regiment was supposed to be decimated as a punishment.

The military authorities tried to curb the ill feelings between the soldiers of the German states without success. A letter written by the Deputy General Command of the first Bavarian Army Corps from 9 June 1916 states:

As a follow-up […], attention is drawn to the ban for all troops on all conversations in pubs or trains which refer to alleged ill feelings or disagreements between individual field units or between the troops from different German states. As these rumours are without any foundation and emerge only due to the idle talk of some individuals who try to show off with their supposed knowledge in the homeland, severe disciplinary action is to be taken against those who initiate these rumours. Furthermore, the army members have to abstain from any comments about the alleged dissimilar distribution of food in the different German states. For these people are not in a position to judge this matter, conversations like these cause nothing but unsubstantiated ill feelings among the population, the more so as the government aims to do everything possible for a fair and even distribution.

Injuries, Death and Killing[19]

In a study on the psychological consequences of war, published in 1914, Georg Wunderle reflects upon killing as the core task of soldiers in wartime:

Every single soldier is the military leader's tool and has to contribute his share with all his strength to realize the commander's will. Breaking the enemy's resistance is in the end the purpose of that will. The most perfect way of achieving this goal is to exterminate the enemy's life. And here lies the soldier's sanguinary duty. It might be easier for him to damage and destroy other people's property, but the basically peaceful man will always have an uncanny feeling about the mass-destruction of the lives of others. He is expected to kill people who never did him any harm, people he never got to know, people who might be hope and support for their families. 'One must not think of all this', declare the older soldiers in particular who have already taken part in combat. 'Otherwise one would not be able to commit a single murder.' This does not really apply to long-distance fighting. To aim at targets that are far away is not a 'personal' matter, so to speak; one does not see the targeted man falling, one does not hear his cry of pain and does not become aware of his death throes. [...] But when he has to butcher people in face-to-face fighting again and again, then the inner, secretive resistance can be gradually overcome by a raging thirst for blood. And the war merely legitimizes violence, and not also brutality!

Many soldiers who arrived fresh at the front could not imagine that they could be injured or killed themselves. Lieutenant Eberbach, who was wounded during an attack on the Western Front, wrote in two letters while in French captivity about the death of a friend and his own injury.

25 October 1915:
I cannot and want not to offer my condolences to the Druffner family, because I cannot and want not to believe that he has fallen. We both always ruled this out for ourselves.

29 October 1915:
[…] I did have a faint idea of returning home not without punishment. And by the way, this was meant to happen, at least I don't know any comrade who has not been killed, injured or taken prisoner. Nonetheless, I had never thought of getting injured myself, that thought gave me courage as well during the last battle. I was even laughing while fighting and was happy that we initially fended off the enemy's assault, and I thought that I would get a decoration after all. Well, now a piece of lead did hit my nose, which is just tough luck!

Walter Ludwig served on the Western Front as a reserve officer from the beginning of the war. As he had had an interest in psychological phenomena, he used his own observations and a survey among a small sample of front officers and other injured soldiers for a study into 'The Psychology of Fear in Wartime'. It was published in 1920. The following excerpts include quotes from his survey:

The most explicit form of hope is a belief in one's own invulnerability. […] 'One can observe some people with a special feeling of security. They tend to think that nothing can happen to them.' 'When I was wounded for the first time at the Somme [1916], I was always convinced that nothing would hit me. And thus I hardly felt any fear even in the worst danger. It was similar with my second injury in Flanders. I had always been able to get away which made me think that nothing really bad could happen to me.' […] 'As far as I am concerned I have always kept the fear distant by telling myself and even having the actual feeling: you are not meant to die yet. Filled with this thought I felt light of heart.' […] People fear severe injuries in particular when they are conjuring up the thought of a permanent disability. To imagine being crippled is enough […] to make death seemingly desirable.

A great role even for people who are far from being malingerers plays the idea to get slightly wounded, without too much pain and permanent damage, in order to escape the dangers and the exertions for a little while. The soldiers call those injuries 'tango shot' or 'Heimat shot'.

The war letter of a medical student who was hit by shrapnel fire during an attack on Belgrade in October 1915 illustrates what soldiers thought in the very moment they were wounded:

When I saw my comrades falling down I thought: Now you are getting your share as well. In the deepest anxiety of my soul I called upon God. 'Oh my dear God, please help, help, save me, have mercy with the shot I am getting.' I am prepared to sacrifice an arm or a leg, I also take a shot in the chest. Considering an abdominal wound I was thinking if my bowels were filled, if I had been eating a lot recently. Considering a shot in the head I told myself that those were usually fatal. One can bleed to death when being hit at the carotid artery. Suddenly I thought about my eyes. If only I'm not blinded. I might be prepared to sacrifice one eye, but rather not even this. If only I'm not blinded. Now you are getting a hit. I am raising my hands towards my head and turn it left. The same instant I feel a terrible hit against my right ear. It is a feeling as if somebody had hit my right cheek with a rubber truncheon. There's a heavy jerk and then a clear crack of bones. [...] On my right side I see a comrade dropping to the ground with a wounded leg. On my left side I see a comrade holding his head with both hands. He has got his share, too. [...] There is blood dripping on my hands, too, and on my coat. When I see it I scream: I am bleeding to death, I am bleeding to death.

Heavily wounded soldiers and those who were arm or leg amputees or blinded usually received only a meagre pension. A return to their old job was often not possible. The authorities in German and Austria–Hungary were keen to reskill them and to find other jobs for them. Excerpts from a list with 'Possible Assignments for Disabled Ex-Servicemen' (1915):

Chemical industry: people without an arm or foot can work as office attendants, gatekeepers or service a set of scales. With certain fingers missing on one hand they are usable for the production of soda, barium-chloride, chlorine sodium bicarbonate etc. as well as in the depot, for transport, in chambers and for work on the yard. [...]

Dyers: No usability with missing arm or underarm (artificial foot with stilt not usable.) [...]

Unskilled labourers: Possible usability with a missing foot, eye or jawbone. [...]

Cardboard-cutters: [...] One eye is enough. Missing left foot would have to be substituted with an artificial leg. [...]

Mechanics: Both arms necessary. Fine-mechanical engineers can have a missing arm. [...]

Photographers: Retouchers or copists can do without a left arm or some single fingers or an eye. [...]

Dental technicians: Has to have both hands, but can have artificial legs.

Rumours about secret hospitals where heavily mutilated soldiers were hidden from their relatives circulated throughout the war. These contained a kernel of truth as artillery shots frequently led to excrutiating facial wounds or to the amputation of both arms and legs (so-called 'basket men'). Soldiers with such severe mutilations were treated in special hospitals and often cancelled every contact with their relatives. The rumours reflected the intensive, desperate hopes of many relatives at home who still hoped to be reunited with brothers, sons or husbands who had been reported as 'fallen' or 'missing'. The Central Police Authority in Bavaria reports on 31 August 1917 about a case it had investigated:

Lately there were some rumours spreading in Eichendorf und the surrounding area about so-called secret hospitals where mutilated soldiers were hidden from their relatives. At the instigation of the Bavarian Ministry of War in Munich, Detective Sergeant Grob conducted an investigation on the spot and established the following facts:

Wilhelm Höringer, single, elementary school teacher, born 28 December 1890 in Eichendorf, son of Michael and Katharina, née Krenn, shopkeepers in Eichendorf, served in the 4th Bavarian Infantry Regiment 7th Company and was killed in action at the Eastern front on 4 September 1916. His sister, Elsa Höringer, single, sales assistant, born 28 October 1897 in Eichendorf, Bavarian citizen, living with her parents in Eichendorf, employed by company Schötz, bank and colonial goods store, in Neumarkt upon Rott from 1 March until 1 July 1917.

According to her statement she learned about the so-called secret hospitals in March or April 1917 for the first time. During a train journey from Eichendorf to Neumarkt upon Rott an unknown person told a story about a family father who had managed to visit his son in one of those hospitals. But on the first sight of his son the father dropped dead due to a heart attack. As a result of this story she got the idea her brother Wilhelm might be mutilated and in one of those hospitals. In the following she wrote three made-up letters in shorthand without signature and circulated them. Transcription of these letters is attached. [...]

By doing so she hoped to find out where her brother was. She could not believe he had been killed in action as it was stated in a note by his unit. It had not occurred to her that she would commit a criminal offence by spreading these rumours.

One of the fictitious letters by her brother, dated 19 July 1917, says:

My beloved sister Elsa!

Today is a day of great joy for me, since my first male nurse is visiting me to write a letter to you for me. You have probably received the last lines we wrote eight weeks ago. Dear Elsa, I will tell you everything and in every detail, but please, you have to keep it a secret. Not long and I have been here for one year. I am longing for all my dear ones and my beautiful Heimat more than I can say. I have lost so much and thank God that I still have a clear mind although I have no hands and feet any more. I had yet to undergo eight surgeries and have now two human parts. I have no difficulties to speak, but I haven't got any ears. Three weeks ago I had my last surgery. Now they can't remove any more parts, because there is only head and torso left. I am not so much in pain any longer, because I always get chloroform injections. Forgive me that I have written to you. But I am much better now. I will gladly bear every hardship, because I probably deserve it. I hope you are all well at home. Sometimes I am in the depths of despair, because I feel like I am living among wolves. I think we are 70 people here who are all said to be dead. Please have a holy mass said for me on 4 April, maybe

I could die soon. Please, dear Elsa, don't let on about your feelings so that nobody gets suspicious. Don't be sad about me, for you can't help me anyway, everything is lost. When I am going to die, you will get my watch and my wallet back. My thoughts are always with you and with the dear Heimat. I would have wished to see the parents and siblings once again. But never ask to see me again, for my appearance is horrible. […] Be consoled and receive all my best wishes, Yours Willi.

Many soldiers developed a habit of writing a farewell note to their relatives immediately before an attack. Sometimes their superiors asked them to do so. The NCO Hermann Droege writes on 7 September 1914 to his bride Ida Mohrhoff:

On the battlefield in the heaviest artillery fire: My beloved, dear Ida! I have no idea if I will still get away alive today. If I do fall, you can be assured that my last thoughts were with you and with my dear parents. It is terrible. The earth is trembling. Today I have really learned how to pray and feel very relieved and I will go into death strengthened and consoled, if it has to be. If I can't write another card, please give my parents notice of this one. […] Yours Hermann

The newspaper *Berliner Tageblatt* published a poem on 4 April 1916:

Death in Battle
That is a rather strange thing
how they go to die in the field!
They sink to the ground in rows
And no grievance is to be heard.
No pomp, no pride any longer!

The reaper's scythe is flashing,
he is striding augustly
and ears and ears are falling.
He is mowing with a powerful hand
until the day has drawn to a close.
Whoever has been ripened for the Fatherland
is sinking and keeping silent.

And there is nothing than mowing.
And once there will be a time,

when death has harvested enough,
then the fallen soldiers' blood will become the bread,
the holy bread that will give the grandsons strength and faith
to build up a new time on the old ruins.

Ernst Zahn

In times of war, soldiers were victims but also perpetrators. The factory worker Erich Schurack writes on 12 December 1916 from the Eastern Front.

Yesterday we have accomplished a very hard blood job, we repulsed two attacks by Cossacks with six machine guns. We got them on horseback in the fog, when they were 500 metres away, and then all hell broke loose for them. Only a few could escape. Two horsemen came as close as 50 metres, their bodies were literally sawn up. Best wishes Yours Erich

E. Reubke, a young soldier, contemplates his duty as a machine-gun rifleman:

It can easily all go wrong, for when they have found out a machine-gun position for a start, they let loose on us with all their weapons, since the machine guns are really terrible arms. One wouldn't know until experiencing the impact of such a weapon working on its most powerful level while lying behind it. The whole work takes place on the ground – mainly these 30 seconds of the most fabulous work and hurry until the machine gun is in position and ready to fire – and then the handicraft of murder starts. It must be a very strange feeling to lie behind a machine gun shooting at infantry troops moving forward. One can see them coming and directs this terrible hail against them.

Some passages in the material collected by the Institute for Applied Psychology refer to the act of killing at the front:

[…] 'the enemy is nothing but an obstacle which has to be destroyed.' […] 'One kills the enemies in a brawl in order to eliminate a danger for oneself, just as one would kill a predator getting in one's way.' […] 'A man during battle is not at all aware that he is killing. […] I have never heard of any bad conscience after the battle, not even among very faithful people. The thought of securing one's own life, of self-defence plays very much a decisive role. Only once I encountered a disposition for brutality, bloodthirst, thirst for revenge, when the entire unit of a Russian battery who had been shooting to the last before surrendering with their hands up were massacred. Then, a German Landsturm man triumphantly showed me his bloodstained bayonet shortly afterwards. I encountered different character-types of officers in the war of position. There are some who would target and shoot Russian units in nearby trenches with their sighting telescope for hours and hours as if they were practice targets in a shooting range. Others however declared that they could not destroy human lives like these if there was no need. The men do not seem to have any moral qualms in this regard.

Methods of Warfare and Impact of Arms[20]

The offensive spirit that was prevalent in the German army and which informed military training tried to achieve results through assault attacks against heavily fortified positions. But attacks without proper artillery support or with the use of bayonets only lead to extremely high casualty rates. Within a few days, companies that had left the garrison in full strength with 250 men were reduced to a mere 80 men or even less.

Until his early death in 1919, Johann Knief was one of the leading members of the left wing of the SPD in Bremen and later a co-founder of the Communist Party (KPD). In a letter written on 29 September 1914 he relays his experiences during a night attack on the Western Front:

'Folks, just shout "hurrah" as loud as you can, then the Frenchmen will run off by themselves', that's how the officers encouraged the soldiers. And they did shout, just as erstwhile the hordes of Hermann the Cheruscan might have been shouting, like real Teutons. Meanwhile, the enemy kept all quiet. Some of the comrades might have believed that shouting was indeed the best assault weapon. [...] The clever Frenchmen allowed our misled troops to approach as near as 50 metres. But then a storm of cannon muzzles and gun barrels descended upon the good men, and it made one think the end of the world is nigh. A thick hail of bullets pattered into the close ranks of the Germans. The emerging confusion blasted all the approaching regiments apart in no time. Everyone was running around, some officers withdrew with the remaining 8, 10, 12 men as the wreckage of their companies. They took refuge far behind the front lines. Now everything is over, I heard a lieutenant saying.

The official war diary of an infantry brigade on the Eastern Front does only note, somewhat laconically, that 'casualties were high while advancing' for a day in November 1914. The private diary of the commanding officer contains this entry:

If the officers would not have been as unskillful and the men not as badly trained in modern infantry combat as they are, casualties like these could be avoided. But nobody has a clue about battling, everybody was running in broad lines right into the Russian artillery and machine gun fire. [...] Company and brigade commanders just gave orders like: Deploy! And then everybody started running and everything was dispersed. [...] It makes me furious!

Dominik Richert, son of a farmer from Alsace who was conscripted in 1913 and commanded to the Western Front in August 1914, describes the impact of one of his first battles in his war memoirs:

I got up. What a sight that was! In front of us there were dead and wounded Frenchmen as far as the eye could see. The dead Germans were still there, too, the wounded were carried away already. [...] Some of the dead men looked awful, some of them lay on their faces, some of them on their backs. Blood, hands and fingers like claws, glassy eyes, distorted faces. Many held their rifles still cramped in their hand, others had their hands full of soil or grass which they had pulled out in their death struggle. I saw a lot of soldiers standing together and walked over. A terrible picture presented itself to me. A French and a German soldier on their knees were leaning against each other. They had pierced each other with the bayonet and had dropped like this to the ground. [...] Courage, heroism, does it really exist? I am about to doubt it, since I haven't seen anything else than fear, anxiety and despair in every face during the battle. There was nothing at all like courage, bravery or the like. In reality, there is nothing else than terrible discipline and coercion propelling the soldier forward and towards death.

During the short period of a war of motion up to November 1914 the soldiers had already been exposed to new weaponry and its impact. From a letter about an air attack that was published in the *Bergarbeiterzeitung*:

[The aeroplane] turned around, and we hoped it would disappear, when it was flying another circuit over our camp. I was standing on the other side of the road from where we were firing at the aeroplane. Suddenly I saw a beam of fire very close to me, then a cloud of smoke and right in the middle of this cloud I saw an infantry man. His body was covered up to the shoulders in this cloud and what stood on his shoulders seemed to be the bloody shreds of a human head. This sight was so terrible, so horrible, that I couldn't sleep the last two nights. There is always this infantry man standing in front of me, without a head and with a bloody lump of flesh on his shoulders instead. I cannot stop picturing this. Later, I had a closer look at him. He was lying on his face, the skullcap was removed, his brain was everywhere and he was covered all over in blood.

Time and again, infantry patrols had to make excursions in order to investigate no-man's-land or to capture enemy soldiers who could be interrogated about the strength and the intentions of their troops. During such excursions, soldiers on patrol repeatedly died from 'friendly fire'. On the night of 11 December 1914, the NCO Strauß from the 15th Bavarian Infantry-Regiment was killed in this way during a patrol. Infantryman Georg Bader, who served on a listening post at the time, accidentally shot him. Statements by Georg Bader from the court-martial file:

Suddenly I saw five upright standing objects in front of me. One of them moved and went towards three separate trees on my left hand side. I thought they were Frenchmen who wanted to intercept the three of us. I called out to my comrades: 'There's one coming over there.' They said: 'I don't see anything' and continued to observe the area. Infantryman Obermeier also said: 'You are just imagining that'.

Being on watch at the three trees is very much dreaded, since the enemy often targets the trees which are visible from a far distance. Some time ago it was told that an enemy's patrol was sneaking up to the listening posts of the 12th Infantry Regiment and stabbed them. These rumours and the pitch-black night made me quite nervous.

Statement of the second listening post:

When still in position I had the impression of Bader being rather nervous. He repeatedly said that he didn't feel like going out there. On top of that, some people scared him saying that one couldn't see anything out there and that the enemy would fire at this spot very often etc.

It is true that Bader was rather nervous then. When we reached the post I noticed that he lay down to take cover immediately in spite of all the mud.

Statement of the company commander:

Bader's apprehension at being followed by an enemy seems to be believable and convincing, because of the way Strauß was going around the standing patrol and because of the extraordinary pitch-black night and the heavy rainfall. It is also true that it is very difficult, particulary at night, to distinguish and identify the often almost man-high twigs of the turnip-shrubs moving vividly in the wind as such. It takes a long and very sharp observation.

The turn of the year 1914/15 and the battle of Champagne in February/March 1915 saw the first massive use of heavy barrage, i.e. the constant firing of many artillery cannon of all calibres for hours. Fr. Langhorst, on service in the rear area on the Western Front, hears the noise of the battle. In a letter on 2 January 1915 he reports:

The roar of guns is often so loud and vivid that one cannot distinguish a single cannon shot. It is more like a rolling noise going on for hours without interruption. This roar of guns sounds terrible, and it makes us think of all the horrible devastation. But then what a surprise to hear the very few, dry lines about these incidents in the Army Command's official war bulletin the following day! [...] The men look simply awful when they come right from the trenches to us to have a rest. When will this devastation of human lives ever come to an end?

The medical doctor and psychologist Paul Plaut, who was himself a soldier during the war, reconstructs a shell strike in precise detail:

The shell explodes in front of me, in the same moment the sound hits the eardrum which starts to vibrate; in the same moment the beam of light of the bursting shell hits the retina, in the same moment I can smell gun smoke, in the same moment I feel that it is necessary to search for cover and shelter, in the same moment I am lying on the ground, literally dug deeply into the soil, and in the same moment I mechanically start to think again: Will the next shot be shorter or longer – shall I therefore go straight forward or turn sideways and go back. All this is happening within a split second.

Since 1916 the war at the Western Front had been characterized by battles of materiel. This term is closely associated with the name Verdun. Between February and December 1916, the battles around the town and fortress rarely ever waned. From May 1916, Christian Krull served at Verdun as a gunner. His assignment was to repair the telephone lines between the artillery positions. On 29 July 1916 he writes:

Shellcraters three metres deep and ten to twelve metres in perimeter are behind and in front of the gun emplacements – it is a real wilderness. The whole big and terrific oak forest looks exactly like the place here around our position. For the first time in ten days there has been nothing but sunshine which makes it easier to bear. But the first weeks have been horrible with this never ending rain creating a swamp everywhere around. One couldn't walk for ten steps without sinking into the mud knee-deep. And in this swamp I was on my feet from morning till night to keep the 10 km of wire lines in order. They were hardly longer intact than one hour, some of them we couldn't find at all. So we were running around, always under the heaviest fire, without any cover at all. Wherever we went, we had to throw ourselves down every moment in order not to be hit. At night we tried to get an hour's sleep in flooded dugouts, while we were covered in thick, wet mud. We could not sleep because of all the vermin, the cold and the dampness, so we dashed over to the cannon and relieved the dead-tired gunners just to get warm. [...] And then the days came, when the Frenchmen had discovered us, when the cannon got direct hits, when everybody helped out and took someone else's place and next to us the burnt, half-charcoaled comrades lay screaming with pain and nobody could help.

An infantryman writes about the battle of Verdun on 2 July 1916:

Arriving in position we lay down dead-tired in shell craters – there were no trenches, no dugouts, nothing of the kind, the area had been occupied just two days before. There we were lying for four days, initially all wet and half a metre deep in mud. Then a heavy barrage started which pushed us from one crater to the next one; the wounded screamed and groaned with pain and perished in misery [...] – there is no way of carrying them back. Shellfire day and night – often there is a hail of 10 to 20 shells every second, one of them would bury us and the next would dig us out again. Our lieutenant was crying like a baby. Well, the men were lying there, here a foot missing, there the arms, completely shredded. God, it was terrible. You can't possibly imagine this horror, nobody can who has not gone through this.

Terrible wounds and injuries were particularly caused by shell splinters. Erich Kuttner, who had served at the front during the war, was a Reichstag deputy for the Social Democratic Party, a journalist and the founder of the largest association of disabled war veterans during the Weimar Republic, the Social Democratic Reichsbund. In an article written in 1920, he describes a visit to a specialist hospital for facial injuries in Berlin:

How many people in Berlin have just the slightest idea that there are still about 20 military hospitals in Berlin with more than 2,000 inmates, filled with victims of the war that ended almost two years ago? And how many of those who know about this have asked themselves how a man's body might look considering that this man is still unable to leave hospital even after two, three, five or six years of medical treatment, and despite the fact that they are not exactly fussy when discharging disabled ex-servicemen. These men are not just war-disabled, they are the war-crushed! [...] The hospital committee, the elected representatives of the Berlin hospital patients, invited me to visit several hospitals. [...] The educational trip started with a provision hospital in the Thüringer Allee, located in remote loneliness far away in the Westend. Nonetheless, it would be worth it becoming a pilgrimage site for all sensitive people, for here one can find people from whom the war has taken the most beautiful and noble part of their body – even if this is a terrible thing to say: men without faces. At the committee's request a man with a bandage right over the middle of his face enters the small office room. He takes the bandage off and I stare in a hole, circular shaped and as big as a hand, from the root of the nose to the bottom jaw. The right eye is destroyed, the left one half closed. While I am talking to the man, I can see all inner parts of his mouth cavity: larynx, gullet, windpipe, like a manikin. [...] But what is that strange hairy lump hanging at some sinews and ligaments and swinging to and fro like a bell clapper in the mouth cavity? Someone explains: it is an unsuccessful nose which was supposed to be put in the poor man's face. They chiselled off a part of the bone at the left temple and put it in the mouth cavity. But because the skin is from the scalp, the nose, hardly grown in, was quickly covered with a lot of hair. It has to come off again and is supposed to be replaced with something else. This treatment will propably take another five years. Five more years! To date the man has had his eighteenth surgery. But that is not a record. Shortly after this encounter I meet people who have gone through 30 or 36 operations. [...] The uncomfortable existence of these war victims is forgotten. [...] In the Westend they show me a collection of plaster busts kept in a hidden nook. They are the plaster face masks of the inmates made when they first came to the hospital. Later on, they will also make masks of the patched up faces and add these to the collection for comparison. Why do they hide these memorials of horror?

During the battle of Ypern in April/May 1915, the German army launches a first major attack using poison gas. Franz Tholl, while in hospital, muses on 10 May 1916 about the use of poison gas:

Hopefully this mass-murdering war will come to an end soon. It is said that the Englishmen had lost thousands of men in just one or two hours after a successful German gas attack and had to carry away their dead comrades in waggons. The devastating impact of the artillery on human beings is supposed to be nothing in comparison with this. The technology of warfare is thus heading straight for the destruction of whole armies 'without bloodshed' by suffocating them or putting them to sleep. What a humane conduct of war.

Infantry man Birzer writes to the farmer's widow Anna Birzer in Haselbach (Upper Palatinate):

In the trench, 20.VIII.17 My dearest mother!
  My heart is very heavy today and I could almost cry, so please forgive me writing to you about my sorrow. In November it will be two years that I have been in this swindle, but I have never come across an

incident like the one today. I don't like talking about it, but I can't hide it any longer. It will show you how they treat a warrior and how his efforts and his many and heavy sacrifices are appreciated. Oh dear mother. Tonight there was a very heavy gas attack from the Englishmen at 2 am when I was on guard. Three gas shells exploded on my left-hand side three metres away. I swallowed a bit of gas before I could put on my gas mask and informed the dugout. Then I went to see a doctor, because they have told us over and over again in the training courses, when you think you have swallowed some gas do go immediately to the doctor. But the company commander did not let me go and see the doctor. Instead, he locked me up. Here you go and see how they act. He would be happy if I were *kaputt*. Then he told me off like no one did before. He called me a coward and a malingerer and did not let me go and see the doctor. Dearest mother, I cannot bear it any longer. If it wasn't for you I would kill myself. The company commander and eight men from the 7th company died from the gas. Many are still suffering from the gas, and many will eventually die as well. It is the same with the 12th company, many are sick of gas. The symptoms very often occur not before the next day making you really sick. Dear Mother! I am happy to be locked up, and when I come out again, I will make a complaint and will register with a different company. But, dear mother, even when you make so and so many requests, the company commander won't give me any leave. I can't think of a suitable name for him, someone like him deserves to be shot. It doesn't matter how many requests you write. You can try and write a request to the battalion or the regiment, but it is completely useless to write one to the company. [...] Don't send me anything anymore, dear mother, I think I will go to hospital. 1000 wishes your loving son, wishes to all.

Birzer's letter was intercepted by field post censorship and an investigation followed:

With reference to: abuse of official authority
    According to the War Ministry Decree from 9 November 1912 No. 24200/10 I report the following: The postal surveillance office of the 6th Army High Command intercepted the letter of infantry man Birzer, 11th Company 6th Infantry Regiment, to his mother. Birzer is complaining about unfair treatment by his company commander. The investigation revealed the following:

On 19/20 August 1917, infantry man Birzer was on guard in the company section on which an attack with gas–shells was carried out. Birzer reported to his company commander, reserve lieutenant Münch, that he had swallowed gas.

Lieutenant Münch did not believe Birzer's report, since he had been standing at a machine gun and rather far away from Birzer and had not noticed any gas. Thus he did not believe what Birzer said, also as Birzer had proven to be rather unreliable on former occasions.

Lieutenant Münch called Birzer a 'malingerer and coward'. He ordered to relieve Birzer and sent him with a paramedic to a rearward platoon. He gave order to be informed if Birzer's conditions worsened. Lieutenant Münch then went to the spot where the gas mines had allegedly hit. There he found Birzer's report confirmed. On his way back, Lieutenant Münch looked after Birzer and gave order to send him to see a doctor since his condition had worsened.

Birzer was admitted to a military hospital. Lieutenant Münch was punished with one day of confinement to quarters by his regimental commander, because he had offended a subordinate with the words 'malingerer and coward'.

I confirm this punishment. Lieutenant Münch is one of the best company commanders of the regiment and has no criminal record.

The report of the Field Post Censorship Unit 40 from 25 August 1917, which also included a bag of letters from Birzer's company and his own letter, states:

The letters at hand were written by troops in combat or stand-by position. They clearly show the mental and emotional impact of the last combat operations. A majority of the letters are dealing with the heavy losses of a company through a gas attack. The general mood has to be considered as gloomy.

With the delivery at hand the daily mail of ten divisions has been checked, and the overall result can be briefly summarized as follows:

The mood of the troops with regard to the military situation is consistently good. The very few discouraging remarks have to be considered as exceptions, and they are juxtaposed with multiple positive comments which demonstrate an unconditional feeling of superiority. The complaints about food, frequently mentioned during the summer, have almost completely ceased. Complaints about the

Images like this one, published in 1915, conjured up romantic notions of volunteering for military service. (See p. 29.)

'What are your reasons to reject my proposal?' 'The same that disposed the draft board to defer your service . . .' (1915). (See p. 30.)

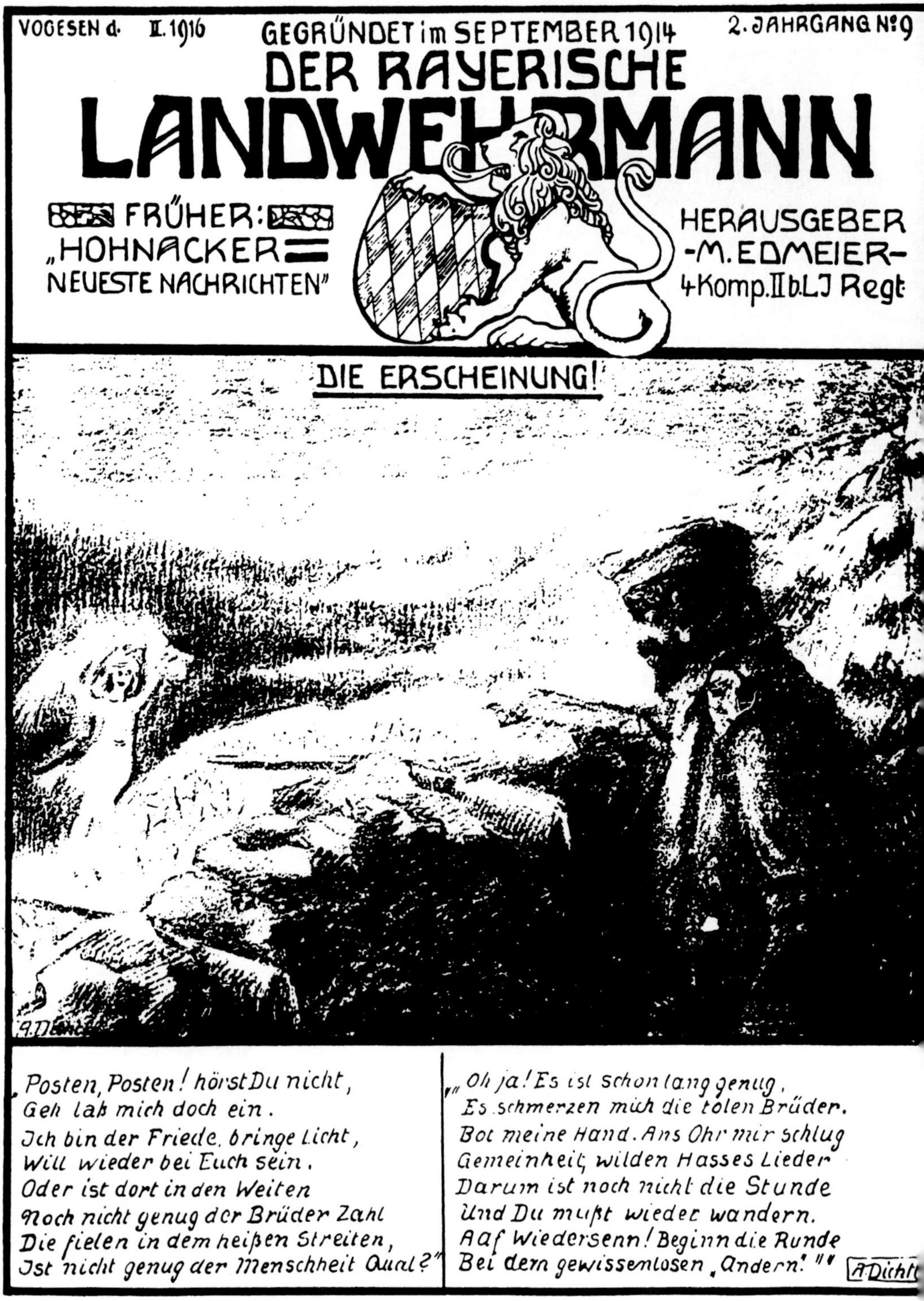

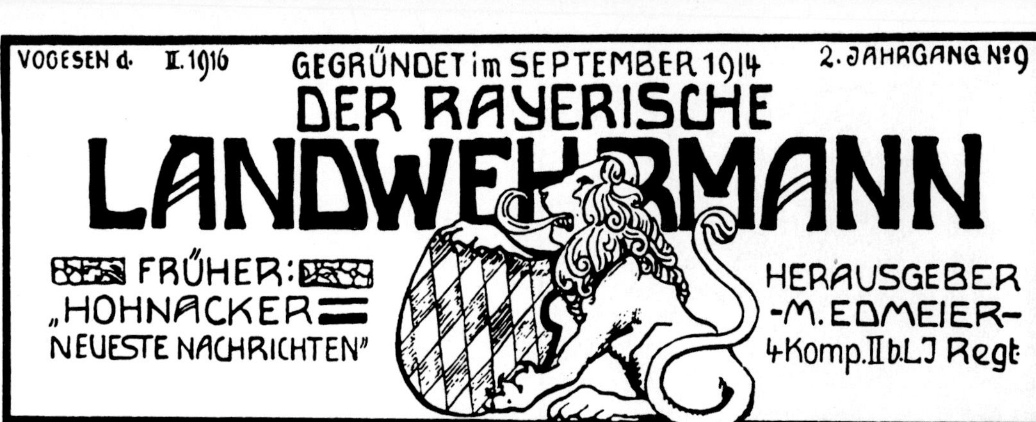

VOGESEN d. II. 1916 GEGRÜNDET im SEPTEMBER 1914 2. JAHRGANG No 9

DER BAYERISCHE
LANDWEHRMANN

FRÜHER: „HOHNACKER NEUESTE NACHRICHTEN"

HERAUSGEBER -M. EDMEIER- 4 Komp. II b. L. I. Regt.

DIE ERSCHEINUNG!

„Posten, Posten! hörst Du nicht,
Geh laß mich doch ein.
Ich bin der Friede, bringe Licht,
Will wieder bei Euch sein.
Oder ist dort in den Weiten
Noch nicht genug der Brüder Zahl
Die fielen in dem heißen Streiten,
Ist nicht genug der Menschheit Qual?"

„Oh ja! Es ist schon lang genug,
Es schmerzen mich die toten Brüder.
Bot meine Hand. Ans Ohr mir schlug
Gemeinheit, wilden Hasses Lieder
Darum ist noch nicht die Stunde
Und Du mußt wieder wandern.
Auf Wiedersehn! Beginn die Runde
Bei den gewissenlosen „Andern." "

A. Dichtl

A Bavarian Landwehr soldier has an apparition of peace.
From the cover of a trench newspaper, 1916.

'Heimatschuss' or 'Blighty'.
Official war photograph
from the collection of the
Bild- und Filmamt (Bufa).
(See p. 133.)

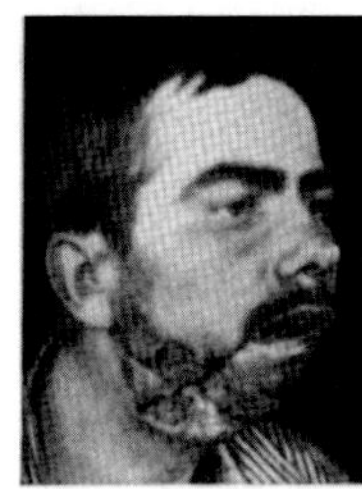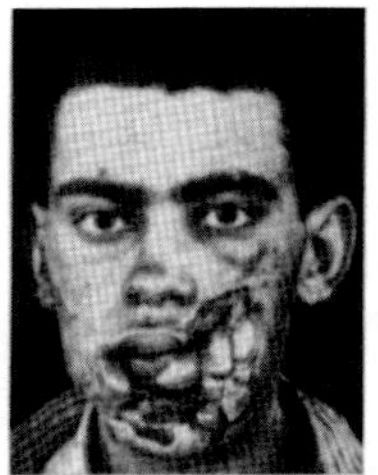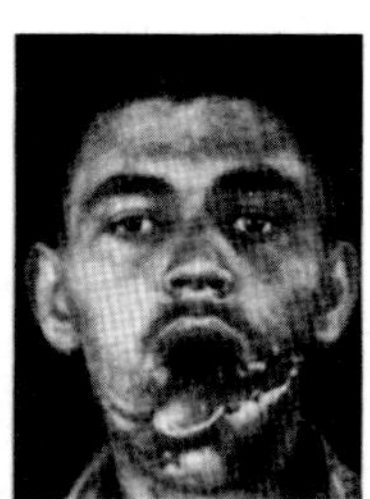

Frische Kiefer- und Gesichtsverletzungen.

These photographs were
meant to demonstrate the
success of plastic surgery
(1916). Similar photographs
of extreme facial injuries were
later used by the pacifist Ernst
Friedrich in his bestselling
book *War Against War* in
1924. (See p. 81.)

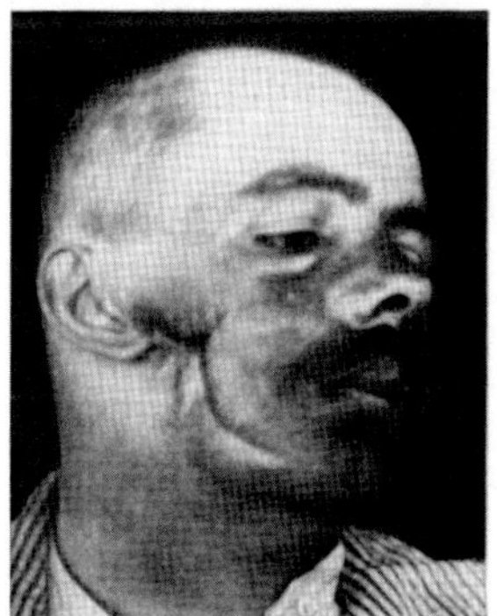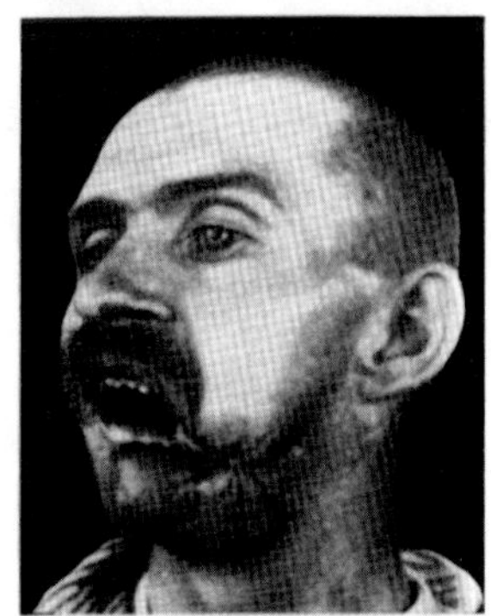

Veraltete entstellende Gesichtsnarben.   Können durch sachgemäße Behandlung verbessert werden.

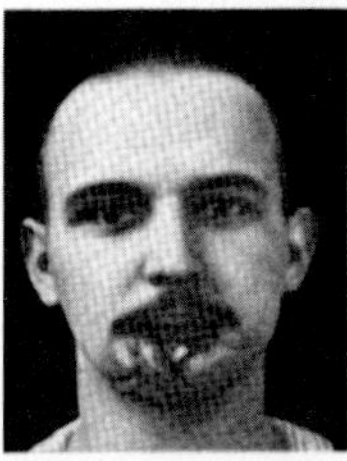

'The Kaufmann-method. The treatment of war neurotics revived medieval torture methods' – caption by Magnus Hirschfeld from his *Moral History of the First World War*, 1930. (See p. 91.)

Heimatsurlaub (Furlough), picture postcard, *c.* 1916. (See p. 117.)

'And Your Duty? Sign War Loans', picture postcard, *c.* 1917. (See p. 138.)

Betreff:
Selbstverstümmelung.

Mehrere von den Feldtruppenteilen als fahnenflüchtig erklärte Mannschaften wurden in irgend einem Lazarett der Heimat mit Finger- oder Handverletzungen aufgefunden. Dieser Umstand legt im Verein mit anderen Beobachtungen die Vermutung nahe, daß sich wiederholt Mannschaften durch Selbstverstümmelung dem Dienste im Felde zu entziehen suchen.

Mit Vorliebe scheinen diese Mannschaften Verbandplätze nichtbayerischer Truppenteile aufzusuchen und sich dann irgend einem Verwundeten-Transport anzuschließen.

Eine Kontrolle im Felde ist nur möglich, wenn die nichtbayerischen Nachbarabteilungen ersucht werden, derartige Verwundete bei Verdacht sofort ihrem eigenen Verbandplatze zuzuführen.

In den Lazaretten des Besatzungsheeres ist allen Verwundungen, die auf Selbstverstümmelung schließen lassen, besonderes Augenmerk zuzuwenden.

J. A.
Kuchler.

'Regarding: Self Mutilation' (1915). Facsimile of the document on p. 133.

Fraternization between French and German troops. Drawing by a French soldier, 1915. (See p. 134.)

An ideal trench, as depicted in an illustrated German dictionary in 1938.

'Firing position at Verdun after move to new position (1916)'. As with the following two photographs, this image is from the album of Theodor Koch and was probably also taken by him. Koch was a platoon leader in the Field Artillery Regiment 33.

'The cannon where I commenced my wartime service (names on the reverse side)'. This photograph was taken in the Argonne forest in 1915. As with many other images in Koch's album, this group shot documented his comrades.

'Tree that was brought down at the kitchen of the 4/33'. Theodor Koch documented the devastating effects of war, also with photographs of graves of his fallen comrades.

'Our Kaiser and the Reichstag 4 August 1914. I recognize no more parties; I recognize only Germans!' (See p. 140.)

'Lord Kitchener produces English armies'. This postcard symbolizes the alleged superiority of a conscript army over a volunteer army. (See p. 65.)

'Made in Germany 1914. German product'. German Anglophobia in 1914 imagined British soldiers as cowards who would be easy to defeat. Some soldiers noted the contrast with their own experiences in their eyewitness accounts. (See p. 65.)

'The Main Strike! Such a sod should have its share! Motto: Honi soit qui mal y pense!'. Combining the motto of the Order of the Garter and an image of a Scottish soldier, this postcard aims to maximize anti-British symbolism. Note the stroke across the postcard, which was added by a military censor. In the early months of the war, military censorship banned many postcards that aimed to debase the enemies, as they would undermine the dignity of the German war effort.

The lion, symbol of Bavarian strength, is eating enemy soldiers. Many Bavarian troops saw Prussian units as inferior in combat performance. (See p. 66.)

endured exertions and the hardship of the service can be found only in isolated cases, complaints about bad and unfair treatment on the part of the superiors are rare exceptional cases.

In general, judgements on the political situation are generally less optimistic. Particularly newspaper articles are explicitly mistrusted. The impact of political agitation is noticeable only in the respect that the opinion that the war is merely continued due to the interests of the big capitalists seems to be widespread in the army. [...] On the other hand, one can observe a strong revival of religious feelings, regardless of the regional background or denomination of the soldier. In general, it is noticeable that army members from the South of Germany are more worried than their comrades from the North. All of them share a strong longing for peace.

Many letter writers do not abide by the ban on mentioning places, in particular when a unit has moved its position. Likewise many people still send food from home to the front although this is also banned, whereas there are apparently less letters from home containing money.

Heinrich Aufderstrasse, in position vis-à-vis an American unit, describes changes in German tactics in a letter dated 14 April 1918. He refers to consequences of 'Principles for the Conduct of Defensive Battle in Position Warfare', a strategy document that had already been introduced in late 1916 and aimed to create a more flexible pattern of defence that granted a higher degree of autonomy to junior officers:

Whereas previously 'Up and close to the enemy!' pushed the trenches closer and closer against the enemy, now the maxim is: to create a glacis of several kilometers between us and the enemy. In pure military terms, both sides benefit from this. The enemy finds it more difficult to get information about the situation behind the front lines because he can't take individuals as prisoners as easily and as often as before. Hence the increase in highly dangerous raids, which are accompanied by extensive artillery fire. Apart from these and from the risky patrols in front of our position at night we benefit from this new system, too, because we have less casualties through infantry weapons. If there were not an increasing activity of aeroplanes and artillery fire in clear weather conditions, one could call it an adventure of thick air. Unfortunately, the amount of cannon is growing and growing. The food provision is not that bad. But it is not enough and after all the exertions we are all worn out like 60-year-old greybeards. The body has no power reserves left. The [SPD] parliamentary party could support the demand that, wherever this is possible for the troops in position battle, similar to the situation during most evenings in the homeland garrisons, the men receive a warm soup in the evening.

The German army employed shock- or assault troops (Sturmbataillone) in the final two years of the war in order to overcome the stalemate of position warfare. With intensively planned and coordinated attacks they were meant to infiltrate the enemy trenches and to pave the way for the following regular infantry troops. A soldier who was drafted in 1917 at the age of 17 to the 1st Bavarian Infantry Regiment writes:

After I had been a soldier for only three weeks, I was sent to Belgium for further training to a huge drill ground. There an assault battalion was assembled, which had the assignment to take important sections of the trench line by storm.

In a very short time we learned how to handle the light machine gun, egg-shaped and stick hand grenades.

This assault battalion had its own artillery. We were trained to penetrate through to the alleged enemy trenches under fire from flat trajectory bullets.

I had not been a soldier for three months when I had my first front assignment, it was terrible. Due to our curtain artillery fire we got into the enemy trenches without any losses. We did not take any prisoners, according to our training we threw hand grenades into the dugouts and fired to both sides with the machine guns.

Often the battle went on for many hours until the enemy trench was free from enemies in a 100 metre stretch. Then we were relieved by our infantry men. Our losses were heavy for we had to fight for every inch of the trench basically in close-range combat. It was not easy for the relief troops, as most of them were seconded from different regiments. The enemy artillery covered the trench section occupied by our troops with fire from every calibre. The survivors had to withdraw and we had to take the same stretch again shortly afterwards.

The shock-troop soldiers were mostly volunteers and highly motivated. Some of the assault battalions provided the core of the counter revolutionary Freikorps in the postwar period. Many declared enemies of the Weimar Republic and representatives of a 'soldierly nationalism' had been officers in shock-troops, such as Ernst Jünger, Walter Beumelburg and Franz Schauwecker. The following excerpt from a doctoral dissertation describes the weaponry used by shock-troops and conveys a sense of their battle force through the brutal language it employs:

The storm trooper was geared to stay flexible: steel helmet, trousers with leather parts, mountain boots with puttees, haversack with an iron ration, two field bottles, wirecutter, gas mask in a box, hand-grenade equipment in two bags, [...] big spade or pick-axe on the back and a carbine over the shoulder. There were two types of hand grenades in use: the stick hand grenade and the egg-shaped hand grenade. The stick hand grenade with combustion time fuze – for clearing up dugouts and small obstacles – and with contact fuze – particularly suitable for the combat with hand grenades, since the grenade exploded on impact. The egg-shaped hand grenade was not suitable for the attack, because it had just small impact and endangered the soldier who threw it. It was more often used for defence. Every man was trained with French and English hand grenades to enable him to use the weapons found in the enemy trenches immediately. [...] On top of that, every soldier was trained to use German, French and English machine guns so that he could shoot in an emergency and fix simple stoppages himself. Every assault company had a couple of trench mortars 16 (called: 'priests') [...]. The combat patrols made their way through the enemy trenches by using the small flame-thrower, in particular against blockhouses and well-fortified nests of resistance. [...] The range of the fire beam was 15–20 metres. Emotional devastation was its main impact.

Emotional Casualties and their 'Treatment'[21]

Already the 'baptism of fire' led to the psychological collapse of many soldiers. Robert Gaupp, the director of the clinic for nervous diseases in Tübingen and a senior military doctor during the war, reports:

When the hospital wards started to fill up with wounded and sick people from late August [1914], there were quite a lot of patients with injuries of the nervous system or brain injuries, but hardly any with mental diseases. This was the situation until Christmas 1914. Only when the heavy artillery battles commenced in the Champagne in

December 1914 and when the artillery superiority of our Western enemies increased to devastating heavy barrage, the hospital trains brought a rather large quantity of uninjured but mentally ill officers and soldiers. Henceforward, their number has increased more and more rapidly. Initially they were admitted in hospitals together with other wounded and sick people as a make-shift solution. Soon this procedure proved to be unsuitable. Special hospitals for patients with mental diseases had to be opened. Since then their number is increasing constantly. A hospital has opened, and very soon it is full and more space must be provided. Now we have the situation that the patients with mental diseases are, in terms of their numbers, the most important group of all sick army members and that the military hospitals for mentally ill soldiers are the only ones that are always fully occupied. [...]
However, troops that altogether amount to several army corps have been withdrawn from front and garrison duty with mental diseases. [...]
The main reasons are fright and fear triggered by exploding enemy shells and mines, by the sight of mutilated and killed comrades, by collapsing dugouts, by the experience of their own injuries or bodily damage caused by blunt items. Consecutive symptoms are the conditions, well known to you, of sudden muteness, deafness or deaf-muteness, of general trembling, the incapability to stand up or to walk, fainting spells and cramps.

Franz Müller writes on 21 January 1915 from a military hospital:

Due to the huge exertions of the last three days in particular, when our trench was literally turned upside down by heavy enemy artillery, I have developed a mental disease. Thus I was carried back on 8 November, two days before the general assault at the whole front. [...] I am up for just a few hours a day, for this bloody illness has affected my innocent legs. The pain and paralysis in my legs and in my right arm make it very difficult to move. Just imagine the giant of 92 kg [about 14½ stones] trudging along like a crab between beds, chairs and tables. It is utter mockery!

The NCO Wilhelm Pfuhl was diagnosed with nervous disease and admitted to hospital in November 1916. He writes on 17 November 1916:

I think rather than the exertions it is all the horrors I have encountered during the last months which has shaken my health so terribly. It seems to me just unbelievable how mankind can slaughter each other in this mutual mass-murder. I cannot praise myself for ever having been particularly robust against the disgusting and horrid, but now I am completely shattered. I am so tired and weak, I would like to go to sleep and not wake up again until there is peace in the country, or not wake up again at all.

A German psychiatrist describes some of the many individual cases of neuropathy he had to deal with. They exemplify the terrible experiences of many soldiers:

Case 421. Officer at the age of 25. Received a through and through bullet wound in the upper arm in 1915. In 1917 dugout blocked by a direct hit. Tried to dig himself out with his comrades. These comrades were slowly losing their energy. They died presumably through suffocation. The patient cannot specify the way they died. He also felt the growing lack of breath. A second shell opened the blocked dugout, which saved the patient. Since then states of nervous anxiety, sleeplessness, nightmares, general nervousness. Patient feels repeatedly breathless, thinks he has to die from suffocation. Three months of treatment without success, therefore moved to a psychiatric clinic. Patient is a strong man, who has always been healthy, intelligent and ambitious before that incident.

Case 504. NCO F., 31 years old, healthy family background, he himself has never been severely ill and has always been fully employable as a miner. Married with two children. [...] In December 1914, he was thrown down (allegedly hurled away) by the blast of a shell exploding very close to him, then he became unconscious. The next day in hospital he was completely confused, did not answer neither when asked nor reacted on eye-contact, staring into emptiness. Had to be fed. Two days later his mind was more relaxed, but he was almost deaf in both ears and absolutely mute. [...]

Case I. Josef B. headwaiter, 25 years old, from the Rhineland. [...] On 5 May 1915, B. was transported directly from [...] to our hospital. According to comrades from the same unit who were on the same transport, B. had been buried by an exploding mine and had only been dug out after two hours. This incident happened on 3 May 1915. [...]

When admitted to hospital, B. was completely disorientated and confused and motorically very restless. [...] B. is terrified by every noise, when brought to his ward, he started whining and screaming. Lying in his bed he was apparently still frightened, he crept under the duvet as if looking for cover against shells. [...] During the night, B. was very restless and nervous, he was screaming and crying, pushing his way out of bed, hiding away and trying to leave the room. [...] According to his wife's statement, B. has always been a quiet, sensible and industrious person without any psychotic attitudes whatsoever. The marriage used to be happy.

Some soldiers suffered from long-term mental diseases when they returned to front-line duty after a first traumatic incident:

Lieutenant Sergeant E., born 1881. On 16 June 1915, severe nervous shock caused by the impact of a shell at very close range. As E. reported afterwards, his entire company had been wiped out. He could not hear anything after the perforation of his eardrum, he could only see how the others ducked down. 'I was running back like mad.' Afterwards he served with a unit for recovered soldiers and returned to the field, now on the Eastern Front in November 1916. [...] He was constantly poorly. His health condition worsened so that he was admitted to hospital again on 4 June 1916. His hearing was back to normal by then, but the patient suffered from noises in his ears, severe headaches combined with a nervous restlessness in general, poor sleep with palpitation of the heart and panic attacks. [...] E. tends to consider military procedures as a personal harassment and is suspicious of his doctor.

Ernst Simmel, who served as a military doctor but was trained in psychoanalysis according to Sigmund Freud, treated shell-shocked soldiers, who were usually called 'war tremblers' as their limbs were constantly shaking. He tried to cure them with hypnosis. Writing in 1919, he describes the reasons for this type of mental disease:

Only someone who has witnessed the events of the war himself or at least their recapitulation under hypnosis can understand the disruptions of the inner life of a human being who is forced to go back into the field after being wounded serveral times; a human being who is separated from his relatives for an unpredictable period of time even when there are important family events, a human being who comes across the beast of a tank or an approaching enemy gas wave and must consider himself to be doomed, a human being who is buried and wounded after the impact of a shell, who lies beneath the bleeding and shredded corpses of his friends, often for hours or even days. And last but not least a human being whose self-esteem is severely damaged by unfair and brutal superiors who have themselves complex mental issues, finally somone who is supposed to keep quiet and silent facing the fact that he as an individual is nothing but an unimportant element of the mass.

'War neurotics' (*Kriegsneurotiker*) was the German term for shell-shocked soldiers. Their 'treatment' included military drills, 'starvation cures', isolation, shoving a probe into the larynx of mute soldiers in order to simulate suffocation, and the application of current impulses. Dr Kehrer, head physician of a reserve hospital at Castle Hornberg, describes the treatment he and his assistant Berthold had developed for shell-shocked soldiers who had lost their hearing:

> Berthold, who picked up all my proposals with greatest diligence and developed them further in a productive manner, treated these cases like this: he would put the blindfolded patient on a daybed, and, under intensive verbal suggestion [i.e. yelling], injected saline solution into the ears and under the skin around the ears, then made, in a circle of 5 cm around the auditory canal, cut-ins with a sterile acus which caused only minimal bleeding, and then applied galvanic current surges of up to five ampere, whilst he ultimately tried to affect the will to regain the hearing [i.e. yelling]. Through the total disconnection of the visual sense the patient had, metaphorically speaking, only one decision left: either to regain his will to hear or to suffer from further and increasing pain.

The medical department of the Bavarian War Ministry issued the following decree in March 1918. It refers to the Kaufmann-method, a treatment named after the Austrian military doctor Fritz Kaufmann who used to 'cure' war neurotics in one session through the application of strong current impulses:

With reference to: Treatment of war neurotics
As a follow-up [...] it is ordered:

> With regard to the isolated cases of sudden death after treatment
> with the so-called sinusoidal alternating current, the further usage
> of this currect for the treatment of neurotics is herewith
> prohibited. According to the general view of the most experienced
> expert physicians in this field, the usage of ordinary faradic
> current with a low voltage is sufficient.

This was a rather belated reaction. The so-called 'Kaufmann-method' had already led to the death of patients much earlier on. Case history of a certain Heidenreich, who served in the 22nd Bavarian Infantry-Regiment:

> On 25 August 1914, the infantry soldier Heidenreich received light injuries to his neck and both arms from shell splinters. Because of an enduring palsy of the left hand he was transferred to the hospital in Zweibrücken run by Catholic nuns on 8 August 1916. There he was treated with the so-called Kaufmann-cure by the assistant physician Dr Egglhuber.
> This kind of treatment, for which at least temporarily good results have been reported, consists basically of an astonishing psychological impact on the patient, whereas the electric current is applied in connection with a military order. [...] During the treatment with electric current H. suddenly stopped breathing and died shortly after from cardiac arrest, which could not be treated although all suitable measures were taken against it immediately.
> The court martial of the 5th deputy Infantry Brigade made an inquiry into the case and finally ruled that the proceedings should be closed, because no sufficient evidence was available that the death of Heidenreich was caused by default of any person who was liable to criminal persecution.

The 'treatment' of shell-shocked soldiers pursued two separate targets: to make them fit for military duty or at least a civilian occupation, or, if that was not possible, to avoid substantial pension payments. During the final phase of the war, these quite obvious aims agitated the patients and their relatives. The medical department of the Bavarian War Ministry writes on 14 September 1918:

The active treatment of war neurotics has caused a lot of substantial criticism, in the public and in parliament as well as in the press. It caused a lot of disagreement and bitterness, and sometimes even justified complaints from some quarters of the public.

This situation is mainly caused by some medical doctors who put too much emphasis in their statements and in their suggestive influence on patients on the issue of cutting off pensions and on unjustified pension payments.

It is unquestionable that rewarding pensions or paying excessively high pensions for neurotics will have negative consequences. But stressing this point in a rather harsh and unreasonable manner will only cause the misleading assumption that all specialist hospitals for neurotics are nothing but an attempt to avoid the payment of pensions or save money paid for pensions.

Therefore, all doctors who treat neurotics have to avoid anything at all that could create the impression of working merely for a financial interest rather than in the interest of the patient and of public health.

Religion and War[22]
In general, contemporary observers assumed a strengthening of religious faith through the war. For soldiers in particular this was regarded as a hard fact. August Messer provides the key reasons in his 'Psychology of the War' (1915):

Apart from emotional blunting there is just one other psychological safeguard against the flood of fear and angst, abjectness and distress caused by the war for combatants and non-combatants: an increased religious feeling. It is an old psychological observation that 'misery teaches us to pray'. But the connection to a superhuman power that is offered by religious experiences does not only have a mental impact when one asks for protection and help in a prayer. It has an important meaning in other respects. It is a deep mental need to search for some kind of value and therefore some kind of meaning in one's existence – at least for all those who do not live entirely thoughtlessly. Since the religious conscience – at least the type we are familiar with – usually does not take this empirical existence as the only one, the other world still offers a chance for the believer to realize the values he is longing for.

The military chaplains of both Christian denominations were quite unpopular among the troops as they supported the war effort and urged the troops to see it through. Members of a Protestant students' association report in their letters:

> The field preachers should at least once not talk about the war, battle, courage, trust in God which will guarantee our victory and about parallels with the Old Testament, but rather about redemption and our destiny to be God's proper children. That is and will remain the key point of Christian religion.
>
> The priest who talks to us behind the lines and thunders against our moral debasement and who has never faced horror and death himself would do better to keep silent and stop talking about the last things as if they were a matter of science. He can never understand us and his consolation is weak and pale like a street song that won't find any response within the soul.

From the letter of a POW who had been exchanged and returned to Germany:

> We attended service almost every Sunday, it was conducted by a French minister who was an army sergeant. The French chaplain read us a sermon which had been translated into German by an interpreter. Style and pronounciation were quite poor. But the content of his sermon was deep and substantial. I can't deny that his words were much more impressive than several sermons of German military chaplains which were more worthy of being called a patriotic address or agitation speeches in favour of the war loan than a Christian sermon.

The pastoral reports of Catholic parish priests at home indicate the piety and religious perceptions of the troops. From the reports of the parishes Höhenstadt and Holzkirchen to the diocesan head office in Passau (Lower Bavaria) from 13 June 1916 and 16 July 1916:

> Last year the military chaplains in the field were praised for their unselfish work and the religious and moral attitude of the soldiers was duly highlighted. But during the second year of the war, some changes have apparently occurred. A farmer's son from the parish whose behaviour used always to be impeccable before the war, writes: 'The

war has stirred up hatred and brutality among the men. The religious and moral improvement that the early period of the war brought to the army has vanished and things are worse than they were before the war.' Another one writes: 'Some time ago praying was very popular, now it is swearing.' Some soldiers on furlough also ventured to make comments about the army chaplains. One said: 'Military chaplains are hardly ever around.' Another one said: 'Chaplains only mingle with the officers, but not with the troops.' 'In the morning a field chaplain encouraged us to hold out undaunted by death, in the afternoon he got drunk and was seen together with a French woman.' About the officers one could hear the following comments: 'The officers have a nice and comfortable life in their shelters. They like to play cards and drink sparkling wine.' Even some women are said to visit them. If these and similar comments are always true, this is beyond our control. But it is enough that such talk and gossip is spreading among the soldiers at the front and at home. A well-to-do soldier writes that there is reason to fear that the war will go on at home, when peace arrives at the front. It will be difficult to keep the soldiers away from deplorable aberration and excess after they have returned from the field.

The seeming lack of success of prayers, the long duration and the terrible brutality of the war have caused many soldiers to doubt god's justice and omniscience so that they do not bother about religion any more. Blasphemous remarks are not rare. Injustice, brutal treatment and unneccessary hardship meted out by the military superiors lead to bitterness among those conscripted to military service, and are also transferred to their families. The irreligious and immoral behaviour of the officers is a bad example and has the worst impact on the troops. But the schoolteachers are supposed to be the very worst! A Landsturm man reports that his company, after being relieved from the trenches, was taken to a theatre play for recreation as shameless as they have never seen before – and all the officers were there as well! Another soldier told us how a faithless lieutenant taught mere Darwinism during lessons in garrison. To proof his point he said: 'Just look at the people and see how many of them have faces like monkeys.' The trust in the superiors is deeply shaken, 'It is all just swindle!' That is the reason why some people do believe even the silliest tales: A soldier on leave told in all seriousness that the German and the Russian Emperors had met secretly and had been drinking together while the soldiers were shooting and killing each other in the meantime. The dislike of the Prussians is so severe that many people consider it better to get together with France. They suspect North Germany to make common cause with England and would betray us [Bavarians]. Even usually reliable men think about the military chaplains who champion the war loans and urge the troops to follow their orders: 'Why have the clerics to interfere in war matters!'

The Swiss ethnologist and folklorist Hanns Bächtold, who had already done research about superstition among soldiers before the war, got hold of a lot of new material for his studies during the war. He gives a talk at the University of Frankfurt on 30 October 1916:

> As the war drags on, the opinions of small religious societies and pseudo-scientific circles are spreading more and more next to the religion represented by the Church. They were received eagerly by some, for they corresponded to the wishes of individuals and of the people as a whole and because they offered answers to manifold questions which bothered people during this time of greatness.
>
> With these new religious communities, some very old ideas and practices that were thought to have been forgotten for a long time resurfaced, mainly caused by the concern about keeping oneself alive. These ideas had held peoples in previous centuries spellbound and were still lying dormant in our people. [...]
>
> The observation of all these mental changes within the population caused by the war is very interesting from different points of view. They offer an insight into the people's inner lives as unveiled as we very seldom get it. For these changes mirror exactly all the fear and the misery and the hope that the war has caused in the people's inner lives, with regard to the whole issue, the nation and their own fate.

A variety of superstitious practices had been used by soldiers since the beginning of the war. These included 'protective ointments' and 'shooting spells'. But the most prevalent were 'chain letters', which were passed on from soldier to soldier, and 'protective shirts'. Bächthold reports:

> The 'chain letters' or 'snowball prayers' saw a revival during the last years before the war. They now play an important role at home and at the front. They have adapted themselves to the war, for they now often read as follows:

'We Germans fear nothing in the world but God. I received the previous expression in order to pass it on. Whoever receives it is supposed to pass it on to friends every night for nine days without signing it. The chain must not be interrupted. The legend says that whoever receives the letter without passing it on will have no luck. But whoever passes it on, will have great joy on the ninth day. This is a traditional custom observed by Germans in every war so that luck would stay with them.'

According to a popular belief held in Baden one would still count as indestructable during the [Franco-Prussian] war in 1870/71 when wearing a shirt woven by a 7-year-old girl, in the same manner as a 'shirt for need' or a 'St Jörgen's shirt' was supposed to protect against misery and danger in previous centuries. Today they are produced in huge quantities and delivered as 'victory shirts in unmatched quality, prompt, cash on delivery'.

Mail from the Heimat[23]

For obvious reasons the relatives at home worried about their brothers, sons or husbands who served at the front. Georg Stempfle from Krumbach writes to his son August on the Western Front on 19 April 1917 – at the beginning of April a great British-French offensive operation had just commenced in the Artois and in the Champagne:

Right now the war is raging terribly again; if you are only lucky enough to get to a spot which is not as dangerous as others. I can't do anything else than praying and commend you for the protection of the dear Mother of God and of the holy Joseph, whom I trust in particular. Have you already received the Holy Easter Communion? Please, never forget to include us in your prayers; at some point there must be an end to this terrible murdering.

A Protestant soldier reports on the mood of his comrades on 15 July 1916:

Nearly all of us are receiving letters from the Heimat full of complaints. A woman moans that she, for example, had to queue in the street in the middle of the night to get some butter. Others are worried about their wives and children becoming neglected and depraved. They have heard and seen a lot. Comrades who have been soldiers for just a short period of time tell about their heroic deeds at home. What are the preparations made to regulate the soldiers' movement back home into their jobs after the conclusion of a peace treaty? In many cases, they will find their jobs occupied by others. Some are expecting riots then, I even heard the word 'revolution' mentioned twice in this context.

What the relatives at home wrote to the front is revealed in letters that were taken from German soldiers who were killed or taken into captivity. British and French planes dropped leaflets above the German lines with excerpts from these letters, in an attempt to undermine the morale of the troops. But this was not the final stage of their propagandistic use. In 1917, German propaganda used some of these letters and urged the 'German Woman' not to write any 'moaning letters' (*Jammerbriefe*). Some excerpts:

Leipzig, 22 August 1916 [...] I do also need some firewood and also coal. When one buys eggs, one has to pay 22 Pfennig each. When one buys a herring, it is 44 Pfennig each, it is such a shame. We get 6 Mark more from the state [in benefits] but the city council takes that away. So there is no point in paying us more. [...], so I hope you will get this letter and can answer my letter and tell me what to do. You can't imagine how busy we are, it is terrible. And then we are not supposed to tell you out there, since we are properly fed up as well. It isn't easy for us either.

Leipzig, 26 August 1916. My dear poor Paul! I have received your card from 20 July. If only this misery that has come upon mankind came to a quick end. Well, there is a lot going on at all fronts now and it will come to an end this very year. We are all fed up here and we all want peace as soon as possible. Yesterday there was a huge meeting in the Albert hall about peace and it said as follows: 'Millions and millions of people have to demand with one voice: It is enough! Will you listen to reason and come back to your senses again! Become human beings among human beings again!' (Storming applause) There were 50,000 people taking part in the gathering. [Between June and August 1916, demonstrations against the poor provision with food took place in some German cities.]

Hochemmerich, [...] If you were here occasionally, you would have been fed up for a long time. I can hardly write it down, for you won't believe me anyway. They have opened a war kitchen [...] and I have to get the meals from there. You can imagine what kind of muck this is! If you were able to see it, you would get an idea what we women are going through. Three pounds of potatoes has to be enough for the whole week, 50 grams fat for each person. The rice we get is full of bugs, it is a shame. Believe me, Tinchen and I, we have had some fine meals! We would have eaten if we had had something to eat. Our main food is bread with cabbage, it is a shame. Just don't be stupid and let them fool you, everything I am writing is the truth, otherwise I wouldn't write it.

Merseburg, 3 September 1916. [...] Beloved dear brother-in-law, if the good Lord would have mercy on us, for I cannot bear it any longer. I have to take care of the four children by day and by night so that they have something to eat. The big boys need a lot and everything is so bitterly expensive. You cannot imagine and I cannot describe it in detail, because you probably would not believe it.

Leipzig, 9 September 1916 [...]. Our thoughts are still always with you. We are delighted that you are in good hands. We are all very well and happy that we haven't been suffocated yet, it stinks everywhere. One is not allowed to make any noise through the trousers, otherwise one arouses suspicion. Everywhere you can feel a guilty conscience. I would have loved to send you something nice, but there is no food left to buy for money any more [...]. Many people have fallen asleep and don't want to know anything about victories any more. When everything is asleep and silent, we will have a reunion: in the mass grave!

Hanover, 10 September 1916 [...] The children are staying with me over the holidays, but they bother me a lot this time. I haven't got down to do anything the whole day long, for I have to go out and get something to eat for them all the time. When some very rare items are suddenly available, it is like organizing a military assault. When I get my ¼ pound of butter to which I am entitled each week, they will even rip off the stuff from me in a rowdy manner. Next time more about this. Hopefully there will be peace soon. Many thousand kisses and best wishes.

A woman from the village Strassdorf in the South of Germany writes in August 1917 to her husband, who is a POW:

I am so sick and tired of human life that I want to cut my own and my children's throat, I am not afraid of committing a sin, after all I am forced by misery. You have to be the most stupid person on God's earth when you have children. They take the breadwinner away from the children and let them starve to death, they are crying for bread the whole day long. For the 33 Pfennig [benefits] one gets for a child they cannot eat their fill even *once* a day. [...] I have got our four little children, none of them can help earning some money. I have to feed them, wash them, have to mend their clothes etc. I have to stand in the street all day long and wait for hours until I get a few things to eat. If one doesn't do it, one doesn't get anything. That's how it is in the villages. Therefore I can't earn anything. The few hundred Mark we have saved, I had to spend over the past three years. Thus, we have to perish miserably or take our own lives. So, don't long to come back to this vale of tears, just be happy in France. Winter is coming fast. They keep saying that soldiers' wives are privileged in getting firewood, but I have already got sore feet from running around, but I get neither a chip of wood nor coal for money. On the contrary, families where the men are at home are not in need. But who cares about a soldier's wife with a lot of little children, she can perish together with her children. And that is all the thanks for a man who has been in the field for three years or in captivity. If you were still at the front line, I wouldn't let you stay there for another day. I'd rather let all of us get shot or send the children to the front lines to stay with you.

The wife of another POW, from the city of Gleiwitz in Upper Silesia, writes to her husband in April 1917:

Dear husband! This is the last letter I am writing to you, because on the 24th I am going to marry another man. Then, I don't have to work any longer. I have already been working for three years as long as you are away from home. All other men come home for leave, only you POWs never come. Nobody knows how long it will take until you come home. That's why I am going to have a new husband. I will give the children to the orphanage. I don't give a rat's ass about a life like that! There is no way to survive with these few Pfennig benefits. At work they have a big mouth about the women. Now I don't need to go to work, now the other man is going to work for me. All wives whose husbands are POWs will do the same thing and they will all get rid of the children [...] Three years of work are too much for the women and 20 Mark war benefit and 10 Mark child benefit are not enough. One cannot live on that. Everything is so expensive now. One pound of bacon costs 8 Mark, a shirt 9 Mark.

Chapter 3

Grievances

As a matter of course, every total war puts pressure on the material resources of a nation at war, and thus has the potential to exacerbate inequalities in society, including in the army. In this respect, Germany did not differ from France, the UK and other belligerent countries. What was different in Germany was the unwillingness of the bourgeois political elites and of the army leadership to implement reforms in the army that would address the most important grievances of the troops and acknowledge them as citizen-soldiers. Quite to the contrary, the gross inequalities and injustices in the army continued until autumn 1918 and laid bare the fundamental reform blockage in the Wilhelmine political system. While private soldiers received 15,90 marks pay per month, a 20-year-old lieutenant earned 310 marks. Inequalities with regard to the provision of food and furlough and the awarding of military decorations, but also the extensive exploitation of their priviliges by officers added to the perception of gross injustice in the army and led to a widespread hatred of officers. As the sources in this and other sections of the book make unmistakably clear, not only senior staff officers or those who served in the Etappe attracted the scorn of the troops, but also and even more so younger troop officers, who were perceived to be both incompetent, arrogant and careless about the well-being of their mostly older subordinates. While military censorship – yet another element of the troops' grievances – was able to suppress an open discussion of these issues during the war, they were the subject of controversial debates during the Weimar Republic. Under the heading '*soziale Heeresmißstände*' (social army grievances), the whole complex of social inequality and injustice in the army was for instance discussed in the parliamentary subcomittee that discussed the 'causes of the German collapse in 1918'.

'The Yoke of War'[24]
From the beginning of the war, letters from the field (Feldpostbriefe) were used as a medium to air grievances. These letters were addressed to relatives, but also to the War Ministries, to members of parliament,

newspaper editors, priests and functionaries in trade unions and political parties, in short, to institutions of public life in which the soldiers trusted and which they expected to work as their advocates. During the early months of the war, many complaints focused on the extent of drill and on other duties that were perceived as harassment. A rather typical example is the following letter, which was written on 8 April 1915 by an NCO in the 20th Bavarian Infantry Regiment on behalf of all NCOs in his company. It was sent to the Catholic priest and Reichstag deputy for the Centre Party, Benedikt Hebel:

I do not complain about the yoke of war, for our God has endorsed it to humiliate the nations. But our company commander's strictness and severity is a heavy burden on us. Recently he told us himself that our nicest days were over now. In the evening of 1 April, we took a forward position for five days. In the area of our company the enemy lines are 40 to 70 metres away. Therefore, the highest safety measures are necessary during the night and half of the company has to be awake. Hence all troops have to be on guard every two hours. During the day, a third of the company has to be on guard and the rest of the troops have to build up entrenchments. That is very exhausting. But one would happily do all this because it has to be done and the enemy is very close. But now there are the days of *rest*, five of them. Thus we arrived in the quarters on 6 April at 11 pm, all dirty, while it was raining. After we had all had our dinner and had eaten, it was around midnight when we could lie down. The next day we had to line up at 8.30 for instructions. At 11.45 am there was a roll call in heavy marching order and woe betide anyone who was still a bit dirty. At 1 pm taking a bath, 3 pm rifle inspection, 3.45 to 5 pm lessons and at 6 pm again roll call with coats. Today (i.e. 8 April) there was company exercising from 9 to 12 am, then lunch, then we had to clean our clothes and equipment, then we had to report for different kinds of duty again until 7.30 pm. And so it goes on and on every day without an hour of rest and relaxation for the men. On one occasion a man came to the roll call wearing a coat that was a little bit dirty. The punishment was two days arrest. That is his reward for fighting for the fatherland right from the beginning. If it goes on like that a great deal of men will be punished for subordination or they will desert to the enemy, bringing shame on the regiment. The troops were much more joyful and courageous if they would be treated differently, if they had more time to rest and for doing things for themselves like washing their socks and handkerchiefs and if they could wash themselves more properly and get more rest in general.

What I have reported here briefly is the truth and nothing but the truth.

I would like to take the liberty of asking you on behalf of all NCOs and private soldiers to take steps and relieve us from this unbearable burden. We thank you very much in advance! May the days of peace come to us soon by Providence of our gracious God! We will all plead for this, at home and in the enemy's country. With rock-solid trust in God we will go on fighting.

Imposing Discipline[25]

Three years into the war, not a lot had changed with regard to these disciplinary practices, apart from the length of the arrest that was imposed. From a letter that was written in August 1918 and subject to postal censorship:

[…] and then the idiotic bullying, the orders from above. They don't know how to bother the ordinary soldiers. When they are relieved from the duty at the front lines and are at rest, they have to exercise for the whole day. That is a grinding like in a garrison. […] We have for instance an order as follows: Whoever comes from the front to the baggage in heavy marching order and is not wearing the carrying strap underneath the shoulder strap, gets 14 days of arrest. Whoever is carrying his rifle around his neck to relieve the weight instead of carrying it like a carbine over the shoulder according to orders, gets also 14 days of arrest. Well, we are all in high spirits here at the front!

When units in the rear area (Etappe) were prepared for transport to the front line, disciplinary measures were applied. Resentment about these procedures was mentioned in letters such as this one by Karl Otten on 27 August 1916:

On Monday: march in review, to be practised every day. On Sunday, standing at attention under surveillance. Who would dare saying we haven't improved! After a long march in heavy marching order, also carrying 210 live cartridges, 87 men were played out in the terrible heat. They were all old and invalid soldiers, 44, 45 and 47 years old. To punish them, a marching club was founded. Every Saturday night, after all the others have gone to bed, the 87 men are marching in heavy marching order through God's glorious nature [...]. Forsooth, they do this whilst the cannon are roaring from the Somme. The life in the trenches is bitter, but even bitterer is the misery burdening the people who are here behind the lines. All men except me and two Silesians volunteered to go into the trenches after being asked. But on 2 September we all will go, including the two Silesians and me, it just keeps getting better! For we didn't volunteer, I was told.

From a field recruitment depot in the rear area Josef Pfaffinger writes to his parents in Oberham, Lower Bavaria on 25 June 1917:

Dear Parents. Now I have to write some lines because I keep telling you to write more often. I would be happy if I received as much as I write you to send. May I please ask for a box of Österreicher Sport [cigarettes], since I have been longing to have some for quite a while. I just wished the war came to an end at last. There is grim pack drill for all, including those who shoot poorly. It has already struck nearly everybody, even me once. [...] I am fit and healthy and hope the same of you. Best wishes from your son Josef

Marginal Misconduct[26]

Even light forms of disciplinary misconduct could result in severe punishment, depending on the mood and character of the superior, and even forms of punishment that were not listed in the military penal code. From a short notice within a memorandum by the Deputy General Command Stuttgart from 15 May 1917 about 'special incidents, wishes, claims and complaints':

Abuse and punishment: A complaint by the wife of pioneer Schäfer, 5th Landwehr Pioneer Company, because her husband has been sentenced to 'two months service in the foremost position' by the company commander because of a marginal absence without leave. The company commander was advised about his incorrect behaviour.

The Alsatian soldier Dominik Richert describes the consequences of stepping out of the marching column on the Eastern Front:

Due to the unbalanced food provision, I suffered – like many others – from severe diarrhoea. […] I asked my platoon commander NCO Will for permission [to step out of the line]. Because he still hated me, he sent me to the company commander to ask him. But the commander was riding at the front of the battalion. Again I asked NCO Will for permission. And because I couldn't possibly wait any longer, I stepped out of the column, put the knapsack, rifle and waist belt down at the side of the road and went into the bushes next to the road. […] Our company commander, a terribly rude person, now came from the front to his company. When he saw my things lying at the side of the road, he snarled: 'Whose things are these?' I shouted from the bushes: 'They belong to me, Musketeer Richert!' – 'Well, come out here!' he shouted. I got my clothes sorted, went over to him and stood at attention. 'Have you asked for permission to step out?' – 'Yes, Sir, I have asked NCO Will,' I answered. 'NCO Will, come over here!' the First Lieutenant said. 'Did this man ask for permission to step out?' […] 'No, Sir!' – 'You impertinent rude bastard!' the First Lieutenant then bawled at me. 'You get five days severe arrest for lying to a superior!' I then wanted to inform him that at least 20 men must have heard me asking NCO Will for permission. I had hardly opened my mouth, when he raised his hand holding the riding whip and shouted: 'Shut the hell up!' I was burning up with anger, but I was entirely powerless. […] For as there was no time to serve the sentence and no proper locality for detention available, those who had been sentenced were tied up with ropes to a tree or a cartwheel. Two hours of being tied up equalled one day of arrest. Therefore I was supposed to be tied up for ten hours.

Peter Hammerer, 38 years old, was a basket-maker from a small village in Bavarian Swabia. During autumn 1916, his wife Rosina was pregnant with her seventh child. A charge report concerning 'unpatriotic conduct' was submitted in March 1916, after an officer had brought complaints about Hammerer's war letters to notice. In terms of character and style, these were very similar to the following one from 3 November 1916, which Hammerer wrote to his wife after he had been sentenced to two months in prison for absence without leave:

Dear wife Rosina, I sent you a card on 23 October and those in the post office Oy in Haslach have sent it back to me and have written on it unknown you are not in Haslach. Is that not a mean lot and they know you so well – you can see what sort of help you have there my dear wife. What sort of misery you are going to have when you go into labour this month and I am not going to be there. No help but the children. And the devil's swindle doesn't stop. Although I think about it all the time, I am running out of answers what to do to you. Dear wife Rosina, here the sons-of-bitches write you're getting so much help and get so much, the swindle nation. Dear wife, just like those crucifix bandits wrote that I wasn't doing anything – just getting drunk all the time.

I'm supposed to give my life here for such bandits. No, they shall give their own lives. I get nothing from them – only harm. Dear wife, let things go their own way – I've had enough. I stayed with you several extra days and now I have received two months jail. It's just as well. Dear Frau Rosina I know my own thoughts. I told it to them in the trial. I want to be let out. I don't want to have anything more to do with this misery. This must be the payment for the years when we were protecting the Big Capitalists, protecting their stuff. Let them protect it themselves and not send people out who have to go out and make a living. I get nothing from them and I want nothing more than to just come home to you. It's been over two years of trouble and misery now for you and the children and me. I have nothing to defend. Now I just want to make my own money, be on my own. I get nothing from them but hunger and misery. They don't give us nothing more to eat than goulash, and there's only potatoes in it – the rest of the goulash, the meat, gets eaten by those who are behind the front. They hold their heads in a way that isn't pretty and get the big money on top of it. Dear wife, you can't imagine how bad it is here for us and every day it just keeps getting worse. It's the same at the front and at home. You saw it in Kempten already. The Big Shots – they have more meat to gorge themselves on than a shepherd could jump over. And out here it's the same. Dear wife, let me just tell you, the ones taken prisoners are much better off than we are here. It's said that he in the 'field' deserves double rations, but has nothing to eat but potatoes and cabbage. It's because of them. They got big money and better food so that they can turn the troops into fools. But that's over. Everybody knows it's a lie, a swindle. Many warm greetings from your dear husband. I hope to see you soon.

The court-martial proceedings initiated in March 1916 as a response to the earlier letter were suspended mainly due to a medical expert opinion from the battalion doctor on 21 April 1916. The doctor uses biologistic and psychiatric language and is keen to differentiate between the physical, mental, social and hereditary elements in Hammerer's personality:

The medical examination of Landwehr man Peter Hammerer, 1st company Landwehr Infantry Regiment No. 12, showed neither physical deficiency nor symptoms of degeneration or anomalies due to a weak nervous system nor neurological deficit of any kind.

Hammerer's physique is well-proportioned, his nutritional condition and his development are good, the sense organs without noticable defect. The knee-jerk was substantially increased when examined which leads to the assumption of an abnormality of the nervous system. An increased irritability is furthermore noticeable, it is accompanied by a facial rash, symptoms that are a sign of congestive blood flow towards the head respectively towards the central nervous system.

Hammerer denies alcoholism and sexually transmitted diseases. He rather explains that he would become violent after having just a few beers.

His sleep, he claims, is very poor and very often he falls asleep not before morning. He would suffer from nightmares very often. Frequently he would have a feeling of vertigo which is presumably caused by the blood flow as mentioned above.

There are some more affirmative indications for the assessment of patient Hammerer's mental condition when examining the family history of the defendant. His father who is also a basket-maker is still alive and is said to be a chronic drinker. He came repeatedly into conflict with the law for getting involved in a tussle. The grandfather on his mother's side is said to have committed suicide, the grandmother is said to have become insane in her last years.

In summary and provided that the given statements are truthful and according to the results of the examination the following must be assumed:

1. Hammerer's education was poor and very insufficient, therefore he is lacking character qualities that are important and necessary for a regular life.
2. Hammerer is an example of a very irritable nature without any educationary and moral stability lacking any kind of self-control.

3. Hammerer has a hereditary handicap from both his father's side directly and his mother's side due to his grandparents.
4. Due to his itinerant profession already pursued by his father and due to his poor education, Hammerer does not have the certain ideals of life which are absolutely necessary for a good soldier's spirit.

In short: Hammerer is an inferior, weak-minded and easily irritable person with a low morale and without a firm view of life and without the sense of duty. These are characteristics that should be taken into consideration in his personal assessment but do not classify him as irresponsible respectively certifiably insane.

Dr Kaindl

Tied Up[27]

'Tying Up' (*Anbinden*) was a punishment according to the 'Military Regulations about the Execution of Sentences' in the field. If an appropriate locality for detention was not available, severe arrest could be carried out by tying a soldier to a tree or a cartwheel for two hours a day. As this form of punishment was extremely humiliating, the military authorities received many complaints. In December 1915, the Prussian War Ministry asked all army high commands whether the punishment was fit for purpose. Those who wanted to discard the punishment were in the majority, but it was nonetheless only prohibited in March 1917. Lance Corporal Adolf Benedict writes to his parents from the Western Front on 26/27 June 1915:

> Today two of our men were punished. The first one was tied up to a tree for two hours for lying and impermissible behaviour against a NCO [...], the second one was tied up for one hour for foul-mouthed comments. This really is a terrible punishment, isn't it?

War volunteer Paul Wittenburg was also tied up in early 1915, as no locality for his detention was available. He writes:

> The prisoner was simply tied up to a cartwheel for two hours. And there I was and had to endure for two hours in deep snow and quite freezing temperatures. [...] I perceived this punishment as slanderous

and was partly angry, partly devastated by the thought of my father who wanted to be reunited with me as a hero and an officer and of my mother who would have certainly pitied me.

Superiors[28]

Many soldiers, particularly older ones, found it difficult to obey orders given by young lieutenants between the ages of 19 to 21, who were, as company commanders, their superiors. They voiced intensive criticism of the social privileges these young officers enjoyed in the German army. A. Reddigond writes from the troop camp Beverloo in Belgium on 28 April 1915:

I am now assigned to a reserve regiment which will shortly leave for the front lines. The second battalion marched out yesterday, I don't know where to. Obviously, no one from the old guys who are 36 to 39 years old liked to go out to the front. The first hurray–ecstasy has very much disappeared. Thus the mood was more than poor. Although some of the superiors started singing, they then stopped. The troops did not join in. You would not believe how much the men hate those who have just become officers, the sergeant-lieutenants and those who serve as officers. A huge majority of them are still paid their entire salary and on top of that their [monthly] pay of 205 to 250 Mark. Furthermore, they get five Mark each day special ration allowance, whereas the troops are actually going hungry. We do have 1.50 Mark per day for food, but that has been suspended for the military training area Beverloo. Now the provisions are in accordance with the food stock that is available. The poor guys who usually have just 53 Pfennig [the daily pay of a private soldier] for food, they are to be pitied. In the morning there is just coffee, for lunch bread – and what a bread – and again coffee in the evening. Bread every three days and twice a week some lard or butter. On top of that the duty. Now you can see for yourself if the rage against the ones mentioned before is legitimate or not. By all means, the situation is unfair and this outrages everyone. It is a common view that the gentlemen just make a huge profit out of the war, whereas the allotted billions should be used more fairly.

Richard Schiller writes on 13 October 1915 to the Social Democratic MP Hermann Sachse about the treatment by the superiors:

What can I possibly tell you about my drill of the worst kind in Breslau? That wasn't any news for you. You have probably received dozens of complaints about the bad treatment of old people. And I didn't want to appear as somebody who is always complaining. I wanted to experience everything, to have it firmly in my mind.

I have led this life now for three and a half months and I am in a good position to judge several situations with much more confidence. The duty we have to fulfil is an especially rich source of experiences. We old guys, all between 40 and 45 years, who have never done military service, [...] we had to learn everything and under the most unpleasant circumstances. [...] And then the treatment we receive. Just one example: A 40-year-old master tailor did not understand an order during the roll call for pay; he asked. Answer: 'Shut your bloody mouth until you have been asked!' When he then repeated his question shyly, he was told: 'If you don't shut up at once, I'll hit you in your kisser.'

A Protestant student who had only risen to the rank of a lance corporal after two and a half years of service writes on 27 December 1916:

During the first months of war, the officers were mainly active or reserve officers who had already received their commission in peace time. These superiors were responsible and strict on duty and comradely and caring after duty. Therefore the relationship between officers and troops was then quite good, often excellent. But slowly this relationship changed for the worse, when the reserve officers trained during the war became platoon and company commanders. They were lacking any sense of duty with regard to the troops. The platoon and company commanders were very strict with the men and observed the rank difference very carefully. They made sure not to socialize with their subordinates without realizing that the same men were supposed to serve their country faithfully, taking great risks and even making the ultimate sacrifice.

Sometimes the distance between superiors and subordinates even became noticable while the men were exposed to enemy fire. In his memoirs, Felix Fonrobert, who fought with the Fusilier Regiment 39, reports about the battle at the Chemin des Dames in August 1917:

The artillery fire never stopped, sometimes it ebbed away just to rise again to heavy barrage before an attack. Our losses increased, even in the sap, the improved connection trench. But there were still some quiet hours offering the chance to get sorted and to get some orientation. Even though I was the commander of a group (the NCOs used to 'piss off' and tried to be detached to another place when we were supposed to head to the front lines), I also had to stand as a sentinel in the sap: The platoon commander, a reserve officer, asked me to do so. He, like many other officers did not show up in the trenches! He even relieved himself into an old steel helmet in the shelter. His orderly had to empty the helmet afterwards.

Blood Sacrifices[29]

Families with many children were sometimes affected in more than one respect by the quickly increasing death toll at the front, for they could lose more than one son and the family father at the front. Thus, the number of complaints from the people increased. The Bavarian Ministry of War issued a decree in October 1916:

In view of the long duration of the war, the complaints from the population and from members of the parliaments multiply. They criticize the fact that the troops are used without consideration of the family background of the soldiers, while some families have already suffered many blood sacrifices. They also claim that family fathers with many children always have to do duty in the foremost front lines. The Ministry of War does not want to close its eyes to the legitimacy of these complaints and attributes great importance to measures that could possibly eliminate these hardships, as it is also in the interest of the state to spare the last sons and the fathers of many children. It is on the other hand impossible to issue general decrees in this respect. Therefore the Ministry of War requests the troops to take the family background of soldiers into consideration, as far as this is possible in terms of military organization, by reassigning or detaching them. Signed Kreß [Bavarian Minister of War]

'Hindenburg's Thanks'[30]

Entirely meaningless orders that put lives at risk created a lot of bitterness. The following report from a postwar trial about the 'stab-in-the-back' legend refers to 'Hindenburg's thanks', Hindenburg's replies to the numerous congratulations on the occasion of his seventieth birthday on 2 October 1917:

Once a messenger, full of indignation, showed me a report he had to carry through the thickest barrage fire after it had been dispatched to the wrong position by another messenger. He came right into the heaviest barrage and looked if this message was really that important. It said: 'Infantry Regiment Kirchbach, 7 October 1917. Regimental order. Hindenburg's thanks are to be cut out of all newspapers and to be posted in all quarters, shelters etc. […]' Because of that order, two men had to go through the heaviest barrage.

A soldier in the Garde-Ersatz-Division notes in his diary on 17 January 1917:

Comrade Ladner, who is lying next to me, told me a 'nice' story from the front lines. His regiment was lying between Douaumont and Thiaumont. One day, one of their lieutenants, it was the 19-year-old Schröder from Kassel, sent an orderly to the front line to deliver a message to another lieutenant who was leading a platoon. The area was constantly under the heaviest barrage. The orderly could not get through and was seriously wounded on his way. When they found the man and opened the important message, they saw an interesting newspaper article which Schröder's friend should read just to pass the time in his forward front position. Just before the orderly died, they gave him the Iron Cross. And this way, a father of three had to pay with his life for Schröder's iniquity.

'Scribbles'[31]

When the deteriorating troop morale could not any longer be overlooked, 'measures' were taken. A good example is this secret order from 6 January 1917 to all company commanders of the Marine Corps, which was stationed in Flanders. The order refers to the peace offer by the Central Powers from 12 December 1916, which was rejected by the Allies:

With dislike I have noticed several scribbles on the walls of the troops' quarters and dugouts at the front line etc., which display a longing for peace. After the enemy has harshly rejected the peace offer made by our highest commander in chief and his allies, peace is out of the question here at the front, facing the enemy. Our slogan is: 'The war to the knife and as our aim the unconditional victory!' Only our complete victory can lead to a German peace. This easy logic should be understood by every man. All scribbles on walls, in barracks or in the trenches are to be removed immediately if they show any other spirit than stubborn fight, assault and a firm will to prevail. The officers have to object vigorously to any weak and unmilitary spirit, where ever it might occur, and they are responsible for keeping up the enthusiasm for war and attack and an undestroyable firm will to win.

The character of these 'scribbles' is also revealed in a letter written in April 1916 by a soldier on the Western Front who was a member of the German National Union of Commercial Employees. He writes to Walther Lambach, the president of this association:

Now for something else! It is said, that fools when able smear walls and table. But why would the king in ancient times have a fool as a court jester? And did the scribbles on train waggons in August 1914 not show the right mood of the population? I was wondering about this when I recently saw the scribbles on the walls of some damaged houses in a village occupied by our troops which said something entirely different than some years ago. Just when I was using a toilet here I was reminded again. I recall the following: 'Down with the officers, these gentlemen are scoundrels'. 'No murdering, we want peace!' 'To die a hero's death isn't of any use for us. That is just hot air.' And a remark underneath: 'You are right, comrade.' There aren't many nice words about being killed in action, anyway. There is a lot of truth in this one: 'Those who praise heroic death in battle should go to the front, there they can find it.' And then: 'Bread gets thinner, butter broader, when will the gentlemen ever get any sense? Everything needs to be shattered first.' 'Dear comrades, our wives are starving, just shoot them. The officers of the German army are the ones who eat everything.' 'We have to fight only for the purse of others. Anything else they keep telling us is rubbish.'

Hunger[32]

Food provision was a key issue and major grievance in the German army. From early on, not only people at home in Germany, but also German front-line soldiers experienced hunger. Private soldier Meier reports in November 1915 from the Eastern Front:

We had to march for 22 to 25 kilometers every day, in heavy marching order. Our weak condition was getting worse due to 'good' food provision day by day. When we arrived at the regiment after 8 days, 200 (out of 600) men were missing. One morning when we were marching off the battalion commander told us that we would probably meet Field Marshall Hindenburg during the day. He requested we pull ourselves up straight. The troops answered with hundreds of voices: 'Hunger, hunger, bread, eating' – and only the gentleman kept quiet.

The extent of hunger in the German army is documented in excerpts from war letters written by soldiers in the Eighth Army in June/July 1917 on the Eastern Front. These excerpts were gathered by a field post surveillance unit and forwarded to the High Command East and to Erich Ludendorff as Quartermaster General. A selection:

2. But hunger leads one to write letters like this one here. I can write nothing but the truth, one suffers from hunger here, it makes us sick. It is not any longer bearable.

3. For how long is it still going on. These thickheads at home, they are to blame. They want a formidable victory. Then they will get more chances and get even richer than they already are. They should come over here and hold their heads between the bullets.

4. Everyone is longing for peace here. It can't go on with the food like this much longer. [...]

5. It is a shame, the food, unbearable. Barley-soup and groats, groats and barley-soup. [...]

8. I don't feel like dying a hero's death any more, or are we rather supposed to starve to death; [...]

14. Everyone is war weary and doesn't bother any more. Hopefully there will be a time of proper retribution, for it is a shame in the face of humanity how they treat the troops. It can't be worse in prison. [...]

20. They drive us out of our minds. And on top of that there is the inner hatred and rage. [...] All my best wishes to the children, who knows, I might starve to death here. The day will come when I will eat my own shit. [...]

30. First they let thousands starve to death and when the people are thus feeling offended, they get machine guns into position to shoot down poor hungry women. It has to be like this in Russia to get rid of the bloody militarism. [...]

Upon receipt of these extracts the Quartermaster General asked the High Command East:

[...] if there is any evidence pointing to grievances of any kind concerning provisions in the Eighth Army.

Hunger was also widespread on the Western Front. Complaints about the poor food provision coincided with and were connected to other grievances. A report on the morale of the troops in the Fifth Army, which was compiled on the basis of postal surveillance, states on 12 July 1917:

By far the most important issue in a soldier's life is food provision. When provisions are poor and insufficient, the soldier will start to neglect his duties and be more inclined to criticism. That became very clear at the end of last year [1916], when the army administration proceeded to eke out the potato rations with turnips. The reduction of bread rations some months ago [March 1917] had an almost unbelievable impact. The most intensive complaints and accusations against the military authorities provided evidence for this. The impact has not diminished until today, on the contrary, every letter mentions more or less vividly the question of provisions. And in their resentment, the letter writers add complaints about further issues which were formerly only mentioned in a more hidden manner and only in a few isolated cases, and all that now in a very aggressive manner. Derogatory remarks about the officers are the order of the day. They are said to have more money and would snatch the best food away from the troops. They and their orderlies would enjoy unbelievable privileges concerning leave etc. [...] Then it goes on with more general accusations. The entire state would be nothing but a tool of capitalism and the usurers etc. The recently conducted prophylactic vaccinations gave a few letter writers even an opportunity to inform the people at home that they had received a jab against 'hunger'-typhoid.

A popular slogan among the troops went like this:

With the same pay and the same food
The war would have been long over.

Johann Brandl, a single baker, writes to a farmer in Vilshofen (Bavaria) on 6 May 1917:

Dear Michael! I am still rather healthy and hope the same of you. Here in the field it is all going down, for the provisions are so small that it is hardly enough for us. The food is really crap, but we have to eat it because it is the only food we get. In the morning and in the afternoon we have to work up to the last minute. They are painstakingly exact in this respect, but they don't care about the food we get. We are climbing up and down the mountains all the time and have got to work as well. And the whole time there is a guard watching us and checking that we work properly. As if we were convicts, they have a warden as well. We are in the Vosges. If somebody has to see a doctor the doctor would always say that everything is all right with him unless there is a foot missing. He wouldn't believe anyone saying that he is not feeling well. It is high time that the swindle comes to an end. I didn't even get furlough when my brother died. That is so sad. But the duty comes first. Best wishes from Johann Brandl, farewell. Every three days we get one loaf of bread. It has to be enough for the next three days. We are always hungry. If the officers would get the same provisions as we do, the war would have been finished a long time ago. I am with the communication unit now. It is the same with honours and promotion. Whoever deserves it won't get it.

Some soldiers did not want their relatives to be worried about the poor provisions and avoided mentioning the topic. From a letter written in March 1917:

I hardly have to confirm to you our very insufficient provisions. But please do not tell my wife about that, for I have described everything to her in the most favourable light possible, in order to calm her down and to prevent her sending anything. She hasn't got anything for herself, but she would scrimp and save everything she could and for obvious reasons I have to prevent her from doing that.

Another soldier wrote directly to his wife in June 1918. But the repeated insistence that he would be fine and the use of dashes suggest that the soldier used a code he had agreed with his wife. This was widely practised when soldiers were aware of postal censorship:

I am happy with the food —— Dear wife, please don't worry about me. Out here we are still getting more than you do. I can't complain —— Dear wife please still don't worry about me, I am still well and there is plenty of food.

The food provision in the rear area (Etappe) and in the officers' canteens differed a lot from the situation at the front. Franz Lauterbach writes on 2 August 1917:

Being on procurement duty for the company I was once – introduced by an NCO who was a friend of mine – able to eat something from the kitchen of the divisional sutler and the army storage depot. There was food available! Plenty of meat. There was white bread with the vegetables. In the meantime, the men at the front with teeth problems don't get any white bread although subscribed by a doctor, but just pan loaf.

If You Go on Furlough[33]

From a 'bulletin for soldiers who go on leave' from December 1917:

If you go on furlough, let all the filth and the sad thoughts remain behind you in the trench! [...] If you talk about your experiences, don't complain that you fared badly. Be rather proud to have accomplished superhuman feats. [...] Don't be surprised when your friends from the pub's regulars' table at home don't take much notice of you! Their hearts got all mouldy from all the waiting and sitting on their hands – Just bring them a breath of fresh air from the front and the humour of the front lines!

Leave from War?[34]

Next to food, the scarce provision of leave was a permanent problem and affected the morale of the troops deeply. A decree of the Prussian Ministry of War from 23 October 1915 shows the scale of the problem:

Several requests, claims and proposals about leave that have been sent to the Ministry show that some men who have been on service since the beginning of the war or who have served directly in front of the enemy for a very long time, have never been on furlough to go back to their often hard-pressed relatives. Particularly older, married soldiers and their relatives perceive this as a hardship.

Usually, two weeks of leave were granted after twelve months of front-line service. But many soldiers did not survive such a long period of service. Resignation crept in. Christian Krull, now an officer aspirant, writes in August 1917:

It will take a while with the leave for which I hoped, I am used to nothing else than coming home every 13 or 14 months, and always during winter time. [...] I became resigned to this a long time ago. I'm not at all bothered.

Against the backdrop of the poor allocation of leave, injustices in the way it was granted were a sensitive issue and caused widespread concern. Many soldiers complained that furlough was granted to the orderlies of officers so that they could bring requisitioned food to their relatives at home. In order to secure a proper management of farms particularly during harvest time, special furlough was granted to peasant farmers, which triggered complaints. Wilhelm Rütjerodt, who served at a reserve unit in Holzminden, writes on 18 July 1916:

The only ones who are not in need here are the farmers. They don't have to restrict themselves in any way and have the privilege to go on furlough quite often. Agriculture is a trump card and is supported in every respect as far as possible. The farmers really take advantage or one can say rather exploit these circumstances. If they are on leave and it rains, they won't come back to the company as ordered, but stay at home. When their leave ends, they come back and request furlough because they couldn't get to work in the rain, they claim to need more furlough urgently which they get again. Anyone who is not a farmer has a lot of work to do, so that the farmers can go home on furlough. The farmers have the fat, for the others there is nothing else for it than to watch how they taste it. The comrades are getting more and more fed up, for they watch the farmers living under conditions that are almost even better than those during peace time. The farmers sell butter to the NCOs for a pre-war price. [...] Whoever is a farmer is eminently respectable, and all those with a properly filled purse are spared and promoted in every respect.

Report of the Bavarian Landwehr Infantry Regiment no. 6 from 11 October 1917:

Furthermore, the present regulation of the precarious matter of furlough causes discontent among the urban population and among small businessmen in particular. Despite insistent instructions, the population fails to see the necessity of privileging farmers due to the economic situation. [...] The ways in which requests for furlough, particularly week-long furlough, are reviewed by the local authorities at home, often based on questionable statements, is in many cases not flawless. It is nothing but natural that the troops are puzzled and bitter, when small farmers are getting several weeks of furlough often more than once a year. On top of that comes the fact that those furlough requests that were approved in the first place and later rejected by the unit cause ill feeling against the superiors who make decisions about furlough, for the troops start to think that their superiors in the field would reject their 'essentially necessary' leave.

Furlough was sometimes only granted when soldiers had signed up for a war loan. The following case became public when someone complained.

Troops were granted furlough to confer with their relatives about war loans. It is true that Lieutenant Ludwig, Field Artillery Regiment 10, a young officer ambitious to serve for the good cause, allowed furlough even for those who declared: they would subscribe for war loans if they got furlough. He has also announced leave to several men to encourage them to do this.

Even in the case of a bereavement in the family, the immediate superior had to give his final OK when leave had already been granted. In a case on the Eastern Front it was reported:

In August this year [1916], there was a message via telegram that the father of one of the NCOs in the company had died. The message already included the permission given by a higher ranking authority for a week of leave. When the company sergeant put the telegram to the company commander and returned to the company office, he repeated the company commander's comment: 'There is no point in going back home. By the time he has arrived there, his father will already be in the hole. He can't see him again anyway. He is just interested in joining in the funeral feast.'

In early 1915, articles in medical journals warned against handing out medical certificates as a favour:

Particularly since the beginning of spring, many women have approached a medical doctor in order to obtain a medical certificate to get furlough for their husbands. [...] Some women whom he [a doctor mentioned in the article] had operated on years ago and cured in his opinion, suddenly showed up again. They referred to the previous surgery and asked for a medical certificate so that their husbands, who had been in the field since the beginning of the war, got leave at last. […] A greengrocer asked for a medical certificate because she went to the market hall every day at 4 am and was therefore unsound. When asked how her husband's leave would change this condition of hers, she answered: 'Not at all, of course, but then he could have a proper rest at home.' Four weeks ago, Doctor Sch. [äfer] recommended surgery to a woman with a slipped disc. The woman asked the doctor if she could get this recommendation in writing, for then her husband would get leave. When questioned if she would undergo surgery then, she answered: 'Of course not, when my husband is coming.'

In the Rear Area[35]

A popular expression at the front highlighted the unfair distribution of medals and decorations:

It is raining bullets in the front line,
it is raining decorations in the rear area.

Franz Lauterbach describes how some units practised requisitions:

That is looting! The Russians could not possibly have been worse in East Prussia. But here comes the best. By command of our company, sergeant Spendel and four men requisitioned eight bags of flour of 50 kg each aside from some other stuff. Three bags were given to the kitchen to be distributed among the troops, but only some of the married men got six to seven pounds. A whole bag of 50 kg each got: 1. Sergeant Wöhnelt who works as a cashier at a gas company in Berlin in civil life, 2. Sergeant Lamm, mill-owner in Grünberg, Silesia, 3. Sergeant Lieutenant Jung, a police officer in Düsseldorf. Two bags were still at the company commander's disposal. He sent the flour away. The flour was usually packed in boxes and sent to Germany with the company commander's notation 'transport permitted'. The sergeant, the above-mentioned Mr Lamm, who was then just about to be dismissed due to his age of 45 years and has left the company by now, managed to sell his bag for 250 M to our battalion canteen. The 1st, 2nd, and 3rd company of our battalion also requisitioned flour, from which our battalion commander captain Gertung has kept 2 bags for himself as well. Mr Gertung is district attorney. He has been in Düsseldorf recently and helped to sentence the poor people who joined local hunger riots.

In particular the officers and civil servants who were employed in the military administration of the rear area (Etappe) in Belgium and Northern France could make a decent living during and from the war. Wilhelm Appens, after the war a local school inspector in Dortmund, served as an NCO in the II. rear area headquarters Charleville in the French rear area. From his book *Charleville. Dark Episodes of Life in the Etappe*, published in 1920:

There were always just a few men in every formation who seriously worked. Most of them were loafing. These spongers were summed up by the expression: 'If only peace doesn't break out!' During the last two years of the war, I have met officers and members of the military administration who visibly turned pale when peace was mentioned. Whole formations were redundant and expensive military measures resulted in nothing but the scorn and derision of the front troops.

Appens also mentions the Voluntary Automobile Corps, basically a chauffeur driven car-pool for officers in Charleville:

These were gentlemen with a strange military rank. They were no officers, but were wearing some kind of a lieutenant's uniform. They had a distinguished or high finance family background. They had the same attitude as the one-yearer's of a feudal guard regiment. Their entire patriotism consisted of nothing but offering their own cars and themselves at the Great Headquarters' disposal. They had some very illustrious leaders at their top: the fragile Prince Waldemar of Prussia and the Prince of Schaumburg-Lippe who again acted as the pleasant philanderer of the ladies in Charleville, just as in 1870 [during the Franco-Prussian war]. No other formation in the Great Headquarters behaved more pretentiously and unworthy than this one, but then no other has been avoided like the plague.

Whoever could, tried to get to Charleville. Even at the time of the Great Headquarters, it was not the competent men, but the most noble men from always the very same noble families who were chosen to serve in Charleville. Whenever one of them had got hold of a place in the sun, he would get his blood relatives and acquaintances to follow him. New positions proliferated like Hydra's heads. [...] During the last two years they have followed this method even more so than ever before. Everybody made a bolt for the back. As in the cinema, there were the best seats. In the front, it flickers.

First-lieutenant Herrmann, serving in a divisional staff, writes to his father-in-law, the Protestant minister Hans Falck, on 7 June 1915 from the rear area on the Eastern Front:

The horseshow has provided a welcome change for me yesterday and today. I have already told Ilse all about it. In some respect, my expectations about the war used to be different. Just imagine: 6 km behind the front, grandstands decorated with flags, music, show-jumping and driving competitions etc. In many respects, an event like this one is a good thing. But in my and several other people's view it is not, for it does no good to the infantry men in the front trenches at all. It might even fill them with bitterness against headquarters and particularly against the convoy-troops who obviously have the greatest opportunity to join in an event like this. But that is an idle consideration.

Prostitutes and brothels were usually only found in the rear area. The military authorities regulated them strictly in an attempt to control the spread of venereal diseases. In the territories occupied by the German army, women prostituted themselves for economic reasons. They were the target of German soldiers, as Heinrich Wandt describes in his booklet 'Etappe Gent', which was published in 1926 and sold more than 200,000 copies:

But the honest soldiers in field grey, who often had been away from mother way too long, did not only want to drink 'een groote pint beer' or 'een warm pottje koffie', they also wanted something for body and soul. Thus they graced first of all the estaminets with their presence, where a reubenesque landlady or pretty daughters served food and drinks.

Next to them or even with them sitting on their laps, they felt comfortable, safe and secure and almost 'like with mummy' or like 'Vadding in France'.

For this reason, a certain establishment in the village of Afsné near to Gent was very popular and had lots of visitors. Its landlord had seven daughters, the youngest 14 year old. [...] The soldiers never called this establishment other than: 'The fourteen buttocks'. Without doubt, it was the most popular pub in the rear area of Gent.

The Social Democrat Willy Hauffe was a scribe in the medical transport unit in the town of Mitau (nowadays the Latvian town of Jelgava). In a lengthy letter written on 15 May 1916 he reports about an 18-year-old Latvian girl who was working in a brothel for German officers:

She looked haggard and aged! I asked her about all sorts of things, because she was quite talkative. Being asked about her husband, she answered bitterly: 'Well! (She took a deep breath and sobbed) If it wasn't war, I had a husband, I were a respectable woman. But it is war, so I am your whore. I don't have a man, so I have to have men for money.' Then she gave me a small blue book, her control book. She worked in the officers' brothel in Mitau. Her fiancé had been a soldier. She was from a little town near Libau. [...] Around here are two brothels in operation, one for officers (8 women), one for the troops (6–7 women), it is 10 marks in the first one, five marks in the second one. 12 marks per day they have to pay for board and lodge etc. Officers are allowed into the brothel for troops, but not vice versa. That is 'war-life'!!!

Heinrich Wandt makes a final judgement about the system of German military brothels:

The German soldiers were surprised by the very large numbers of women and girls who prostituted themselves. They did not take into account how [German] militarism with its systematic brutality had disgraced these unfortunates and did not leave them any other choice, if they did not want to starve to death, for the long war had robbed them of any other way of earning a living. Terrible and massive was the suffering of those men who were putting their lives on the line at the front and died and got crippled for the madness of war. But even more terrible and massive was the mental suffering of women and girls, and most terribly and massive was the suffering of those penniless women in the occupied areas.

Complaints and Censorship[36]

Until April 1916, when centralized postal surveillance units were introduced, letters from the front were read and eventually censored by the immediate military superior. The historian Martin Hobohm, who later investigated the causes of the German collapse in 1918, was an ordinary gunner on the Western Front during the war. He describes the consequences of an order about the censorship of letters in his unit:

> I can remember very well how we were feeling in spring 1915 in our recruitment depot. Most of the men were average family fathers from Berlin. When we were told to hand in only open mail, because our letters were to be checked, every one of us had a very strange and bitter feeling. For the second time we felt torn away from our Heimat, we felt disgusted watching this sergeant reading our letters to our wives at home. One was amazed and puzzled and as a free citizen one felt as if someone had pulled the rug out from under oneself.

An article in a newsletter featuring military decrees states in February 1917:

> Quite often, there are complaints about violations of the secrecy of correspondence. In particular, older married men are bitterly offended by the way their letters are checked without appropriate consideration of the secrecy of correspondence in the company orderly room. Even intimate family matters are divulged and turned into a laughing stock. We request headquarters and formations to make provisions for the censorship of letters, so that only officers are to be called in to conduct the surveillance of letters and people who can safeguard the secrecy of the messages they have to check due to their civilian background and their reliability, as well as due to their discretion and age.

A soldier on leave writes in February 1915:

> Dear Parents. Today I would like to send you a detailed letter, because this one is not a 'field post letter', but an ordinary one which is delivered by the civil post service. [...] Dear Mother, please don't be upset because I told you that I do not need any more knee warmers. You also complained that I don't let you know more details about my health. Please consider that our letters are always checked. Knowing that

someone else will read the letter, one does not want to tell everything, even if it does not cause any offence.

Letters that were addressed to members of parliament were sometimes the subject of specific checks. The military apparently feared that they would contain complaints that it did not want to be revealed in the public parliamentary debates. From a letter written in 1916 to a Social Democratic member of the Reichstag:

Please accept my apologies for intentionally not adding M.d.R. [Member of the Reichstag] to the address on the envelope. I am convinced that no letter would reach you uncensored in this case.

On the other hand, soldiers expected negative consequences if they received letters from a member of parliament. Dr Max Süßheim, a member of the Bavarian diet, explains in a speech in May 1916:

It is a very strange phenomenon that members of this house were asked by men in the field army not to use official parliament envelopes when corresponding with them. Apparently there are special reasons for this request. The relevant soldiers who were expressing this wish are under the impression that they will get into trouble with their superiors when corresponding with a member of parliament. [...] These wishes demonstrate clearly the severe mistakes made by some military authorities.

From a decree by the Bavarian War Ministry on 19 February 1916:

The Ministry of War received complaints that in several formations superiors ridiculed their inferiors who received letters with an added 'Mr' to the address on the envelope.

I request to put a stop to any rudeness of this kind, because it is offensive and therefore particularly condemnable at the present time when all different groups in our army stand together regardless of their social standing or age.

On 4 March 1917, the Quartermaster General issued a decree on postal censorship which was (perhaps deliberately) open to interpretation by military units in the field. The decree issued on 29 April 1916 to which the Quartermaster General refers had introduced censorship through centralized postal surveillance units:

> In case of objections against field post letters on the grounds of article 2 of the decree of the Chief of the General Staff of the Field Army from 29 April 1916 – M.J. No. 36061 – it is imperative to protect the interests of national defence and other general interests. Therefore it is impractical to be too narrow-minded in the scrutiny of letters and to stop letters containing general complaints about poor provisions, duty on bank holidays or general expressions of ill-humour or discontent. The private exchange of ideas between front and home should not be interrupted if possible. On the other hand, it is certainly justified to take action against the letter writers in case of undoubted damage to the interests of duty, severe violations against military discipline, provocative and severely discouraging comments. Letters in short hand are banned within the army postal service.

The postal surveillance units of the Fifth Army on the Western Front adopted the following practice:

> All field post letters of every division entering the formation of the army for the first time will be monitored most thoroughly and repeatedly during the first days. Usually, several objections occur, followed by the punishment of the particular letter writers. After a short while this practice has spread by word-of-mouth in the formations. The men are warned and will be more careful now when writing about military matters to the Heimat.

Some soldiers used codes they had agreed with their relatives in order to relay unfiltered information about their well-being. Many others gave their letters to comrades who were going home on leave, so that they could be delivered by normal postal services. If discovered, these soldiers were sentenced to severe arrest. From a decree of the High Command of the Fourth Army in January 1916:

> It was ascertained in one army that soldiers going on leave took a huge number of letters back to Germany, affixed stamps and handed them in for the distribution by the ordinary civil postal service in order to avoid censorship. Very often these letters contain military secrets. Therefore

it is forbidden to pass on letters to soldiers going on leave so that they use the ordinary postal service, and it is forbidden to take those letters. The soldiers going on leave are to be searched to implement this ban.

Many of the complaints mentioned in the letters were actually legitimate in the context of the military procedures provided for complaints by troops. But not only soldiers but also members of parliament, such as the above-mentioned Social Democrat Dr Max Süßheim, knew:

The entire military complaints procedure is meant to convince soldiers that they should refrain from complaining at all. The iron discipline, the uncontested power of the superior over his subordinates, the ban on every refusal whatsoever, even in cases of physical violence [by superiors], the demand of unconditional obedience, recollections of incidents oneself or others have experienced explains very well why the men fear that a complaint would do more harm to them than to their superiors. [...] Everyone who is familiar with the army life knows that a man complaining about his NCO will be heavily maltreated by him afterwards.

The journeyman butcher Michael Kappelmeier, infantryman on the Western Front, experienced possible repercussions following a complaint. Möggenried, a master joiner from the Bavarian town of Sonthofen mentioned in the following letter, actually passed on Kappelmeier's letter, but not to a member of parliament, but to the Bavarian War Ministry. In January 1915, Kappelmeier was sentenced to one year's imprisonment for 'smearing a superior'. The fact that he had tried to make his case public aggravated the sentence. The letter to his former master, a Mrs Burger in Sonthofen, was the key evidence during the trial:

Dear Mrs Burger! [...] Apart from that I am thank God still well. We have to bear a lot here. I haven't taken off my clothes during these five weeks. We sleep in the open field, mostly without any straw. Then you understand what life means. For three weeks we have continually been in the trenches around 70 km north of Paris. Believe me, Mrs Burger, now a meat loaf would be quite nice. But there is sometimes nothing other than grenades and when we come back, very often everything is cold, for the field kitchen of the tenth company is just a mess. We have nothing else other than reserve officers here any more. Well, officers?

They don't deserve to be called officers, for they are nothing than fools. The other day we got a barrel of wine for the company. The field kitchen had to put half of the barrel into bottles, so that the reserve officer gentlemen had something to drink. And that is called comradeship. As a result, the sergeant was drunk as a monkey when he came along with the field kitchen the next day. But we would be happy to get anything to eat at all. Naturally, he did not come before night, although he could easily have driven over during the day. Thus, any pleasure is lost. But we do it all for the fatherland and for God. Please could you ask Möggenried if he could inform a member of parliament. It is the same story with the military postal service. Of course, the sergeant will pass the letters [from home] on only if he wants to. We out here cannot do anything about it, for we are threatened with being shot immediately. He has certainly done the fatherland a good service. Other companies receive gift parcels, in the tenth company they are sold anyway. We have to pay 10 pfennigs for the worst cigars, and then it is a mercy to get one at all. It is too bad, but all true.

It should also be considered what a humiliation it must have been for an artisan with a stainless reputation like Kappelmeier that not only was his complaint not investigated, but that he was even sentenced to a prison term in the process. Something similar happened to the NCO Johann Wilhelm Entz. Following the letter he wrote to his wife on 20 July 1917, he was sentenced to one year's imprisonment for 'insult' on 20 February 1918. From the incriminating letter to his wife:

Expecting that you have received all my mail, I would like to give you a little impression of our military life which is unfortunately very much glorified by the newspapers. I just wish one of those scribblers would stay within the range of grenade fire for a couple of hours and eat from our field kitchen just for a month. Fortunately there are still some newspapers that make any effort to point out some grievances. But the newspaper proposes, the superior disposes! You would think our living conditions would improve the longer the war goes on, but alas, far from it! Since nobody at home has the slightest idea, how the gentlemen superiors who are all former school teachers dare to behave. [...] It is all true, what a member of the Reichstag or the Landtag recently said: If the troops get all the provisions going out for them, they would all have enough. But until the provisions have arrived at the front, bit by bit has been taken away. It is a shame how much is left for the men at the front. [...] It is a mistake that the same NCOs responsible for food provision and the same provision's officers are sitting on these posts since we left for the front. They have good connections and clients at the rear area. They are forced to resort to shabby tricks, for they all made themselves quite comfortable in the rear area, and the women cost money as well. The amount of stuff pushed into these holes and still to be pushed in the future, is just amazing. The Bavarian Minister of War recently wrote he would interfere with an iron hand to abolish grievances like that. Has the man got sore hands in the meanwhile? I bet! He may go and see for himself the difference in the provisions. But alas, decrees by the Ministry are apparently only issued to be evaded in defiance.

Anonymous Letters[37]

The many obstacles soldiers faced when they wanted to log a complaint led them to search for another outlet for their discontent. As a result, more and more anonymous letters were filed both at home and at the front. The following from November 1915 was addressed to the Reich chancellor:

When will this murdering come to an end? The price increases are unbearable. Anyway, our field-grey soldiers have to suffer terribly from ill-treatment by sometimes more than snotty superiors. Thus, every single man states that he would rather be a prisoner of war than to fight for a fatherland like this. The whole company has to suffer constantly only because there are just a few bad elements. Our husbands say that this is the justice in Germany. They say we shouldn't grumble about the enemy, for they certainly don't grind their men behind the lines as our husbands are grinded. For example, an acquaintance who was wounded and has returned home, got a stone thrown at him by his sergeant. The reason was that due to his ulcerous legs he could not walk as quickly as this stableboy of a sergeant wanted him to do so. That's how they treat our German men in their own fatherland. And how are the sons of the noble men doing? They get engaged, they are always with their wives and children. The Empress goes into the field if she feels the need to do so. They take everything away from us. For what are our husbands fighting? We wives know it, it is not for us. Afterwards, we will be worse off than before. Thus down with the war, otherwise there will be a proper revolution. We want our husbands back. One woman speaking for many others.

Anonymous letters also reported grievances in specific military units. The letter writers knew that they were not using the official channels. From a letter with complaints about a Landsturm battalion in Nuremberg sent to the Bavarian War Ministry in November 1915:

Against my will and my further opinion I am forced by the military penal code and the regulation on complaints procedures to make complaints and objections about the unbearable situation in the local Landsturm Infantry Battalion Schweinauerstrasse without giving my name. I am forced to adopt this method of complaining which I have always considered as condemnable under normal circumstances. But if I complained with my full name, the relevant Landsturm soldiers and NCOs would be known and possibly be punished for evading the official channels. But following the official channels there is no way that the relevant troops get their rights, for the major and his adjutant will make sure that no complaints will be passed on, unless the troops are hindered from submitting them in the first place.

Chapter 4

Refusal and Disobedience

Unlike in the French army, which was severely hit by mutinies in the aftermath of the failed Nivelle offensive in April 1917, no major incidents of collective disobedience occurred in the German front-line army until autumn 1918. Nonetheless, the increasingly war-weary German soldiers could refuse or dodge their military service in similar ways as their counterparts in other armies. Fraternization, tacit agreements to 'live and let live', self-mutilation, the simulation of mental-health problems or desertion were the most widely used options. German soldiers could not only defect to the enemy, an act that was fraught with risks, not least the threat of being shot by either the enemy or their own troops. They could also desert to the neutral countries of Denmark, Switzerland and the Netherlands. According to contemporary figures and estimates, about 30,000 German soldiers fled to these three neutral countries during the war. It is much more difficult to establish the number of those soldiers who tried or were able to desert to the enemy lines or to the rear, hiding in the Etappe or on German territory. These difficulties are partly due to the attempts of officers of the Imperial army and subsequently of the Reichswehr to whitewash the court-martial system during the war. It must be assumed that incriminating evidence about the number of desertions and issues of the death penalty for desertion was destroyed during demobilization and the revolution in 1918 or was not properly scrutinized in the Weimar Republic. Actions like these were part of the attempts to exonerate the Imperial army, and the front-line troops in particular, from any culpability for the German defeat. Despite these problems, an informed estimate can put the number of desertions in Germany (including those who fled to the neutral countries) up to July/August 1918 at about 100,000. In a mass army that mobilized millions of men, this was still not a major problem that undermined the whole disciplinary system. But by the summer of 1918, desertion was also more than just a negligible quantity, indicating that war-weariness motivated an increasing number of soldiers to contemplate and practise individual forms of refusal.

Injured Soldiers Going Back Home[38]

During the initial months of the war of movement, the front troops were advised to send injured soldiers quickly back to the rear area. At this time, so-called 'Patient Collection Points' had not yet been turned into tight filters which could prevent soldiers from heading further back and getting home to Germany. Thus, many injured soldiers were able to be admitted to hospitals in Germany. From a decree by the Prussian War Ministry from 6 September 1915:

Recently, a number of army members had to be punished for absence without leave. They had been referred to other military hospitals and, instead of arriving there immediately, they had first visited and stayed with their families for quite a long time. In many cases they have been entirely respectable soldiers up to this point who had been severely wounded in the war and who were only enticed by their longing for their families.

It can be assumed that these men were not sufficiently aware of military hospitals being official positions for them in terms of paragraph 64 Military Penal Code and that thus failing to appear there deliberately has to be seen as an absence without leave.

According to the circumstances and with regard to the severe sentences given during the state of war, the War Ministry considers it as advisable to give the men detailed instructions.

These cases were also considered in medical journals. The deputy head physician of the first army corps, Dr Herhold, writes in a supplement to the journal *Munich Medical Weekly* in October 1914:

It is even more fatal to discharge slightly wounded men individually at their own request and allow them to go back home and to see any doctor there. Naturally, these men will stay with their relatives and are hence beyond military control. They often do not know where to go after being cured. Thus, they are initially lost for the field army. These mistakes of discharging slightly wounded persons were made mainly by voluntary aided military hospitals. But also some ambulance-train platoon commanders gave several slightly wounded men permission to leave the train before it arrived at its destination. It is the duty of all medical doctors and of all hospitals to report all men and NCOs presenting themselves individually for bandaging to the next reserve military hospital or to the next district commander and to state their regiment and place of residence.

The great enthusiasm of our youth that we witnessed at the outbreak of the war ensures us that our men are eager to fight and will get back to the front after their wounds are healed. May everyone try and help to keep up this enthusiasm by considering what was mentioned above.

Self-Mutilation[39]

Some soldiers inflicted injuries on themselves in order to escape the war. A decree by the Bavarian War Ministry states on 29 January 1915:

Several men who had been reported as deserters by their formations in the field were found with injuries to fingers or hands in some military hospital in the Heimat. In view of this fact combined with further observations it seems to be likely that repeatedly men tried to evade service in the field by mutilating themselves.

From the memoirs of Felix Fonrobert:

In mid-March 1916, I was jolly well fed up. I called in sick. The field hospital was in a mill that had been closed a long time ago, near by our hutment. It was on the second day of my stay, the medical officer happened to be there for an examination. Suddenly a shot was fired right in this room full of several sick and wounded men. The bullet went into the wall without hurting anybody. But no, someone was moaning: 'My foot!' He was lying next to me on a cot with a paillasse sack. The bullet had shattered his big toe. I had seen that he had done it on purpose – and kept silent. It had happened when he was cleaning his rifle. That was my answer when the medical officer demanded clarification. The wounded man went to hospital. He got himself a 'Heimatschuss' [blighty wound]. Cases of self-mutilation like this one were not unusual at all.

Excerpt from a court-martial sentence:

In the criminal case against Friedrich Sautter from Blaubeuren, musketeer of the 3rd company 124th Infantry Regiment, presently in the military hospital II in Ulm, charged with self-mutilation etc., the court martial convened on order of the court of the 1st Deputy 54th

Infantry Brigade in the garrison of Ulm delivers the following sentence after the meeting from 12 November 1915:

The defendant is sentenced to three years in prison, as well as the degradation accorded to a soldier of second class for committing the crime of self-mutilation during his duty simultaneous with the offence of leaving his post in the field without authorization.

Fraternization[40]

The son of a peasant farmer describes developments that reached their climax in the Christmas period of 1914 in a letter written on 13 December 1914:

Dear Mother! Tonight we are lying comfortably in our stony caves. And although we often have a hard time, it is always followed by some better times. The weather here is quite mild. There were some days with light frost. Let's hope it won't rain a lot, that is the worst for us here on this loamy soil. The men from the 13th [regiment] from Münster are in the trenches on our left side. They are just 15 metres away from the enemy at some points. During the day, the French officers are away, and then there is no shooting. The sergeants on both sides are sitting on top of the trenches and having a conversation. The men are exchanging cognac and cigarettes. The Frenchmen also handed them a letter asking our men to surrender, since the Russians were already in Berlin. One of the men from the 13th could speak French. He explained to them how things were. They shrugged their shoulders and were surprised. The men from the 13th will be relieved by the 56th, then maybe things are getting serious again. These are just some details, but they are all true. At Christmas we will be relieved for 20 days and will be brought back to reserve positions during that time. That is going to be a lovely time of peace and quietness, because we haven't been away from the roar of guns since 2 September.

The fraternizations between German and French and British troops respectively during Christmas 1914 were a remarkable phenomenon. For days, the soldiers met in no-man's-land, exchanged gifts, sang Christmas carols and buried their dead comrades. Carl Zuckmayer reports in his autobiography:

In the Christmas days of 1914, the soldiers in the trenches to the west of Roye, which were very close to each other, stopped shooting during the night, which was quite common at all quiet front lines. Instead of hand grenades, they threw parcels with sausages and chocolate over the hay-wire circuits. At a Hesse regiment a German patrol started a conversation with a French one. They shook hands and invited each other over into the shelters. The Germans brought beer and booze, the French wine. Naturally, this happened without the officers knowing – until one night a young lieutenant on his round found some cheerfully banqueting Frenchmen, who had unstrapped and put their rifles in a corner, in the shelter of a German squad. Out of stubborness or out of a sense of duty, he detained them and had them hauled off as prisoners immediately. That was the end of the short fraternization.

Incidents of fraternization endangered a crucial requirement for the continuation of war: the enemy images of the troops and their combat motivation. A total of 70,000 copies of a trench newspaper were distributed to the troops in the Fourth Army. It featured the following article in early 1915. It refers to 'Michel', a nickname for the typical German and a symbol of German national identity:

But hell, no, for our German soldiers the Frenchman is no comrade, as he is fighting shoulder to shoulder with English mercenaries and some sort of African scallywags against us. And we do not want to lapse back again into our old, trustful, easily forgiving, stupid 'Michel' spirit. We should not believe in the possibility that there ever will be a real fraternization between Frenchmen and Germans. Fortunately, the sentimental ingratiation between the trenches around Christmas is over. Now the slogan is again: Let him have it! That does not only apply to the moment of receiving the order to march forward, but also for the long hours of mental preparation. Michel, stand firm! [...] This is a fight to the finish, the struggle for life. Go on then, Michel, give everyone a smack in the kisser who wants to have peace too early. One can only get on with the Frenchman when he and his army is defeated and defenceless.

Fraternizations also occurred over the Christmas period in 1915. On 7 December, a lieutenant writes from the Western Front:

Dear parents! At the front line, there is a huge fraternization going on. Frenchmen and Germans are standing between the lines or even in the trenches in small and big groups. They exchange wine and cigarettes, have a conversation and even take photographs of themselves. Even officers join in. I have never seen anything like this.

At many of the more quiet stretches on the Western Front, occasional fraternizations could turn into more extended forms of mutual agreement to 'live and let live'. Otto Weber, after the war a member of the veteran's association in Buchloe, states in a recollection written in 1928:

The first Bavarian Army Corps was engaged in the 'Autumn Battle at La Bassee and Arras' (according to the official expression) on 12 October 1915 to ward off the most recent French major offensive. The right wing was standing near the Loretto Height in front of the sugar factory of Souchez. In the beginning we had some highly unpleasant days, without any trenches and obstacles, but we were supposed not to budge an inch more. Then we started again to build up a network of trenches. From the midst of November, it rained relentlessly. The trenches, which had been built up with a lot of effort, collapsed. Very often it was impossible to use them any more. The dugouts were completely filled with water and mud, if we did not go on dragging buckets of water out of them or pumping them dry. We built up barricades and traverses and dammings with filled sandbags in the soil, we worked day and night, it was all in vain. [...]

Our position with the 1st Infantry Regiment was situated on the right wing of the army corps on the hill right in the west of Givenchy and was about 60 to 80 metres away from the French position. The French tried to get closer, building up saps and combining them with a trench, until they got a new position. We did the same thing. This way, we got as close as 30 or 40 metres in some places. Since it was raining constantly, we could not stay in the trenches any longer. Therefore we had to leave the trenches. Shooting was out of the question, for our rifles were completely covered with mud so that we could not open the bolt any more. It was the same with every man on guard. During the whole time on position everyone was covered in sticky mud from head to toe and of course constantly wet as well, so that one could hardly recognize his best comrade. Fortunately, it was the same for the French. Several times we could hear a voice from 'over there' or a head appeared: 'Comrade, no more bumm bumm!' Naturally, we agreed. But even if we moved more openly out of cover, the relationship towards the enemy remained still very tense anyway. One day I witnessed for example how a French post shot one of my comrades. We were both carrying explosive material into the first trench in broad daylight. We were walking outside the trench side by side, when the Frenchman shot my comrade. When we protested indignantly towards the French over there, one of the Frenchmen apologized that the shooter was a very young lad and that it would not happen again. We could communicate with each other, because some of us could 'parler' in French and some of the Frenchmen could speak broken German.

One day in mid-November, a Frenchman shouted over to our man on guard – I happened to be in the dugout –: 'comrade, tonight here explosion!' We immediately reported this to our company commander. But he said: 'Don't believe them. They only want us to leave the position, so that they can occupy it afterwards.' When it was getting dark in the evening, we started to feel rather anxious and thought that the French could have been honest with us. At about ten to nine the same Frenchman appeared again and came very close. He held up ten fingers and shouted with urgency: 'Comrades, only 10 minutes left, then explosion, everything kaputt!' The post informed all men very quickly and we rushed out of the dugouts in a flurry of excitement. Again, the company commander was informed quickly, but unfortunately in vain again. Our fear increased more and more, the Frenchman certainly just wanted our best and we were sitting on the edge of a smoking powder keg which could explode any minute. The same voice rang out this moment, now even louder and more excited: 'Comrades, only three minutes left, then explosion, then everything kaputt!' As quickly as possible the company commander (I think it was Captain Hartmann) was informed. Eventually he ordered us to leave the position, but to fight the enemy immediately and throw him out of the position, if the French did occupy it. Which meant to occupy the right and the left flank immediately. That was our relief. We had hardly left the endangered stretch of the trench, when masses of earth were thrown into the air. The French infantry kept quiet. Only the enemy artillery started a fire of destruction. When it got quieter, everyone, Germans and Frenchmen, who had put their rifles in pyramids behind the trench crawled out of our cover, viewed the resulting crater on each side and talked to each other. Some of us swapped cigarettes and tobacco for bread, cognac etc. Some days after this explosion, there was an explosion planned on our side. Self-evidently, we informed the Frenchmen this time as well. But the Frenchmen did not get permission to withdraw, the trench exploded and they had 16 casualties. We watched them digging out the dead and wounded. This way, the best local friendship had developed between deadly enemies. On both sides, we worked openly to maintain the saps and were on guard like before – only we did not shoot, and that was a feeling of relief for every soldier in the trenches. A comrade told me that a French officer came over to one of our officers. They said hello to each other, talked for a while, took some photographs of each other and then the Frenchman said goodbye in a friendly way and left.

For obvious reasons concerning discipline and fighting spirit, the higher command posts did not appreciate these tacit understandings. One day in December, a comrade told me that a higher ranking officer on his round through our position had witnessed many of our men standing outside the trenches, talking to the French. At one point, Germans and French who were only 4 to 5 metres apart, had built up barricades with sandbags outside the trenches. The officer was indignant about this behaviour. When some short shots fired by our own artillery hit our trenches as soon as we showed up outside of them, we suspected a high-level order. One had to accept this measure as justified from the viewpoint of our military leaders, but we severely regretted that the time of comforting peace was over. At the end of December 1915 it was again a question of life and death and the death of war continued to rule the regiment for another 2¾ years.

Against the War Loans[41]

Germany financed its war effort to a considerable extent by borrowing money from the population. Altogether nine war loans or war bonds were offered for subscription during the war. The middle classes in particular subscribed to war loans. They hoped for good interest rates and early repayment. This way of funding the war was based on the assumption that victory would be secured. The defeat in 1918 laid bare the extent of the inflationary process triggered by the lack of appropriate taxation. During the war, each invitation to subscribe to a war loan was accompanied by intensive propaganda efforts, and refusal to support the loans was carefully registered. From a secret appendix to the war diary of the Marine Corps in Flanders in October 1916:

Authorities at home have learned that members of the field army –
either being on furlough or in their letters to the Heimat – vividly
agitate their relatives against subscribing to the fifth war loan on the
grounds that a poor subscription result would finish the war quicker
than a positive one. One cannot condemn these unbelievable actions
thoroughly enough. All superiors have to make sure that they instruct
their subordinates in this respect.

The Bavarian Ministry of the Interior made similar observations in two
reports dated March and August 1916:

The district authority of Wasserburg has just informed us by telephone
that it was repeatedly observed that war letters have provoked a
negative mood against the subscription to war loans. Information on
cases had been received when soldiers wrote to their relatives like this:
'Do not subscribe, when the Reich has not got any money left, the war
has to stop and we will come home sooner.' The ministry has been
informed about similar observations from agricultural circles.

The president of the administrative district of Svabia and Neuburg
states in his weekly report dated 21st of this month: 'Shortly the new war
loan will be offered to subscription and the advertising campaign is going
to start. The people in charge of advertising the last war loan thought it
was a severe obstacle that soldiers agitated against the participation in
war loans verbally and in writing. The soldiers declared not to subscribe
to finish the war. One could think that the military commanders are
supposed to take remedial measures. This problem will occur without
any doubt in the case of the new war loan to an even higher degree if
nothing is going to happen.' There are further district authorities that
have repeatedly informed the Ministry of the Interior about similar
observations during the subscription for the previous war loan.

On 20 September 1917, August Holder published a poem about the
seventh war loan in the *Württemberger Zeitung*:

Autumn is upon us and brings a lot of blessings,
The rooms fill with oil, with must and wine;

And a flood of money streams through the dry country
to reward industry and hard work, to pass from hand to hand.

But where ever it comes to a halt, this is the rule:
it is to be given to the Reich as the seventh war loan!

On the same day, the Landwehr soldier Georg Weile, while on furlough in Friedrichshafen, wrote a card to Holder:

In response to your lovely poem in the *Württemberger Zeitung* No. 220 I like to suggest you refrain from publishing such things for your own sake. Even if you are again as absentminded or of an unsound mind as here, you cannot expect to infect others with your illness. You idiot. Attach this card to your mirror so that you won't forget!
[on the reverse side:] We wish peace!

'Shirkers'[42]

Adolf Armbrust, a master quarryman from Geroldsheim, serves in the Bavarian 15th Infantry Regiment. He is dispatched to Mannheim to collect sales articles for the unit on 1 November 1917. He decides to desert the colours and sends the following letter to his unit. In this letter, he refers to a speech made by Kaiser Wilhelm II on 4 August 1914, in which he declared: 'I recognize no more parties; I recognize only Germans!', thus declaring the so-called 'fortress peace', the suspension of domestic political strife in favour of a unified war effort:

Ludwigshafen upon Rhine, 15 January 1918. To Provisions Officer Strobel.

Having arrived here today, I am surprised to learn that I am accused of absence without leave. But have I been intentionally absent from the army? I believe not. I just assert the claim to the legal right applying to every free German citizen to go where ever I want to. I am entitled to do so all the more according to the Emperor's words from 4 August 1914. According to these words, parties do not any longer exist but only Germans. But has that been the case during this war? Never before has the cleavage within the people been greater and more pronounced, but also never visible in a more reckless manner than precisely during this war. Has not every poor man the same right to exist as the members of the financially better-off circles? This is certainly true from a so-called humanitarian point of view. But where is a sense of humanity and equal rights to be found among the upper strata of the people? Nowhere, from my point of view. If the working people in particular were in possession of their undisputed right to maintain their existence and livelihood, the differences between the classes were much diminished. Most pronounced is the difference between poor and rich in the army. Does an ordinary soldier here have any right which he is capable of defending? No, there are only duties and duties again. And why is that? And for what reasons are all rights of the common soldier disregarded? There will probably never be a clear answer to this question, which is not only asked by me alone. Why did they impose such terrible sacrifices and heavy burdens on the more humble people during the war? The answer will certainly be: On the grounds of defending the fatherland. But have all the countless blood sacrifices really been necessary to come to the point we have reached today? Is the success that has been achieved substantial enough to ease the sufferings and privations, not to mention all the losses? We, the members of the working people, are supposed to be happy with the explanations they have given to us. Hopefully, this useless murdering is coming to an end soon: Hence, I personally did only what every 'free German citizen' is entitled to do. I took the justified liberty of doing what I did and will do so in future. When somebody asks me: 'But what if everybody acted like that, what would happen with Germany?' I answer: 'Why don't they stop the murdering which is so useless and such a great offence against the lower strata of the people?' According to the official army regulations I have committed a criminal offence, according to my own consideration I have not. I have thrown off the duress pressing on me and freed myself. I will also take care that I'll stay free. Until you will have received these lines, I will have moved beyond the Dutch border and will remain there also after the war. I do not feel like receiving a severe punishment after they have already violently taken away my rights for long years. Sincerely, Adolf Armbrust.

(Adolf Armbrust successfully deserted to the Netherlands. On 16 February 1919 he acknowledged the suspension of the court-martial procedures against him.)

Many soldiers used the geographical proximity of neutral countries, the Netherlands, Switzerland and Denmark, and withdrew themselves from military service by crossing the border and entering these countries. Lieutenant Sengmüller at the border station Ermatingen reports to the German embassy in Berne on 8 September 1917:

I consider it my duty to inform you in particular about the increasing number of German soldiers deserting to Swiss territory within this border area recently. During the last days, three men deserted near Schaffhausen, one man near Constance, last night a sergeant Knecht, Infantry Regiment 114, swam across Lake Constance and arrived on land here in Ermatingen.

A lieutenant notes in his diary a conversation in April 1917:

Recently, Mr Quendt visited me when I was on observation post. [...] He told me that he was with the mortar troops-communication unit. [...] He also told me about the two deserters who wanted to run over to the Frenchmen in the morning at dusk. However, they only reached the enemy hay-wire circuit, because either the French misunderstood them or they were noticed by our own men. At the hay-wire circuit, they threw themselves provisionally into cover. Our artillery, machine guns and officers shot at them in vain, even mortars took part on our side. They got close, but could not hit the lads. It did not stop all day long – a good punishment for the traitors. At nightfall, a voluntary patrol from our side went over to them and met them. One of the guys dared to throw a hand grenade at his own fellow countrymen. Thereupon he was shot. The other one surrendered and was sentenced to death. A plea for clemency was submitted for him. Then, news about more defectors arrived. The plea was rescinded and he was shot. He was impertinent as he faced death. Some similar incidents happened on various occasions so that they have withdrawn the men from Alsace. I have no idea if this is justifiable. However, the deserters we have heard of were no Alsatians.

According to official figures published by the Reichswehr during the Weimar Republic, only 76 soldiers were sentenced to death for desertion during the war, and only 28 of them were actually executed. It is, however, highly unlikely that these figures are correct, as Reichswehr officers had a vested interest in painting a rosy picture of the court-martial system in the former Imperial army. The following excerpt is from the war chronicle of the Catholic priest Karl Lang, who served as a military chaplain during the war. At the end of February 1917, he was called to a regiment that was on duty near Koworsk in Russia. Lang was asked to offer pastoral care to a soldier from Alsace who had been sentenced to death for an attempt to defect to the Russian lines:

In the gleam of the lamp, the officer is pronouncing the sentence. I am watching the scene from outside through the lower window. In the end, he [the convict] is supposed to sign the sentence. He refuses. Crying and broken-hearted he is stammering: 'I don't deserve this.' After that, back to the dugout. We settle his last matters. I dictate him a farewell letter to his parents. He gives me 80 Reich marks in gold to be sent to his parents. Then we pray in front of the Most Holy Sacrament [a consecrated wafer] in a folder which I had leaned against a sill. It was the altar. [...] Then, they bring some civilian clothes he has to put on. He is still only wearing his military cap on his head. At 6.15 out of the dugout. [...] Into the luggage coach. I am the first entering the coach. Philipp is following me. A soldier with a rifle loaded with live ammunition is sitting next to the driver on the coach box. [...] Heavy snow flurry, we are driving with galloping horses. Like a child, Philipp is laying his head in my lap. As good as I can I make him sit upright again. Like this, we are driving for half an hour. Then Stop! and we get out of the coach. An entire company of soldiers was standing there in heavy marching order; they were all from Alsace and supposed to be deterred. As soon as I had left the coach with the poor man, a voice was yelling very loud: 'Here comes the traitor!' It is the regiment commander. As I am passing by him with Philipp, the commander is whispering in my ear: 'Hurry up, Father! One has children oneself, too!' 'It will be quick as far as I am concerned.' There at the railway embankment is a freshly peeled pole sticking in the ground! Behind it is the coffin. They tie him to the pole. He refuses to get tied up. I cajole him into getting tied up, for Christ's sake. Then he lets it happen. [...] They even take his cap away to make him look like a man without honour. [...] Just now I hear the commander of the execution squad quietly counting – 1, 2, 3. Then eight shots are fired, eight bullets knock the man down. I say a few words, we pray the Lord's Prayer; then I have to inform the superiors on behalf of the court that he repented his deeds and asked for forgiveness. On our way back to the cemetery, the court officer said: We know that 10 per cent of the executed soldiers are in fact innocent, but we have to be that strict, because otherwise we could not fight the war any more. Philipp was buried outside the military cemetery. The dead man's last words were: 'My poor parents.'

On 25 August 1917, Otto Biegner, a building locksmith from Munich, is sentenced to six months in prison for absence without leave. On 12 August

1917, he wrote the following letter to his sister Anna. It was intercepted by the postal surveillance unit in Metz:

> Dear Sister! I am in Metz and have a stopover of several hours. I know what I have to do in order to shirk [military duty]. You don't need to worry about me for the time being. I will write again soon. Hopefully I am lucky this time and have more success. I am of good cheer and don't worry about anything. Either I receive a blighty wound or I will shirk anyway. I am not prepared to risk my neck for the damned Prussians and big capitalists any longer. Please, don't write for the time being, for I don't know what they will do with me out here. Send my love to Josef and Father, Yours Otto. Best wishes to Fanny.

The farmhand Karl Böck had been a soldier since 1915. In late March 1918 his regiment was about to be sent to battle, for him a reason to abscond on 1 April 1918. On 7 April, however, he was arrested in Hirzon. From his statement in front of the court martial on 28 August 1918:

> I left shortly before the transport departed so that I did not have to go to the front. I believed that I would never reach the front lines but would be killed by a grenade or any other weapon while advancing. The reason why I stayed behind was fear of personal danger. I also expected my comrades to make fun of my cowardice after my return.
>
> I departed from my company on 1 April 1918, for the enemy artillery had been shooting close by and had already caused casualties. It was true when I then stated that I hoped to come back to the unit when it would be quieter after having served my sentence. I believed that the division would be out of the great battle and in a quieter position, until I had served my sentence, therefore the danger would not be so great anymore.

Brief arrest sentences were an appropriate method for many soldiers to escape from the front and have a period of rest. The military authorities thus tried to make sure that arrest sentences were served directly behind the front lines. In September 1916, they created 'Military Detainee Companies' for the same purpose. These units were used for construction and entrenchment work in firing range of the enemy. In the autumn of 1917, about 10,000 soldiers served their sentences in these units. Jakob Wirth, a farmhand from Oberambach (Upper Palatinate), writes to his brother on 9 December 1915:

I would like to let you know that I am just serving an arrest sentence. We have been out there in position and I have been away from my company for four days. They've told me that I won't get away with anything less than a year. It would be fine with me if I had to serve the sentence right now, for I am fed up with being in position. Otherwise I am still fine and do hope the same of you. I send my love, your brother Jakob.

Georg Heinle, a farm labourer, writes on 28 July 1917:

Dear Fanny! You asked me to tell you if the war is over soon. Unfortunately it has been starting all over again up there in Flanders. There are eight French squadrons in Flanders, one behind the other, to launch an offensive. That is what all the French prisoners of war state. I also have to let you know that my arrest is over now. This was really a rest for me. Now I am in my right mind again, for I was quite confused recently. I enjoyed being in arrest in St Juvin so much that I'd rather go there again right now. My best wishes to you and Willi from Schorsch. I hope I will see you soon!

Peace for Days and Weeks[43]

Apart from open fraternization with enemy troops, the soldiers had other, less spectacular forms of refusal at their disposal. Tacit agreement with the opposition troops to 'live and let live' was one of them. The Chief of the General Staff of the Field Army issued a decree on 28 November 1914:

We have received several communications from the front and from newspaper articles showing that at some points on our forward front lines where friend and enemy are very close to each other, some kind of fraternization between these two parties has emerged. Even mutual agreements to stop shooting have been reported. These events involve an extraordinary danger. The strong will of every single man to fight the enemy with all his power at all times and everywhere must not be reduced. If we want to be victorious – and we want and we have to prevail – then we have to look after the previously good martial spirit of our men. Even the war of position, where it might currently take place, has to aim everywhere for the extermination of the enemy. Incidents like the ones mentioned above have to be observed carefully by the immediate superiors and ought to be prevented with all our strength.

But until 1916 the situation did not fundamentally change:

> Notes from the Heimat show that conversations between troops on furlough give the impression that at some stretches on rather quiet fronts some kind of tacit agreements with the enemy are in place. Particularly where units have been facing each other for a rather long time they agreed not to shoot at each other, because they were 'all just family fathers'. It is said that in some cases where the trenches were quite close to each other, soldiers threw newspapers over to the enemy lines in a comradely manner.
>
> Even though I generally do not attach too much importance to this kind of idle talk, which I mainly attribute to misguided exaggerations by troops on furlough, they do go around and spread and are easily believed, and they do give a wrong impression of the earnest attitude that is prevalent out there in the field.
>
> On the other hand it cannot be denied that irregularities like this on the part of some loose and weak people do happen sometimes at quiet fronts after a long period of war behind the back of the superiors in some unobserved moments. Therefore I ask again (see my writing from 28 November 1914, M.J.No. 10406) to prevent any contact with the enemy by taking appropriate drastic measures.

The sapper K. Betsch writes on 24 February 1916:

> During the day there are a few hours of shell-fire and mortar-fire. There isn't a lot of rifle fire to hear. If we don't shoot, the enemy won't shoot either and vice versa.

Adolf Benedict, a private first class, reports the following incident in a letter to his parents on 16 June 1915:

> We are positioned quite close to the Frenchmen and rather often we throw them over some [crossed out: sweets] and get [crossed out: chocolate] in return. The Frenchmen also throw over little pieces of paper telling us to expect a storm attack and asking us to open more intensive fire in order to prevent the attack from happening.

In a letter written on 17 June 1915 he adds:

Today the Frenchmen threw over a note with the following words: 'Don't shoot. Old troops.' [...] Indeed there was not a single shot fired during that night, except of artillery fire. One could think I am on a summer holiday given the way I am living in position here right now.

Faced with a tight disciplinary corset, soldiers came up with other forms of temporary disobedience. Dominik Richert was leading a group of machine guns at the Somme in late April 1918. When he learned that they were ordered to return to the front without rest, he and his men considered alternatives:

By chance I saw a bucket half full of very poor booze next to the field kitchen. I told both soldiers immediately: 'I know a way out!', got my mess tin and dipped it inconspicuously into the bucket with booze. I had almost two litres in my mess tin. Then we went into the bushes and with an intense distaste we got drunk to an extent that we could not stand up or walk any more. We staggered back to the company and were lying down on the ground. Then the company had to line up. The sergeant read out the order. He noticed immediately what was wrong with us when the three of us did not get up, but he did not say an awful lot. Lieutenant Strohmayer on the other hand, who had just taken over the command of the company, did not stop telling us off. Then NCO Peters stood up, got a big spade and staggered against the lieutenant. Raising the spade he shouted: 'If you, Mr Strohmayer, give us another order as stupid as the one last night, I'll beat your brains out!' The lieutenant reached for the pistol, but he stood back every time until Peters tipped over, fell down and remained on the ground. While the company marched off, we three heroes were lying asleep in the woods.

In the rear area and in the garrisons at home, other methods were used. Men serving in replacement units used court-martial procedures to delay being sent to the front. From a decree by the Prussian War Ministry on 29 December 1916:

Several Deputy General Commands brought up the issue that troops who have a court-martial investigation pending against them try intentionally to prolong the proceedings by means of cleverly taking advantage of legal respite, by applying for a motion to take evidence or by resorting to legal remedy in order to delay or prevent their return to the front.

An Opinion Poll[44]

In the spring of 1917, the *Kölnische Volkszeitung*, a newspaper edited by the Catholic Centre Party, collected signatures for a *Siegfrieden*, a peace based on a German victory that would entail the annexation of large territories in France, Belgium and Poland. As a response, the Social Democratic newspaper *Münchener Post* (*Munich Post*) urged its readers to send in signatures for an 'immediate peace', and received many letters from the field army. From a memorandum by the press department of the Bavarian War Ministry, 15 June 1917:

The editorship of the *Munich Post* presents randomly picked samples from the letters it has received at the free disposal of the War Ministry.

Already now the number of letters has increased to several thousand. We have received so many of them that we could not record them in the books. Individual letters often had sheets with 200 signatures enclosed. There was not one letter that contained threats with regard to a loosening of discipline or a refusal to perform duties. It is noticeable that people from rural areas are very strongly represented among the signatories. The letters can be deemed to bear witness to the views held in large parts of the field army.

Excerpts from the letters provided by the *Munich Post*:

Everyone mutually strives to continue this war of complete destruction, until everything has degenerated into languishing state. It is out of the question that the victorious nation will get financial compensation for the loss from the defeated nation or nations. We will have to face costs that are yet unforeseeable. What will it cost just to support the cripples and the surviving dependents of the servicemen at least to some degree? [...] No enemy can convince us that we will be the defeated nation. It is very clear just by looking on a map that we have the better chances. But it is also clear that certain industrial entrepreneurs have accumulated huge amounts of capital through the war, that usury and exploitation of the working classes are in full flow within all countries, whereas others perish because of physical weakness and the young generation loses so much of its strength due to the continuous malnutrition that it will never recover. 'Russian means' have to be used to stop the clamour of those mercenaries acting on behalf of the big capitalism who are suggesting that Germany would perish without compensation payments.

Hopefully somebody will shut up the Rhenish Centre Party newspaper properly. I am from the Rhineland and used to be an admirer of that paper. But the black press and party have ignominiously abandoned the working and the lower middle class in times of need. I have been at the front since the beginning of the war. As far as I know the soldiers' opinion, *nobody* wants the peace suggested by the Kölnische Volkszeitung, but rather the one favoured by the *Munich Post*.

Wide circles of the population turn towards the Social Democrats with their last hopes, as they are disappointed by the attitude of a large part of the bourgeois press.

I can confirm that 99 per cent of the soldiers in field-grey uniform would vote for an immediate and permanent peace as suggested by Scheidemann [Philipp Scheidemann, head of the Majority Social Democrats, became synonymous with an immediate peace 'without annexations and contributions' since the party had adopted this position in April 1917], if they would allow a poll in the field.

We have been collecting signatures for a peace without annexations in the area of our company and got 32 so far. Following a complaint the company commander initiated a great interrogation, without success. Speeches followed claiming that we were liable for prosecution for collecting signatures. *We* are prohibited from enlightening our comrades on behalf of humanity! Do we not deserve anything better after these three years than such an unjust treatment?

I am currently with a larger observation command in position at ... When I let my comrades read the *Munich Post*, they were all and *without exception* in favour of the peace without annexations.

In only a few months this terrible murdering of humans will have lasted for three years. But nonetheless, they still hesitate to fulfil the true wish of all the peoples, the wish and the longing for an immediate peace, for a peace that does not humiliate any nation. A very high percentage of the German people are aware of the fact that no nation will get out of this battle as a victor without sacrificing the last bit of the people's strength to an insane policy of conquest. Even the victor would be defeated. All the troops out here agree with our people in the Heimat concerning the aim of an immediate peace.

We only regret that the *Munich Post* cannot hand out enough sheets of paper to the front soldiers so that everybody can be polled. We do not know anybody in our battalion who would not agree. We strongly wish to inform the widest circles of the population about the mood of the front soldiers. Even those who used to consider themselves opponents of the Social Democrats only a short time ago now feel a deep longing for world peace. Everybody is overcome by the longing for peace, regardless of occupational background. Only professional members of the military can get enthusiastic about the so called 'Hindenburg-peace'.

Prisoner of War[45]

To be taken prisoner became a legitimate and welcome aim for many soldiers. Josef Stigl writes from Nevers on 8 April 1917. His letter is intercepted by postal surveillance:

My very dear parents and siblings! I am content with my lot, for I know exactly how life is in the trenches. There is no need to tell me, since I have been out there long enough and had to suffer a lot. Thank God that I am healthy and happy to be here in France. I haven't been the first nor will I be the last to become a prisoner of war. I am healthy and have all my limbs which is the main thing.

From a letter excerpt in a postal-surveillance report from August 1918:

If nothing else has happened to him, he most certainly is a prisoner of war. Then he might occasionally be much better off than being on our side. You can watch and see how well off the prisoners of war are in Erfurt. It is all bad lies what the newspapers write. Many of my comrades have brothers who are prisoners of war and they are all doing fine. They send pictures of themselves and say that they have never looked better in their whole life. So please, don't worry so much. I'd like to say that the entire infantry wants to desert, if they only always could. And they do it whenever they have the opportunity to do so. Many soldiers want to defect to the enemy and don't have the opportunity, they envy their comrades who are prisoners of war and they say that they wish to be one of them, too. They were just lucky! If only we had been where they were in position, then we would be prisoners of war now, too. Yes, it is like this. You cannot image how relieved the enemy prisoners are when they come over to us. It is the same with our soldiers, they are happy when they get over there.

'Riots'[46]

In his war memoirs Dominik Richert clarifies an understanding held by many soldiers:

> If one refuses obedience, one just gets shot. If one does obey, one might get shot as well, but one still has a chance to survive. Consequently, one obeys, even though very reluctantly.

Nonetheless, smaller acts of disobedient behavior occurred quite often. Felix Fonrobert describes an incident that happened in late 1916:

> Leaving the Vosges, we came into the area of Soissons. After some weeks in the trenches, we were once again at rest far away behind the front. This rest was unfortunately interrupted too often by stupid exercising and marching. One day during a longer marching rest, we got the order to sing off the top of our heads. Lieutenant-sergeant Terlunen, a very brisk superior, acted as conductor and he did it namely his way. He said: 'Listen everybody! We are singing the *Deutschlandlied* ['Song of Germany', a patriotic song written in 1841 and adopted as the national anthem in 1922] now – step up whoever does not know it!' How surprised the good man was when twelve men pretended not to know the song. Now he shouted extremely angrily: 'Whoever does not know this song, is nothing but a dirty dog in my eyes!' And what happened next? It was almost unbelievable, but something very anti-militaristic followed: Since four of those who did not know the 'Song of Germany' stepped up towards the sergeant in a quite agitated manner and shook their fist at him. In a threatening voice, the leader of the four said: 'You'd better watch it, man, don't you call us a dog again!' Our 'hero' became quite pale, tried to calm down the angry men and sent them to their quarters. They were sent to the garrison and, as we learnt later on, it was made clear they should not be punished!

Fonrobert also discusses May 1917, when he was posted to a garrison near Düsseldorf:

> One day in May 1917, some people in higher positions had thought of something special for us! They woke us up bright and early in the morning. Each of us got 25 live cartridges and we were marching

towards Düsseldorf! On our way, a major on horseback joined up with us. He delivered a little speech saying among other things that we would be passing by an ammunition factory where workers were on strike. We should sing out loud to threaten the workers. In the meantime we knew how the land lay! None of us even thought of singing. On the contrary, some critical opinions were audibly voiced! Then we marched into the barrack yard of Derendorf, but still without singing. There was something happening! Many officers, some wearing a Pickelhaube [spiked helmet], and a lot of police were gathered. After we had lined up, a higher officer of the garrison delivered a speech describing the situation from his point of view. But how surprised the gentlemen were when they heard us heckling that we would not shoot on the people! The gentlemen looked sheepish. After the address we were dismissed for the time being. Some of us went in front of the barrack gates and talked to the wives of the striking workers. They told us that the strike was first about higher wages, secondly about the so-called 'Hindenburg donation'. This food donation which was then propagated at the time was supposed to be for the workers' benefit, but they never got anything due to corruption in the higher echelons. We told the women and men in plain language that we would show our solidarity with them and that nobody would shoot at the people! We told them to spread this information. After some hours the campaign fizzled out and we went back to Kalkum.

On 2 May 1917, the Deputy General Command of the XIVth Army Corps in Karlsruhe reported riots and many cases of absence without leave that had happened between 26 and 28 February at a replacement battalion that was due to be sent to the front. Although this had been promised, the men had not received furlough before commanded to the front. The report vividly describes a type of incident that took place elsewhere on many occasions between November 1917 and January 1918 when troops were shifted from the Eastern to the Western Front after the armistice with Russia:

In the morning of 28 February, the transport was lined up on the barrack yard to get ready for marching out. The men were grumbling openly while lining up and did not hide that they were moving very slowly on purpose. They scorned the company commander who was hurrying them along. The troops did not stop grumbling even once the battalion commander had appeared. They demanded furlough und pushed their rifles on the ground. After turning away in groups for decampment, somebody shouted out loud: 'First group halt! We don't want to go to the front lines!' Then, the whole platoon came to a stop. Their superiors could only make them follow the band marching ahead after they had urged them repeatedly. The march to the railway station was a complete mess. The men were laughing and hooting constantly and were shouting to the civilians who came along. On arriving at the station, most of the men refused to go on to the platform. Some of them threw their rifles and knapsacks on the road. It took at least 20 minutes until the last men were rushed to the platform. They also refused when they had to board the train. Most of the troops first hesitated and entered the train only after a great deal of coaxing over some time. Some of them left the train straight away, some were just messing around, were climbing on the running board [...] and more of the like. Six men did not enter the train again at all but let it depart without them. They were subsequently arrested. The riots continued during the train ride and particularly at the stations. When the train stopped at a food supply station, nine men departed unnoticed from the transport und went to a nearby village.

Measures[47]

Even at the front it was possible to abscond for a while. The 4th Infantry Brigade reports to the 2nd Bavarian Infantry Division about the battle of Verdun:

It is impossible to execute police service immediately behind the foremost firing lines. Besides, this is not that necessary, because only very seldomly troops run off from the front lines backwards. But this will happen with the replacement troops. These men are getting lost between the reserve positions and the front firing lines. It is safest to collect them in the gorges in front of the reserve positions and send them back to their units. This is the duty of permanent patrols. Every soldier who is not wounded and is coming back from the front lines has to have an identification card. In the camps, military police patrols are necessary. They have to bring every soldier who does not belong to the unit currently in the camp to the camp commander. He has to take care that the men picked up are sent back to their units. It was striking that a growing number of only slightly wounded or sick men got rid of all their weapons and equipment before showing up in the reserve position, the longer the assignment became and the more the amount of reserve troops was increasing. The police force had to take action against this as well.

It was necessary to check the forward trenches for soldiers who had not gone 'over the top' during an attack. Specially selected soldiers, usually officers or field policemen, searched for them. Such a 'battle police' was also in action behind the front lines. From an order issued by the 13th Army Corps on 24 November 1916:

1.) From 26 November, the front trench of the second reserve position will be declared as military police line in order to contain absence without leave from the unit. […]. All men coming individually or in groups without commander from the front and crossing this line towards the East, have to identify themselves with an order written by their superior. 2.) The divisions have to install passage posts only at certain points along this police line. The unauthorized crossing of the line between the posts is to be forestalled by patrols. 3.) In addition, patrols are to be ordered between the police line and the line from Metz-en-Couture over Gouzeaucourt to Heudicourt in order to control a) the dugouts of unoccupied positions, b) the stops and routes of advance of the field kitchens, c) the cellars and dugouts in villages to the east of the police line. 4.) The military police patrols assigned to the local commander's offices are to be provided with extended assignments.

Direct disobedience at the front – refusal to obey orders, defecting to the enemy or desertion to the rear – brought life-threatening risks. A soldier who defected to the enemy could be shot by his own or by enemy troops. The same could happen to those who would allow themselves to be taken prisoner. Decrees threatening the death penalty were repeatedly read out to the troops. Their non-observance makes clear that morale deteriorated rapidly from the early summer of 1918. On 25 June 1918, Ludendorff urged the superiors again to bring the following 'sharply' to the attention of the troops:

1. Every defector to the enemy will be punished with the death penalty when returning to Germany.

2. All his domestic assets will be confiscated.
3. He will lose his citizenship. His relatives will lose their entitlement to receive benefits.
4. If he is under suspicion of treason, which will be already the case with the admission in one of the so-called privileged camps [Allied prisoner camps for deserters which offered more freedom of movement and better food provision], charges for treason will be pressed.
5. Amnesty or limitation of time is not to be expected.

During the final months of the war, an estimated number of 750,000 soldiers in the field army absconded from duty. Many of them were among the rapidly increasing number of lightly wounded or sick soldiers and simply flooded back to Germany, either by foot or by boarding a hospital train. Others took a more active role in their desertion and were hiding in the Etappe in Belgium or Northern France. The repeated orders by the War Ministries and the Army High Commands which tried to control the situation became increasingly threatening both in their tone and with regard to the measures they announced. The following decree by the Prussian War Ministry was issued on 5 November 1918 but refers back to earlier decrees, indicating that mass desertions had commenced in late July:

The present situation of the war is demanding the most drastic action against the so-called shirking (absence without leave, desertion, cowardice, self-mutilation, endangering the military in the field, insubordination in order to evade battle), namely in all units of the field and the replacement army, not only in the foremost front line or with field convoys, but also in units at rest behind the front, in the Etappe and the other occupied areas as much as in the reserve and other units in the Heimat. Referring to the decrees from 22 July 1918 M. 7385/18 C 4, from 15 August 1918 No. 9036/18 g. AM and from 24 August 1918 No. 254/18g C 4 it is generally requested

1. to impose the heaviest penalties for the offences mentioned above, if necessary even degrading punishment, in particular the renunciation of civil rights, and the death penalty.
2. to instruct all superiors repeatedly about their right and duty to use their weapons in order to enforce obedience to their orders in cases

of urgent need and extreme danger. As pointed out in the previous decrees, these requirements will routinely be satisfied in cases of the refusal to go to the front lines or into position, in cases of leaving the position against order and in front of other men, or generally in cases of explicit insubordination or of plain insubordination combined with the existence of the danger that mutinous agitation could be spread, if other means to enforce obedience are not at disposal or are exhausted.

It is of specific importance that the military police units not only in the area of operations but also in the Etappe and the other occupied areas are most accurately informed about these authorizations in order to be able to take drastic action against those who are in breach of their duty and roaming behind the front.

War? Without Me![48]

Some soldiers simulated mental problems in order to escape front duty. They tried to convince medical doctors, whose expertise was used in court-martial procedures, that a plea for 'non compos mentis' was justified. In the following case, a soldier had already been sentenced to one year in prison for absence without leave, but then his sentence was suspended and he was sent back to the front. He then pretended to be Sherlock Holmes, the famous detective who was also popular in Germany, in an attempt to get discharged. His case history, written for a medical examination, reveals his true motives:

I have to be a free man. While I was trained to be a musketeer fit for the trenches, it was quite all right, for I could go home every Sunday. But that was over soon and I went into the field. There I was voluntarily seeking death, for I feared to become crippled. Now I will never go back out there, since I know for certain that I won't come back. When we were in Belgium, I suddenly could not take it any longer, therefore I left again. The whole military stuff seems to me exactly as if I were with the voluntary youth force [*Jugendwehr*]. I am boiling over with rage, only if I have to salute. That is all childish rubbish. Anyway, the war is a foul thing in itself. They have got everyone in a nice mess, and we have to face the music now. As I see it, they can have their war if they want to, I'm not bothered. I never wanted the war. They should not have bothered me. But now I am not supposed to be a free man any longer, that is the main thing. [...] Now I am supposed to be with the Prussians and to risk my head for no purpose whatsoever. If I am dying a hero's death, my parents will lose any support. If I get crippled, they even have to care for me. Even though I used to be good for nothing, now my love for my parents is stronger than the love for the Emperor and the Reich. If I get crippled, I will be everybody's fool. And indeed, I do not feel like going this way. But we haven't got that far yet in Germany that one could translate the pious saying of 'The Lord has taken away, blessed be the name of the Lord' and say instead: 'The Nation and the Emperor have taken away, blessed be their name!'

(This soldier was subsequently declared a 'highly inferior psychopath' and as 'persistently unfit for any form of military service'.)

From the case history of another soldier who malingered a mental disease, albeit somewhat less successfully:

Case 22. S., committed absence without leave twice. His psychological motivation is clear. Seemingly abnormal state of mind as long as in pre-trial custody. Therefore referred to observation. Gives the impression of being perfectly stupid. Repeats every question asked by the medical doctor like a complete idiot. Answers only after the question has been repeated several times. Thinks visibly very carefully about how to answer. Stresses that he is a retard since a fall on his head a few years ago and that he is not any longer aware of what he is doing. [...] Acts ostensibly in a childish manner. Then again cheeky and provocative. It is assessed that his behaviour outside of the medical exploration is completely different, that he acts perfectly normal and is not retarded at all when mingling with other soldiers as soon as he has the opportunity to meet them. [...]

Diagnosis: without doubt simulating the mental state of a retard, in this case without hysterical interaction and without psychopathic characteristics in the strict sense. (Has been sentenced in the main court-martial trial on 27 May 1918. Has given up his simulation completely in the meantime.)

Chapter 5

The End

Against the backdrop of a previous substantial decrease in the morale of the troops, several key events influenced the perceptions and expectations of the front-line troops in 1918. The first was the mass strike by industrial workers in January. It was mostly rejected by the front-line soldiers. They thought it would jeopardize the chances for peace as the result of a successful spring offensive. The second event was the spring offensive itself, which began on 21 March and injected a new motivation and offensive spirit into the troops, as they hoped it would finally put an end to the war. After repeated German offensives had failed and the offensive movement had come to a halt, the beginning of the French counter-offensive on 18 July was the third and final crucial event in 1918. It marked another, and this time final, decisive swing in the mood of the German troops. The majority of them, with the one major exception of soldiers and officers from a middle-class background, now understood that the German war effort was bound to fail and defeat only a matter of time. This insight motivated a partial radicalization of the political expectations for a postwar settlement, mostly among working class soldiers who expected and prepared themselves for an overthrow of the monarchy and a revolution. More crucial, though, was the widespread individual refusal to sacrifice one's own life in the dying months of the war. This motivated several hundred thousand front-line soldiers – estimates vary between ¼ million and 1 million, with 750,000 being a widely accepted figure – to shirk their duty and flood back to the Etappe and eventually to German territory. Beginning in August, this mass action of individual soldiers ultimately undermined the fighting power of the German army on the Western Front. The doyen of German military history, the late Wilhelm Deist, has described it as a 'covert military military strike', covert because censorship of both war letters and newspapers was able to suppress full public knowledge of these events until the armistice. As the public was deliberately misled about these military reasons for the German defeat, the ground for the denial of the 'stab-in-the-back' legend was prepared.

Towards the End[49]
From letters by Hans Spieß, a soldier from the Upper Palatinate in Bavaria who served in the 5th Reserve Cavalry Rifles Regiment. The excerpts reveal his anxieties and experiences, but they also mark steps on the way towards the end of the war.

To his parents, undated, presumably 1916:

I wrote you a letter a few days ago, but it didn't go through. I was brought before the company commander today. Some of our lance-corporals are going to Hammelburg for further training [NCO training] soon, I can give them a few lines for you to take with them. We are in a very dangerous position here. There is already a whole graveyard of heavily wounded men in the forest. You cannot imagine the feeling when you are lying in the range of aerial mine fire. The Frenchmen bring mines over more than three cwt big [almost 24 stones]. If one of those hits a dugout, it crunches ten men without leaving a single limb in one piece. It is so sad to watch and see all that. All the nice villages are piles of rubble now. In the previous position we were lying with our rifles in a church that was shot to pieces. Nearby was the graveyard. Then the artillery started firing right into the graveyard, so that the bones were flying around and into our faces. The worst and most moving of all is when one's best comrade is getting torn apart, and one is supposed to leave him next to you until it is dark. Then he can be buried. I already sent you some pictures with views of the area. Our position is not far away from that. Please don't be upset now and don't forget to pray then we will meet again. This is not a war any more, it is just murder, who is to blame for that.

To parents and siblings, 25 June 1916:

How are you all? You probably don't know what to pack [i.e. harvest] first with this fine weather. But just do one after another and don't get annoyed, for you are quite well off, because you still have something to eat, unlike us. All things from the parcel are gone and now I don't know what to do. I do have some money, but this money I can't eat and there is nothing to buy at all in the whole of Grafenwöhr.

To the family, 26 October 1916:

> We will come in a position within a few days from where we still have to march for four hours until we'll reach the [front-line] position. There are aeroplanes around in the air all day long and shrapnels coming behind them. It looks beautiful if one doesn't mind. It is very hard to transport things, for there are high mountains. The horses are backing down so that we don't have a choice other than to push the wheels ourselves. But one gets used to everything. The only good thing is that there is nobody better off. My dears, I can't write everything, for we are not allowed to seal the letters. They are to be read by the regiment first.

From the Vosges, 28 December 1916:

> Dear parents and siblings! Because I just have the opportunity I'd like to write you a little letter. I can't help it any more. I have got to write about how I feel. I know that I am not allowed to write it down, but I believe I will feel better afterwards. The Christmas holidays are just over now, but I couldn't notice that there were holidays at all. We had been relieved from the position on the 23rd. On Christmas Eve I had to be on guard and spent the Holy Night and Christmas Day being on guard. But on the third bank holiday I had to go back to entrenchment work. A dugout is to be built and the ground is all stony. I like working and you know that I am used to hard work, but here I have to go slowly. After half a day's work I am so weak I can't lift an arm. It is unbelievable that one can possibly take any more, for in my entire life I have never seen food like this. In the morning there is boiled water called coffee, for lunch once in a while and nearly invisible a bit of meat, but mostly meatless, and always yellow and white turnips, but so overcooked that even our pigs at home would not eat them. I have no idea why that is. At the squadron where we eat when being in position the food is blameless. The weather is always wet here and I am still suffering from pneumonia. Just be glad that you don't have to go through something like this and be happy with everything you have. But I also have to tell you that I was very happy with my gift for Christmas from the company. My dears, I really thought that it would come to an end this time, but it won't. One just has to go on and hope. It can't be long. Therefore the dear mother should not be worried. There would not be enough paper around here to write down

everything I would like to tell. Thank God, I am still well and hope the same of you. I will end these lines and hope that this letter will reach you fit and healthy. All my love from your son and brother Hans. Farewell until we meet again. Answer soon.

To the parents, 12 March 1917:

I received the parcels No. 11 and 12 yesterday and 13 and the letter and the card today, many heartfelt thanks. I am so happy, for mother is submitting a request, I can hardly write. One has to be clever. Some requests are granted for just three or four days. The reason is that it is my turn this spring, for otherwise it would be autumn. I have handed over a letter for you to those comrades who went back to Hammelburg, but you haven't told me yet if you have received it. I was also very happy to see that mother has got benefits for me. Well, mother does not give in. Mrs Aschaffenburg has visited you, too. It is difficult for her now. F Schlaffer wrote me a letter that he is not well. All the young guys are going to be broken in the military. I know what it is like as a recruit. All cards are photographs of the area around. I've seen it all, but I would be happy if I just had to look at it. What do you think, when will I be lucky sometime and get furlough, should I drop by in Aschaffenburg on my way home? I reckon they wouldn't like it.

To the parents, 1 April 1917:

I fare quite well and get along all right with my master [Spieß has become batman]. We can go wherever we like, I am always with my master and thus I am always in good quarters. Sometimes it is a lot of work, but you have to do your duty anyway and in any other position as well. I also have to cook and serve in the officers' mess. My dear mother will appreciate the new duty for she doesn't have to worry about me any more. Some men have started to go on leave. I could go soon as well, but what am I supposed to do at this time of the year out there [i.e. at home]. The weather is always bad, so I could not help you out very much. Moreover, I have been with my master for such a short time that I don't want to leave him so soon. For if I ask him he won't probably turn me down.

To his mother, 16 August 1917:

I have heard how it goes with the crop and that you are threshing already. I am happy to see that you can manage on your own. Hopefully, I will be home next year to help you. But it doesn't look too good, what do you reckon? There must be an end at some time, even the Thirty Years War was over once. And again you have had two deaths in the neighbouring village.

To his mother, 2 September 1917:

I can't complain at the time being, for I fare so very well with my master. Now you don't have to worry about me at all. And even if there is some fighting, I'll just stay away. You have been lucky with the pigs in the stable, hopefully they will all come through.

To his parents and siblings, 16 December 1917:

Dearest parents and siblings! I received your little letter yesterday and the parcel with meat and two apples today with greatest joy. Many thanks for that. Again, the letter was full of news which I really like. I am waiting to see what will happen with the ceasefire in Russia. I believe that it will all be over next year, then we can celebrate Christmas together again. You must forgive me, but as long as I am at rest there will be less mail, for I have the horses here as well. There is so little time to write letters each day, but otherwise it is all right here. Next to my quarters is the church and many pubs behind it. One doesn't know where to go first. Don't be upset, I have been in church nearly every day. It is not for the sermon when we go, for the priest speaks nothing but French. That's it for today, all my love from your son and brother Hans.

To his parents and siblings, 31 December 1917:

[…] what do you think, will we have to spend the new year in the trenches again? I don't think so. I can't imagine, one gets so cold-blooded and so indifferent. One doesn't even take notice of the grenades any more. It happened to me today. When I was on my way to the regiment, a grenade hit ten metres behind me. It was more luck than judgement, hopefully it will be the same in the new year. I wish you could have seen me running and ducking my head, you would laugh, too. Everybody can run in this situation even if he is extremely lame. Otherwise it is not dangerous here. But recently they sometimes shoot with gas grenades. It doesn't matter, the revenge will come soon as always. Don't worry about me, I am not so stupid, once it gets uncomfortable, I'll just slip away and hide in the deepest tunnel that the hero's death will never reach. It is all right being with this regiment. They can't do much with it though and it is unbelievable how many young men are here and have to stay for such a long time fighting in this war of position. Do you know what they are always talking about in the trenches? They say that we haven't seen the bloodiest days of the war yet. I nearly believe it myself, for they keep on bringing new supplies out here, always the newest thing. Our only comfort is our hope that some day there must be an end.

To his sister, 12 February 1918:

I nearly forgot, today is Shrove Tuesday. Maybe we will eat the sausages together next year, if everything turns out fine in Russia. It is every nation's turn, one after another, right as they have started. It all depends on the results of the spring offensive, the entire Western Front will be shaken. We are prepared like never before. If only it was over already! For two days there has been such artillery and mine fire that one doesn't know if there is any justice at all, or not. It would be much easier to bear, if we didn't have to watch the poor men dying here. I can tell you, whoever survives all this, is a really lucky guy. But nobody will come out of this without strained nerves. But even if I tell you things like this sometimes, please don't worry about me. I am not the one who is always seeking for the front line. I can do without any iron crosses, I rather prefer to be alive. But alas, everybody has to do his share, and we do resist, for being a prisoner of war is again not a solution […]

From June 1918, Hans Spieß served with the 2nd Bavarian Infantry Division, Machine Gun Marksmanship Unit 2, 3rd Company. To his parents and siblings on 3 July 1918:

Our division alone lost 3,400 men and 1,100 horses during these attacks which also caused a lot of damage over and above. The aeroplanes had destroyed our baggage train. We had to survive on horse meat and with the help of what we took from the dead men. Just try to imagine this. We built up cover for our rifles with the corpses. You should smell the odour of it. Nobody can be buried. Anyway, the horses! There are corpses lying around who were killed four weeks ago, and then the heat! It is enough to drive one to utter despair. There is no quietness behind the lines in the rear any longer. The aeroplanes are swirling up everything. Then we were moved and got another position further right at Movel, but there we fared badly. Then we came out of there and were sent to the Somme at St Quentin on the 18th where we have been staying for one week. For lack of men we were withdrawn and since the 1st we have been here in Parzeville. You can imagine the amount of marching we had to do. 40 kilometers every day. Since we've been in Nuremberg, I haven't taken off my boots or uniform clothes. Yesterday was the first time since then. This time we will come even further away, for we are getting loaded for transport. I always try to think that it isn't too bad as long as one gets the head through unscathed.

In August 1918, Hans Spieß is promoted to NCO. To his parents and siblings, 16 August 1918:

[…] otherwise I am still healthy and hope the same is true of you. It doesn't look too good any longer with the war. Quite a lot of us have been taken prisoner of war, around 80,000 men. The same amount of men are said to have laid down their arms. All my love from your Hans.

To parents and siblings, 27 August 1918:

Resl wrote to me that you are already done with harvesting. I'm happy to hear that. I would like to be home now, for I know I could help you a lot with threshing. Believe me, it is getting boring out here, every day the same story. There is a lot of work to do right now. All positions are gone and have to be built up again. We are lying right in the open field. I don't have to work and be on guard any more, but I have to be there all the time. The further reserves we are getting are just children. They cry and scream for their mother when they have to go out into the fire.

To his parents and siblings, 10 October 1918:

[…] the war can't last much longer, we are always moving backwards. We are busy holding up the enemy troops, they are attacking us every day. You can imagine how many of our men that does cost.

To his parents and siblings, 21 October 1918:

> My dears. Today I have got a minute and can write a few lines for you. I am presently still alive. I can't tell you what is happening here on the German side. There is no quiet moment any more. We had to move back more than 100 km within a few days. Whoever can't run, is taken prisoner. Please don't be upset. There's nothing we can do. There are no men left. It won't take long this way. All my love your Hans.

(Hans Spieß died from a shot through the heart on 22 October 1918.)

Rural Homesickness[50]

Peasant farmers in particular suffered from homesickness, especially during harvesting and seeding time. Two letters written in March 1917 demonstrate the extent and form of this homesickness. Letter by Josef Beigel, peasant farmer in Malschenberg (Baden) in the southwest of Germany:

> Written 20 March 1917 Dear Wife and Children, I'm letting you know that I am still hale and hearty and hope the same is true of you. But dear wife, I don't know why it is that I don't get anything [any mail] from you. I am always worried about you and the dear children. Why don't you let me know how you are doing at home? Tell me if I have upset you and by what? I could cry. Or do you think I am going to be on furlough? It just takes time. Only five members of the company are allowed to go home, that's why it takes so long until one may go home. I have already been feeling homesick for a long time, but it doesn't happen. My present company commander is not like the last one. I have to go through a lot and must keep silent. It is just hard when one is already that old and has to obey the young ones. Dear wife, the dear Lord will once show mercy with those unjust things and the time will come again when nobody gives us any orders anymore. It makes me sick and tired of living. My dear wife and children, if only I could be at home with you! I would be happy to work if I were just with you. We will wish all the best. We just can't help it. One cannot make any plans because nobody knows what will happen. If it goes on like this with food it will create a hollow feeling in the stomach. It is bad here and they say it is the same at home? If they go on taking everything away from you [a reference to delivery quotas and requisitions, elements of a controlled economy that agitated many farmers], then you won't be

able to do the work any longer. Leave the work and just do the most necessary things. I have noticed myself that when I am working I am always hungry. Just bouillon, the devil may take it! And we are not supposed to get any [food] parcels from home anymore. I don't care! With the soup alone, war will soon be over. So please answer me, tell me what is wrong! It is time to go to bed now. Good night and sleep well. Best wishes from your husband. [...] I've got an ulcer on my bottom again and can hardly sit or lie down and I'm supposed to ride a horse. It was my fête-day and I was thinking of you, my heart shrank. If you don't get any letters, dear wife, then something has happened.

Letter from Alois Deuringer, farmer from Göggingen, to his wife:

15th letter, in position, 25 March 1917, 10 a.m.

Dearest Lina! I received your lovely letter yesterday. My thoughts are always with you my dear ones. While being on guard during the night I think of you being safe at home, during the day I think of you working. I have been looking forward with intensive longing to seeing you very soon. Have just been at the company report and spoke to the First Lieutenant about seed-furlough. He told me that he would by no means grant me any furlough at all. Nevertheless, you will know what you have to do. Maybe this war will come to an end at last and I might come home healthy, then I will know what I owe to the state, or rather the dear fatherland. I am doubtful about what I am these days; it is too bad that I haven't studied zoology more properly. Please tell me, what the people we have talked about have told you. Don't risk your health, just do what I told you. [...] Don't bother too much, just send me something if you can. If you don't have anything to feed the calves with, see if you are allowed to cut the oats. [...] Again winter has come back here, but that's all right, it's fine to break us, but after the war the common soldier will get up and dare to tell the truth. That's the way it goes when people don't have faith anymore. The most stupid calves even feed their slaughterers themselves, but that's not the last we have heard of that. When it is time for the field work, start around the house and go on working the fields further away afterwards. I can tell you more later on. But why shall I always write about work; it just comes to my mind that I am a soldier and that I have been paying the state a considerable amount of money in taxes for 14 years. O what a joy to be a soldier and to have all these things around. That's just what I needed.

Order the newspaper again for three months, but don't forget it. And tell me if you receive all letters which I have numbered for that purpose. Have received the last 5 Marks, too. The envelopes in which you have sent me the money are not transparent. 5 Marks every week; that will do. Don't bother grandmother, your eyesight is good enough, but two [probably meant: four] eyes see better. However, it's an advantage to be stupid. Now I send my love and many kisses to all of you, Alois.

Discipline and Politics[51]

In a reserve hospital in Bavaria, an NCO responsible for the Patriotic Instruction Programme reports on 'often repeated questions' from the troops in November 1917:

Often repeated questions. 1.) Is not Germany itself to blame in the first place for the outbreak of the war due to its military armaments policy. 2.) Would it not have been possible to prevent the war by giving in diplomatically. 3.) Is the money we have paid for the war loans not lost, for the loan papers have not been delivered yet to the subscribers. 4.) We fight only for the upper ten-thousand. 5.) The German worker will still remain in his miserable situation in spite of all the nice speeches. 6.) The government does not dare to take drastic action against the war usurers. 7.) Emperors and Kings (monarchical constitution) are out of date – Republic. 8.) The German militarism is the greatest enemy of individual freedom, one is treated like a slave. 9.) Why does the government not act more rigorously in dealing with the Fatherland Party. 10.) Prussia's influence on the other German states is too strong. 11.) Concerning food supplies, Prussia should be supported by the occupied nations and not by Bavaria. 12.) Great fear of the future taxes. 13.) We already would have peace now if only Prussia had wanted it. 14.) Why do we need Alsace-Lorraine? 15.) Patriotism would not have vanished, if only the pay was higher.

Attempts to tighten the discipline through extensive drill regularly led to cases of maltreatment by superiors. From a decree by the Bavarian War Ministry, 8 January 1918:

The Chief of the General Staff of the Field Army, being informed by the enclosed writing, has expressed his appreciation for any effort of the home reserve formations to attach greater importance to the elevation and consolidation of discipline.

Unfortunately, several crude riots of late combined with incidents happening in the streets every day have increased the impression that the troops' discipline is declining to an alarming extent the longer the war continues. I do know that not only members of the replacement army but also front soldiers on leave act like this, the latter as they feel detached from any supervision while being at home. And I do not fail to recognize the extraordinarily severe problems in maintaining tight discipline under the particular circumstances of our present time. Nevertheless, following the request of the Supreme Army Command I consider it my duty to direct the attention of all commanders to the elevation and consolidation of discipline within the replacement army.

We know from experience that pressure of superior authorities regarding this problem usually has the result that the formations try to achieve more discipline by additional exercising and a stricter treatment of the troops; this is regularly followed by an increasing number of cases of complaints because of improper treatment. I request to prevent this forcefully. I leave the choice of means by which to elevate discipline to the judgement of the commanding generals.

An ombudsman for the Patriotic Instruction Programme in a regiment in Neu-Ulm in Bavaria reports on 27 December 1917:

As before, officers' experience is that the men do not want to go back in the field. As their reason they cite time and again: 'But we only fight for capitalism anyway.' Indeed, it is impossible to reason with opinions like that. The ombudsman can here only persuade at best, but not convince.

Towards the end of the war, most soldiers in the field rejected the aggressive nationalist policies of the Pan-German League and of the Fatherland Party. A member of the Social Democratic transport workers' union writes:

Many people at home believe that the Independent Social Democrats have just a few supporters or none at all. To my own surprise, things are completely different here. Whenever I had the opportunity to talk to soldiers, I met opponents [of the Majority Social Democrats]. Most of the soldiers don't think that our comrades in the Reichstag act as aggressively as they should. The stalled negotiations with the Russian representatives caused depressive feelings, for it was everyone's hope that our government would now show that it does not have the intention of annexing other countries. But it is crystal clear for everyone watching the negotiations that the contrary is the case. – All soldiers condemn the workings of the Pan-German press and the people in Germany who agitate for annexations. Most of the troops are of the opinion that all editors or publishers who are in favour of the Pan-German policy should stay in the trenches just for one month and they would change their minds. – Everyone has taken the government's promise 'We are not driven by the thirst for conquests' at face value, at least yet. But now, after the negotiations in Brest [peace talks in Brest-Litovsk from December 1917 to March 1918 where Germany dictated harsh terms to Soviet Russia] most of the people have changed their mind. Many believe that this fact has a strong impact on our soldiers' eagerness to fight. Moreover, the majority knows what it will be like for a warrior when they launch an offensive. But if the offensive is launched by us, then our soldiers will badger the enemy, particularly when it goes against the English.

Another member of the transport workers' union writes:

Bit by bit, it is dawning on even the thickest soldier that dirty tricks have been played on him. There are only proletarians fighting at the front. One does not find any of the money people or their sons here. Pp. Especially the people who are exempted from military service are the first to shout for the Fatherland Party.

The son of a peasant farmer writes on 21 April 1918 to Georg Heim, the leader of the Bavarian Christian Farmers' Association and right-wing Centre Party politician:

The unequal pay against the backdrop of the amount of work is what upsets the soldiers the most. Among other things, officers are not on watch neither during daytime nor at night. One could rather consider it as equitable if the relation of pay was the other way round. I have seen officers who were carrying their knapsacks on their own backs, but I met more who expected that somebody would carry their stuff even if it was very light-weight. Anyway, one gets to contemplate many ideas during the war. One thinks this and that and then sometimes something else. If we had only politicians at home like Hertling and Chernin [Count Hertling, the German Chancellor since 30 September 1917, and Count Czernin, the Austrian Foreign Minister who had delivered a memorandum on a peace settlement to his monarch on 12 April 1917], the soldiers in the field would not be so often filled with discontent. They trust rather these people than the loudmouths in the newspapers. Members of the Fatherland Party are the biggest traitors of our fatherland. The leaders of that lot belong in prison. They are ruining the courage of the front soldiers with their loud-mouthed demands. All soldiers are of the opinion that no part of our fatherland should be lost. But the masters with the big money control the governments in every country. Their high demands avert any possibility of starting negotiations. They want to expand the national territory, compensation and all sorts of things. If only these people had nothing more than 70 Pfennig a day and could see shell splinters flying past, some things would be different. It is hard to describe the damage created by the war in religious terms. It seems as if they have thrown down the sixth commandment to the pigs as fodder, not to speak of any other commandments.

In February 1918, the head of the Patriotic Support Association, a pressure group for patriotic instruction organized by both Protestant and Catholic priests, sends a letter by his brother, 'a common peasant', to the authorities:

If only the war came to an end! It will soon drive me crazy! There I am sitting out here keeping up the patience for another half a year and another one, hoping that it will come to an end, but all in vain. If only the gentlemen of the Fatherland Party had to go into the trenches, it would be peace probably much sooner. All my love, from your brother Otto.

Reports – From the Bottom Up[52]
The deferential attitude of many officers motivated them to dispatch misleading internal reports. Thus, the war weariness of the troops remained largely unnoticed until the end of the war. From a letter by General Ludwig von Gebsattel to the Bavarian War Minister on 27 June 1917:

I have accumulated many experiences during my spell of duty in the field during the past 29 months without interruption. These experiences, and the numerous reports and personal messages I filed during this time confirm that there have been indeed very often false reports made by many units, with regard to all sorts of topics, even ones with very severe content. I am firmly convinced that several severe defeats we had to suffer during this war were caused by such false reports. [...]

From the very beginning of the war one could recognize, feel and sense very soon that higher and very high positions of authority took reports that relayed inconvenient facts very badly, for they did not suit the plans of the authority or person in question. The reporting authority or person was accused of being a merchant of doom, a pessimist, to be lacking in energy or even worse, was heavily criticized and in some cases even bluntly told that they could not be employed in such a position when acting like that, and the like.

From a booklet published in 1920 that criticized the 'stab-in-the-back' legend:

Following the lead of the higher commanders, this overestimation and the inability to allow criticism infested the army down to the NCOs, to the company sergeants and to the squad leaders and averted truthfulness and doubt. That made it happen that the reports from several sections of the front to the higher leaders always sounded optimistic about their own situation, about the spirit of the troops. These reports would be again further summarized and in some cases even more sugarcoated during this procedure and then finally announced to the public. Until the very last days of the war, no other general than Ludendorff was allowed to inform the government, for others might have reported the situation in a different, less favourable way. And when Prince Max of Baden resolutely demanded and was able to hear other army commanders following the requests of the political leaders, Ludendorff resigned.

The 1918 January Strike[53]

Between 28 January and 4 February 1918, up to a million industrial workers, also in the armaments factories, were engaged in a mass strike. The January Strike also had repercussions on the Western Front, not only because up to 50,000 of the striking workers were subsequently drafted. The field post surveillance units closely observed the impact of the strike. Against the backdrop of an imminent offensive, which many soldiers hoped would bring peace, the strike was rejected by many front-line troops. Letter excerpts from a surveillance report for the 5th army:

The war won't be over a day sooner because of that.

As they already say in the newspapers, there is a lot going on in Germany. But they should keep quiet just during these few weeks until the war is over. For if they don't want to work any longer they can come here. We would rather like to go home and work, since this is our fourth year that we have been out here.

They are on strike in Berlin. They want more peace and more bread. There will be cuts in our rations as a result.

What will it be like in Germany with the strikes going on? I have little hope that this will shorten the war, for militarism is too strong in Prussia.

In my opinion, the strike is a big mistake, for if the people of the enemy nations don't do the same, it will just be to our detriment, since it will only encourage the enemy governments to carry on fighting.

It came to nothing with the strike. This stuff is no good anyway. You see, now the foreign countries think we are finished.

Hopefully the riots will help in all countries to finish it at last, since the government has now to accept that the people are fed up with the war and that continuing the war further will come to nothing. Because even the planned offensive will not bring us peace, if it can't be gained by other means.

I just regret that they didn't continue the strike. All comrades were happy with the strike. I think there won't be any peace before the front soldiers start to go on strike.

Everyone is talking about the great offensive. It will and has to succeed.

I think it will be quite a spectacle when it starts. This time Michel will make a good job of it and will smash everything that stands in the way. If only the idiots at home had not stabbed us in the back with the strike. Such a**holes!

Last Hopes – Last Offensives[54]

Lance corporal Gettmann reports on 2 January 1918 in a letter from the Western Front:

> There is only little fighting in our present position, which means currently, for our Army Command is planning a lot for the Western Front in 1918. For all I have learned – and one learns a lot over the phone as a telephone operator – we will try to break through in the West and thus to compel our enemies to an early peace.

On 21 March 1918, the German offensive in the West is launched. Some soldiers are reminded of the beginning of the war:

> It's the first day of spring today and not only this. Since 4 am the cannon have been roaring without a pause. Well, my darling, it is war again and I guess the quiet time is over. […] There is feverish acitivity all over the place and the street scene is as lively as during the first war months.

From the monthly report of an ombudsman for the Patriotic Instruction Programme in a Landsturm battalion in Bavaria, 23 March 1918:

> Of course, now every hope is based on the coming offensive in the West which is expected to bring an end to the war. It is clearly observable that these expectations dominate everyone and do not give any room for any short-lived ill feelings at all.

With the advance of the German armies, the offensive brought a return to the war of movement. Voices like this one from an NCO on 5 May 1918 could be found in many letters from the front:

> This 'forward' every day has an encouraging and stimulating effect on the soldier's mind, which has dried up by the all too long period of the war of position, for it raises new hopes that the newly started war of movement could bring the final decision, the much-longed for return to the Heimat, to the dear family, to the familiar peaceful work. And this wonderful award beckoning full of promise from far away, strengthens body and soul and makes the unsettled and disorderly life here with always the same images of misery, sorrow and worries easier to bear.

But the advancement, up to 60km into positions held by French and British troops, also detached the most advanced troops from their support lines and brought them into an uninhabitable landscape. The farmer Franz Xaver Bergler writes on 12 April 1918, the day when he died in battle:

> We have been back in position since 3 April and are still here. Right in the midst of a completely devastated area, everything is shot into pieces, only grenade craters are left. We haven't even started yet advancing against the English. The Englishman is just firing against us with his massive grenade fire all day long. [...] Now we have been sitting in this position for eight days, often covered in mud and dirt up to the knees. We are freezing during the night and have no shelter. Or we are lying in an old tunnel, so tightly squeezed against each other that all limbs hurt terribly.

'Victory Frenzy'[55]

The expectation that the offensive would bring an imminent victory, widespread among the troops, also raised the prospect of a sudden turn in morale in case the offensive failed. In a letter written on 1 May 1918, the Social Democrat Heinrich Aufderstrasse offers a lucid forecast of future developments:

> Now this is how I imagine peace, if nothing unexpected turns up: Ludendorff and Co. have done a great service to these developments, but concerning their own plans a very dubious service when they brought army and people to believe confidently in a great unconditional victory during the last months. Today, 80 per cent count on the 'certain and complete success of our weapons in the West'. The present *victory frenzy* is almost comparable with that during the first months of the war. That is the case here and that will be probably the case at home, too, as far as I can see from the newspapers [...]. Are there any real facts as a foundation? [...] Our discipline is such that *anything* can be done. Give up any possible thought that the army would not carry on at some point in spite of that discipline. If the superiors are tough on the men, you can see orgies of drill. Old and young men, athletes and cripples, they are all shaken after being yelled at. Right here on the spot one could not possibly see a greater difference between the strictest obedience to all orders and the big talk

in the pubs about: 'I thought they could kiss my arse' – 'I stayed calm' etc. Only 1 per cent at best can rightly show off like this when they are not with their superiors. [...] Ludendorff and Co. *cannot do otherwise.* If they do not force through a victory, *what then???*

Let's assume the following: the next offensive operations will bring success but not a decision. After some months, everybody is out of breath and it all stops, stops! But as sure as fate there will be a hangover as big as Michel's current victory frenzy, which was artificially stimulated to the highest degree. The insight will follow that one cannot force through a complete victory. Then – in July or August, maybe a bit earlier or later – the time has come for the supporters of a negotiated peace. Already today, only patriotic deadheads believe in the success of the submarine war. How do Ludendorff and Co. then still plan to put the people off, when all believable possibilities to achieve victory are gone. Then Scheidemann and Erzberger will have the most fertile ground. [...] As far as I am concerned, there is still a slight possibility of Ludendorff succeeding, but I rather reckon there will be a dead spot after some months. But I expect the party leadership [of the Majority Social Democratic Party] has taken this already into account?

I understand and *have accepted* that I have to wait here for the rest of the war. But I am not disheartened, for by my calculation the slaughtering will be over in the foreseeable future, in autumn at the latest.

'Hangover'[56]

The rapid changes in the morale of the troops since 18 July, when the Allied counteroffensive commenced, confirmed Aufderstrasse's forecast. For many soldiers no longer a victory, but only defeat now seemed able to guarantee a peaceful end. From a letter written on 13 October:

How will I be relieved when the roaring sounds of battle are replaced by a ceremonial silence. And when we have times ahead which are ten times worse, yet they surely cannot be worse than the four years of disconcertment of the mind.

A letter intercepted by postal censorship stated:

The main thing is that the swindle and the murdering has an end. We do not have to care whether we stay German or become French, we are now finished anyway. You at home will have an even better insight than we out here. If it does not come to an end right now, there won't be nothing left of Germany at all.

At this point, the soldiers did not any longer care about postal censorship and possible punishment. From a postal censorship report written in August 1918:

It is by the way remarkable that letter writers, after having recently vented their anger in most drastic form, often add: 'I know they are checking my correspondence, but just let them read this, this way they will at least learn the truth.'

Soldiers used increasingly extreme methods to withdraw themselves from service. From a decree by the Bavarian War Ministry, 29 May 1918:

It has been noticed here that agents are sold to soldiers on trains which are supposed to cause leg ulcers. These soldiers try to elude being sent out to the front by using these agents. The train patrols and line commander's offices are to be instructed accordingly.

From a report about the morale of a battalion, 11 September 1918:

An absolutely reliable helper, a teacher by profession, gave a couple of talks on his experiences and suffering as a French prisoner of war in front of some companies at the request of the battalion. He had returned to the battalion as an exchange prisoner. The talks were good and only an advantageous impact on the audience was to be expected. Indeed, they caused a vivid conversation among the people. Though the speaker afterwards felt compelled to report that the questions and enquiries of several comrades who asked him after his talk hardly gave rise to any doubts that these men wanted to find out about the best way to get taken prisoner without any risk and attracting attention, and how to act as a prisoner in order to be treated well.

'Sucked Dry'[57]

Allied propaganda used the rapid deterioration of morale in the German army and called on them to desert or refuse orders. From a leaflet that was issued in September 1918 and signed by an Association of German Democrats in French Captivity:

Comrades! According to some comrades who have defected to us, troops of several regiments (including the 41st and 43rd East-Prussian Infantry Regiment) have refused to be sent to the Somme front and to be slaughtered for the benefit of the company Hohenzollern, Father and Son and Co. The incident had quite an unhappy ending for the persons concerned. The machine guns were stung into action and some more German proletarians died as victims of the Prussian militarism. [...]

Comrades! Whoever is sick and tired of being a bullet trap for the old and the young Hohenzollern while his relatives at home are pinched by usurers and sucked dry, come over and join us. But follow the example of our oppressors. Whenever they are not completely in control, they deviously use trickery, lies and fraud. They lie to you, promise furlough, victory, imminent peace, free suffrage and God knows what else, as long as they fear the masses that you are. But as soon as they have singled out one of you, as soon as they are the stronger side, they will put you on court-martial, send you to prison or shoot you like dogs.

Show them that you can be as clever as they are. Agitate secretly. Inform your comrades, but only refuse obedience and blow away the officers, if you feel confident and if they can't retaliate.

(A call to defect followed, and a password was given: 'Republic'.)

Heinrich Aufderstrasse reports in a letter written on 27 August 1918:

Three-quarters of the men here wish an end, no matter how. It is only discipline keeping them still together, no more ifs and buts of politics. Enemy aeroplanes drop brochures about Potsdam, the Emperor, the beginning and the current situation of the war. We send anti-English ones over in small hot-air balloons. There was not a single deserter from the Entente as long as I have been here, but some of our men defected. The enemy has given us 'Republic' as a password for defection. Is it really possible to hold the front incessantly under these circumstances? I have severe doubts about this.

The final downturn of morale could neither be averted by disciplinary means nor by the belated promise to improve officer–men relations in the army. The following letter by a major, published in the newspaper *BZ am Mittag* on 18 October 1918, must have had a cynical ring to front-line soldiers:

The long years of war have cooled the enthusiasm of 1914 slightly. But there are still incidents with an uplifting impact. For example, in my regiment the gentlemen have promised voluntarily in these hard times to eat the same food as the troops and together with them, and not to enter a shelter but to bivouac within the front lines and to always be in touch with the men. [...] This was necessary, for due to the war of position and the concrete shelters for the officers we have become slightly effeminate and the mutual trust between troops and officers has been dampened. But this has come to an end now.

'Peace at Any Price'[58]

Excerpt from a report of the postal surveillance unit of the 6th army, 4 September 1918:

War weariness and depression are general phenomena. The letter writers have accepted for themselves the naked truth that: 'We can't be victorious' and partly even combine this statement with the opinion that Germany must be defeated. A certain number [of letters] state that it is vital to stay put, and some lines demonstrate, alongside the many who express their ill-humour and dissatisfaction, loyalty to the King and unwavering love for the fatherland, which is worth all the sacrifices. The number of letter-writers who openly wish death on the fatherland, is, however, not much smaller. They say: 'Possible further German successes can do nothing but prolong the war. A defeat would bring us the much longed for peace!' 'It is the same pay, no matter if we are under French, English or German domination after the war.' [...]

The opinions about the war and the causes of the war appearing in the letters are amazing. They say for example that the purpose of the war is to eradicate the working class, in other cases the Mittelstand [middle estate – *Stand* denotes a traditional form of social inequality based on shared habits and codes of honour, which is distinctive from modern notions of class], and that the war was started for this reason in the first place. The ordinary people who are reflecting on questions like this do not take into consideration that the educated estates of academics, higher civil servants etc. earn in many cases less than a worker in a factory which is vital for the war effort these days. On the other hand, there are quite a lot of level-headed people with a middle-class background who are worried about the subsequent economic effects of today's unnaturally high wages, particularly for young workers.

Almost none of the letters mentions any sense of patriotism at all. According to the overall impression created by the checking of the letters, there seems to be a certain sense of shame in putting a patriotic idea into words. Some letters are based on the view: 'Whoever shows a robust patriotic faith, has a vested interest in the war and will therefore profit and benefit from it.' On the other hand, the war weariness is so intense and the indifference towards joining to serve the good cause is so pronounced that the men wish to lose for example a left arm or to get similar injuries in order to evade the 'useless murdering', as they put it in their letters. The individual's interest in the war has taken a back seat; nearly all men are of the opinion: 'I'm shirking the front as good as I can!'

From the letter of a soldier, 15 September 1918:

Now we have begun to retreat at the whole front, not because we were forced to do so, since the German is too good a soldier to be forced to do that, [...] but because our fighting troops do not want to hold out any longer. Why should one sacrifice oneself, for what? Perhaps for the sake of the fatherland and its most holy goods? No, they all buried their patriotism a long time ago. They do not want to fight in a war of conquest any longer [...]. This is the view shared by 95 per cent of all branches of service in the field.

Captain Loose of the General Staff reports to the Army Supreme Command about the morale in the Army Groups Gallwitz and Duke Albrecht, 5 November 1918:

The commanding generals and the chiefs of the groups Maas-West and Argonne as well as the chief of army-detachment C have declared that they can hardly vouch for the morale of their troops. The mood here is very low. The troops are not any longer eager to fight. Maas-West and Argonne blame the physical breakdown for the disastrous mood. Yet in Metz, on the other hand, it was a regiment that was not under severe strain which has mutinied. It is impossible to show pictures of the Emperor, Hindenburg and Ludendorff in the cinemas. People are booing. It is said that on the appearance of a picture of Hindenburg in one particular corps area there was shouting: 'Turn off the light, get out the knives, two mess kits to collect the blood!' A band was playing

'Germany, Germany, above all' and people were shouting at them: 'Put down the brass trumpets!' etc. Thus the reversal of mood is indeed in many cases caused by a moral breakdown.

In the area of the army group Albrecht, the mood is generally unstable, in some cases bad. Anyway, a rapidly declining mood can be observed here as well. The troops wish for peace at any cost.

According to numerous accounts, the mood at the army groups is by and large so bad that the troops will not continue to fight if we do not achieve peace immediately. We will then have the revolution in just a couple of weeks.

From an anonymous letter to Chancellor Georg Count Hertling, written in August 1918:

Your Excellency will kindly allow the signatory to point out the following: I had the chance to talk to a soldier on the Western Front, who was on leave, about the last offensive which has been to our disadvantage. In this connection, the soldier told me that it was bound to happen like this. The soldiers do not want to fight any longer, they rather defect and let themselves be taken prisoner. Whereas the combat troops have to starve, the officers are indulging themselves behind the front in luxury, also with women, namely the younger gentlemen. These issues have caused severe resentment among the soldiers with the result that entire companies and batteries have refused to fight. I had my doubts about this scandalous story and approached further soldiers on leave and even NCOs who confirmed the very same thing. Even if these stories are only partly true, they are outrageous and must not be concealed from the Army Supreme Command. Therefore I would like to make Your Excellency aware of these incidents, for a situation like that can easily lead to a disaster. [...] With true love for the fatherland.

From a booklet published in 1919 by a publisher close to the Independent Social Democratic Party (USPD):

After having indulged in illusions for 4¼ years, after having postponed the hope for the promised end from month to month, after having taken heart from one slogan to the other to hold out at the front and at home, the new catchphrase of the 'national defence' was not going to work anymore with the masses. Everyone wanted peace. Even the most daring soldiers out here and those without any worries did not want to get killed right before the end. Ludendorff resigned on 26 October. Nobody believed honestly in any military successes. Naturally, the resistance against the stormy advancement of the enemy was growing weaker. Thus, the lines were tottering at many points where they would probably have been able to hold in military terms. The panicking of the higher authorities increased the chaos. Never before had orders and counterorders rushed one after another in such a confusing manner. No sooner were divisions deployed than they were withdrawn again. Others who had just been relieved were thrown into battle again. The result was forced marches every day. Commanders and troops never came to rest. The officers shook their heads, the troops were swearing.

But nobody considered the defeat as his own defeat, but rather as a defeat of the old system. The withdrawal was welcomed as a march back home. There was just a wistful glance on some faces when they passed some famous places which were once conquered with blood of many comrades.

Later on they tried to play off the 'brave front soldiers' against the soldiers in the rear area and the sailors by suggesting the latter would have stabbed the former in the back and would have prevented them from resisting the enemy. They forgot and wanted to forget that also among the front troops in early November the mood was indeed ripe for the revolution.

From a booklet that was published in 1920 and aimed to rebut the 'stab-in-the-back' legend:

The majority of the exhausted troops was willing to hold out as long as the men deployed in the gruelling war of position along most of the front sections could follow their comrades in their mind's eye violently charging and attacking with promise in other places of combat; as long as there was the most minute possibility of finishing the war and returning to wives and children soon. Whoever did not witness these months among the combat troops at the front lines, whoever did not watch the old and young soldiers from the twentieth reserve, making desperate efforts to construe the prospect of an early end due to the smallest political or military incident, whoever did not witness the impact of the debacle of the summer offensive, accompanied by hopes so high and indeed by the very last hopes, on the masses of the troops, who did not observe mistrust and desperation increasing all of a sudden to an enormous extent now, did not notice the hatred against the leaders that was exploding like a darting flame: whoever did not witness these things should refrain from judging and condemning!

All diseases broke out then at a great rate, similar to the epidemics of the middle ages. The morale disintegrated completely, after bits and pieces had already crumbled away. While the masses of soldiers on leave were crowding the back area, while the continuous train transports from the front were getting more intensive and rushed from day to night and from morning to evening, while there was chaos going on within the leading military authorities which could only have happened to a completely puzzled and surprised army commander, there were already soldiers who went on absence without leave and looted the provision trains.

Radicalization[59]

During the final months of the war, radical expectations for postwar change emerged. In January, rentier Schütz reports to the 2nd Army Corps in Stettin:

I herewith report to the General Command that I was recently listening to conversations in waiting rooms and train compartments, repeatedly overhearing soldiers who bluntly declared that they would take revenge after the war for all the injustice on the part of their superiors by starting a revolution. [...] I was travelling from Mikolaiken in Eastern Prussia to Arys. There were some soldiers in the compartment together with two civilians, a female teacher and myself. The war and its bad economic side-effects were the subjects of the conversation. A young soldier sitting next to me, who was according to his own information from the industrial area in Rhineland–Westphalia, also expressed his opinion about the revolution which will happen after the war. He said that he had provided himself already with weapons for this purpose, army revolvers with sufficient ammunition and hand grenades. I asked him if it was possible to take away weapons and ammunition without being noticed by the superiors. He replied that this could be done without attracting attention with both our own army revolvers and the captured enemy revolvers. One could easily take those home unnoticed. It was also, he stated, easy to take home hand grenades after unscrewing the stick so that the different pieces would simply fit in one's pocket. In his home area, every soldier going on leave would take home weapons like these.

On 12 March 1918, the observations of the rentier Schütz led to a decree by the Chief of the General Staff:

A letter to the Royal Prussian Ministry of War has informed me that soldiers on leave have openly discussed a revolution for the time after the war. Thus a soldier who is allegedly from the Rhenish–Westphalian industrial area and travelled on a train, declared that in his Heimat soldiers who were on leave would bring weapons home for this purpose. It would be easy to take home both German or captured revolvers and hand grenades dismantled into two pieces.

I request to give the order to search thoroughly luggage and clothes of a random selection of soldiers who go on leave. It will be possible to do so during bathing and delousing. Every breach of the regulations is supposed to be punished severely. But above all I ask all superiors who witness or learn about such condemnable talks by chance to take drastic measures immediately.

Epilogue

A Plea[60]
One of the many war widows, Maria Geiger from Leutkirchen in Württemberg, writes on 12 May 1918 to the Kaiser:

> Your Excellency! I would like to address a plea to Your Excellency if I may. That is to say, my husband had been at the front since 2 August 1914. He has participated in everything in his active Infantry Regiment 124 without any injury. Then he was killed for the fatherland on 22 March during heavy fighting on the Western Front [...]. Thus, Your Excellency, I would like to beg most humbly if Your Excellency could be of help in transferring my husband's corpse back home, for we would love to bury our unforgettable husband and father in the Heimat. I am penniless and can't possibly afford the transfer, since the costs are too high. For my husband had been in the service of Your Excellency for 42 months and had had to suffer terrible exertions, so I take the liberty and address this plea to Your Excellency that Your Excellency might be of help that I can get my good husband's corpse home for just a small cost. Since it is a great sacrifice for a happy family to lose the breadwinner on the field of honour.

(The office of the Lord Chamberlain for the Kaiser forwarded this letter to the 13th Deputy General Command in Stuttgart, which asked the widow on 5 June 1918 to submit a further, formal request. It cannot be verified from the archival record if this was successful or not.)

Glossary

Alldeutscher Verband	Pan-German League, a radical nationalist pressure group founded in 1891.
Besatzungsheer	Replacement army. All military units on German territory, particularly those that trained military personnel that were sent as replacements for corresponding active units in the field.
Einjährig-Freiwilliger	One-year volunteer. Young men with a high-school diploma could sign up for military service as a one-year volunteer. This would cut the period of service to a half and allowed them to lodge privately. The 'one-yearers' had to pay for their own subsistence and also their equipment, indicating that this was a privilege not only based on formal education but also on affluence. After their one year of service, one-yearers could advance to the rank of reserve lieutenant. Due to the heavy losses of the active officer corps in the first months of the war, one-yearers who had been promoted to reserve officers were the immediate superiors of many soldiers in the German army. Their lack of accomplishment due to the reduced period of training and their lack of empathy due to their middle-class background was the subject of intensive criticism from private soldiers.
Etappe	Rear area. In the widest sense commonly used by many soldiers, the Etappe was all territory that was out of the firing range of the enemy artillery. In a more narrow sense, it was the territory between the operational area of the field army and the occupied territories or German territory. The Etappe provided supplies for the field army and was under the

	command of Etappeninspektionen (rear area inspections) of the armies and Etappenkommandanturen (rear area commands). Different terms of military duty and livelihood led to a deeply felt alienation between front troops and the mostly Landsturm troops and the officers who served in the Etappe.
Feldgraue	Field grey was the uniform colour in the German army from 1907. During the First World War, Feldgraue (i.e. soldiers in field grey) was used as a synonym for the troops in the field.
Feldwebelleutnant	NCOs who performed the duties of officers without the certificate were made Feldwebelleutnant (Sergeant-lieutenant). Thus, they still ranked below the lowest rank of reserve officer and were only second-class officers, a fact that contributed to the widespread perception that the officer corps was a separate caste and endowed with unjustified privileges by the monarchical state.
Heimat	Literally, home or homeland. In a more technical or geographical sense, Heimat could denote Germany or German territory, as opposed to the front, Etappe and occupied territories. In letters written by soldiers, it would usually denote their place or region of residence, a familiar place they longed to return to. The romantic connotations of this sense of Heimat are impossible to render in English, not even through the term blighty, which was in some ways the equivalent among British troops, although Heimat is strictly focused on the regional and not the national identity space.
Landsturm	The Landsturm comprised reservists above the age of 40 and those who had not been drafted for military service before the war.
Landwehr	After two years of conscription, men who were eligible to the draft had to serve in the reserve in peacetime for two years. After that they were moved to the Landwehr, which consisted of a first tier with five years of service, and a second tier with three

	years of service. In peacetime, Landwehr soldiers were called to exercises once a year. During the First World War, Landwehr-units consisted of Landwehr soldiers up to the age of 40.
Oberste Heeresleitung (OHL)	Army Supreme Command. Upon mobilization, the Chief of the Prussian General Staff was declared the Chief of the General Staff of the Field Army. The OHL had supreme command over all military operations.
Patriotic Instruction Programme	When a growing number of soldiers on furlough started in the summer of 1916 to agitate against the war loans issued by the government, the military authorities began to discuss propaganda efforts among the front-line troops. Reacting to the Interparliamentary Peace Initiative by the Reichstag majority parties in July 1917, a systematic programme for the Patriotic Instruction of the troops (*Vaterländischer Unterricht*) was rolled out both at the front and in the replacement army. Specifically designated Aufklärungsoffiziere (enlightenment officers, so the official euphemism) organized a programme of lectures by pastors, politicians and academics and the screening of films in order to convince the troops that the war had to be continued until a German victory had been secured. The affinity of the Instruction Programme to the policies of the Vaterlandspartei provoked a backlash among the troops, who mostly either resented or simply ignored the programme.
Stellvertretendes Generalkommando	Deputy General Command. With the declaration of the state of war on 31 July 1914, the deputy commanding generals in the 21 army corps took over the tasks – mainly recruitment and supplies – of the army commanders who left for the front. Together with the fortress commanders, the deputy general commanders as military commanders also took over the domestic executive authority, with wide-ranging powers with regard to the war economy, censorship etc.

Vaterlandspartei	German Fatherland Party, founded on 2 September 1917 as a backlash against the peace resolution that was passed by the majority parties in the Reichstag on 19 July 1917. The Fatherland Party opposed any attempts to conclude a peace based on compromise and reconciliation. Its main aim was to propagate and demand a Siegfrieden, a peace settlement based on a German victory which would imply widespread annexations and a shift to authoritarian domestic politics. With its aggressive nationalism and anti-Semitism, the Vaterlandspartei was a direct ideological precursor of the Nazi party.

List of Abbreviations

A.K.	Armeekorps (Army Corps)
A.O.K.	Armee-Ober-Kommando (Army High Command)
BArch	Bundesarchiv Berlin-Lichterfelde
BA/MA Freiburg	Bundesarchiv/Militärarchiv Freiburg
BHStA/IV	Bayerisches Hauptstaatsarchiv München /Abt. IV: Kriegsarchiv
BHStA/V	Bayerisches Hauptstaatsarchiv München/Abt. V: Nachlässe
Btl./Batl	Battalion
Div.	Division
G./Geh.	Geheim (Classified)
Gen.Kdo./GK	Generalkommando (General Command)
GLA	Generallandesarchiv Karlsruhe
HStA/MA Stuttgart	Hauptstaatsarchiv Stuttgart/Militärarchiv
Inf.	Infanterie (Infantry)
KM	Kriegsministerium (War Ministry)
K.M.E.	Kriegsministerialerlaß (War Ministry Decree)
Komp./Kp.	Kompanie (Company)
Ldw.	Landwehr
Lt/Ltn	Leutnant (Lieutenant)
M.G.	Maschinengewehr (Machine Gun)
O.H.L	Oberste Heeresleitung (Army Supreme Command)
R./Res.	Reserve
StAH	Staatsarchiv Hamburg
Stellv./stv.	stellvertretend/stellvertretendes (deputy)
U.O.	Unteroffizier (NCO)
Verhandlungen Landtag	Verhandlungen der Kammer der Abgeordneten des Bayerischen Bayerischer Landtages. Steno-graphische Berichte. 36. Session, 1912/18, München

Verhandlungen Reichstag	Verhandlungen des Deutschen Reichstages XIII. Legislaturperiode/II. Reichstag Session, 1914–1918, Berlin
WUA, Gutachten Hobohm	Das Werk des Untersuchungsausschusses der Verfassunggebenden Deutschen Nationalversammlung und des Deutschen Reichstages 1919–1930, 4. Reihe, II. Abteilung, Bd. 11/1, Gutachten Martin Hobohm, Soziale Heeresmißstände als Teilursache des Zusammenbruchs von 1918, Berlin 1929

Notes to Introduction

1. See the reproduction at: http://germanhistorydocs.ghi-dc.org/sub_image.
   cfm?image_id=17271 (accessed on 24 August 2009). For context, compare
   Detlef Hoffmann, 'Der Mann mit dem Stahlhelm vor Verdun. Fritz Erlers
   Plakat zur sechsten Kriegsanleihe 1917', in: Berthold Hinz, Hans-Ernst
   Mittig, Wolfgang Schäche (eds), *Die Dekoration der Gewalt. Kunst und
   Medien im Faschismus* (Gießen: Anabas, 1979), pp. 101–114.
2. Bernd Hüppauf, 'Langemarck, Verdun and the Myth of a NEW MAN in
   Germany after the First World War', *War & Society* 6 (1988), 70–103. On
   Ernst Jüngers' war novels see Roger Woods, *Ernst Jünger and the Nature of
   Political Commitment* (Stuttgart: Heinz, 1982).
3. See Richard Bessel, *Germany after the First World War* (Oxford: Clarendon
   Press, 1993), pp. 274–282; Karin Hausen, 'The German Nation's
   Obligations to the Heroes' Widows of World War I', in: Margaret Randolph
   Higonnet et al. (eds), *Behind the Lines. Gender and the Two World Wars* (New
   Haven and London: Yale University Press, 1987), pp. 126–140.
4. Cited in Bessel, *Germany after the First World War*, p. 283.
5. The most detailed account is now Boris Barth, *Dolchstoßlegenden und
   politische Desintegration. Das Trauma der deutschen Niederlage im Ersten
   Weltkrieg 1914–1933* (Düsseldorf: Droste, 2003); see Jeffrey Verhey, *The
   Spirit of 1914: Militarism, Myth and Mobilization in Germany* (Cambridge:
   Cambridge University Press, 2000), pp. 219–223; more generally see Robert
   Gerwarth, 'The Past in Weimar History', *Contemporary European History* 15
   (2006), 1–22.
6. Carl Zuckmayer, *Als wär's ein Stück von mir. Horen der Freundschaft*
   (Frankfurt/Main: Fischer Taschenbuch Verlag, 1969), p. 198.
7. George L. Mosse, *Fallen Soldiers: Reshaping the Memory of the World Wars*
   (New York/Oxford: Oxford University Press, 1990), p. 7.
8. Ibid.
9. Ibid, p. 10.
10. Walther Lambach, *Ursachen des Zusammenbruchs* (Hamburg: Deutsch-
    nationale Verlagsanstalt, n.d. [1919]).
11. On Lambach and the DHV see Larry Eugene Jones, *German Liberalism and
    the Dissolution of the Weimar Party System, 1918–1933* (Chapel Hill/London:
    University of North Carolina Press, 1988), p. 318; Carole E. Adams, 'Anti-
    Semitism in the Political Culture of Wilhelmine Germany: The Case of

White-Collar Workers', in: John Milfull (ed.), *Why Germany? National Socialist Anti-Semitism and the European Context* (Oxford: Berg, 1993), pp. 61–74. The membership figure in Jürgen Kocka, *Facing Total War: German Society, 1914–1918* (Cambridge, Mass: Harvard University Press, 1984), pp. 78f.

12. See Lambach, *Ursachen*, pp. 23, 25f., 32f., 56f.; on the institutional structure and the failure of the Patriotic Instruction Programme see Benjamin Ziemann, *War Experiences in Rural Germany, 1914–1923* (Oxford/New York: Berg, 2007), pp. 68–71, 152f. The positive assessment by Alexander Watson, *Enduring the Great War: Combat, Morale and Collapse in the German and British Armies, 1914–1918* (Cambridge: Cambridge University Press, 2008), pp. 81f., is not based on sufficient evidence.

13. Cited in Lambach, *Ursachen*, p. 59.

14. Quotes ibid., pp. 111, 21f.

15. See Bernd Ulrich, *Die Augenzeugen. Deutsche Feldpostbriefe in Kriegs- und Nachkriegszeit 1914–1933* (Essen: Klartext, 1997), pp. 257–259.

16. Ulrich Heinemann, *Die verdrängte Niederlage. Politische Öffentlichkeit und Kriegsschuldfrage in der Weimarer Republik* (Göttingen: Vandenhoeck & Ruprecht, 1983), pp. 177–185, quote p. 180.

17. Ibid., p. 189.

18. See Das Werk des Untersuchungsausschusses der Verfassunggebenden Deutschen Nationalversammlung und des Deutschen Reichstages 1919–1930, 4. Reihe, II. Abteilung (WUA), vol. 5, *Verhandlungsbericht: Die allgemeinen Ursachen und Hergänge des inneren Zusammenbruches*, 2. Teil (Berlin: Deutsche Verlagsgesellschaft für Politik und Geschichte, 1928), pp. 262–335.

19. See Ludwig Bergsträsser, 'Front und Friede', *Vossische Zeitung*, 31 March 1926.

20. WUA, vol. 11/1, *Gutachten Martin Hobohm, Soziale Heeresmißstände als Teilursache des Zusammenbruchs von 1918* (Berlin: Deutsche Verlagsgesellschaft für Politik und Geschichte, 1929). Compare Bernd Ulrich and Benjamin Ziemann (eds), *Krieg im Frieden. Die umkämpfte Erinnerung an den Ersten Weltkrieg* (Frankfurt: Fischer Taschenbuch Verlag, 1997), pp. 85–88.

21. On Hobohm's biography and political activism see Hans Schleier, *Die bürgerliche deutsche Geschichtsschreibung der Weimarer Republik* (Berlin: Akademie Verlag, 1975), pp. 531–574.

22. Wilhelm Deist, 'The Military Collapse of the German Empire', *War in History* 3 (1996), 186–207; see also Ziemann, *War Experiences*, pp. 73–110; Scott Stephenson, *The Final Battle. Soldiers of the Western Front in the German Revolution of 1918* (Cambridge: Cambridge University Press, 2009).

23. See Ziemann, *War Experiences*, pp. 73–153; Aribert Reimann, *Der Große Krieg der Sprachen. Untersuchungen zur historischen Semantik in Deutschland und England zur Zeit des Ersten Weltkriegs* (Essen: Klartext, 2000).

24. Hermann von Kuhl in a meeting of the subcommittee in 1926, cited in Ulrich, *Augenzeugen*, p. 251.
25. Hermann von Kuhl in 1926, cited ibid., p. 249.
26. See Markus Pöhlmann, 'Yesterday's Battles and Future War: The German Official Military History, 1918–1939', in: Roger Chickering and Stig Förster (eds), *The Shadows of Total War. Europe, East Asia and the United States, 1919–1939* (Cambridge: Cambridge University Press, 2003), pp. 223–238. On the politics of the archive see also the brief remarks by Peter Fritzsche, 'The Archive and the Case of the German Nation', in: Antoinette Burton (ed.), *Archive Stories. Facts, Fiction and the Writing of History* (Durham/London: Duke University Press, 2005), pp. 184–208, here pp. 193f.
27. Ulrich, *Augenzeugen*, p. 249.
28. See Ulrich, *Augenzeugen*, pp. 39–168; Ziemann, *War Experiences*; compare also Reimann, *Der Große Krieg*.
29. Philipp Witkop (ed.), *Kriegsbriefe gefallener Studenten* (Munich: Georg Müller, 1928). This edition was translated into English in 1929, and recently edited again as Witkop (ed.), *German Students' War Letters*, trans. by A.F. Wedd (Philadelphia: Pine Street Books, 2002). On the publishing history and reception of this collection see the detailed account by Manfred Hettling and Michael Jeismann, 'Der Weltkrieg als Epos. Philipp Witkop's "Kriegsbriefe gefallener Studenten"', in: Gerhard Hirschfeld and Gerd Krumeich (eds), *'Keiner fühlt sich hier mehr als Mensch ...' Erlebnis und Wirkung des Ersten Weltkriegs* (Frankfurt: Fischer Taschenbuch Verlag, 1996), pp. 205–234; see also Wolfgang G. Natter, *Literature at War, 1914–1940. Representing the "Time of Greatness" in Germany* (New Haven: Yale University Press, 1999), pp. 90–121.
30. Hettling and Jeismann, 'Der Weltkrieg als Epos', pp. 207f., 210, 212.
31. Ibid., pp. 220, 223–225.
32. See for instance Modris Eksteins, *Rites of Spring. The Great War and the Birth of the Modern Age* (London: Black Swan, 1990), p. 277.
33. Ibid, p. 275.
34. On the idiom of French peasant farmers, see Annick Cochet, 'Les paysans sur le front en 1916', *Bulletin du centre d'histoire de France contemporaine* 3 (1982), 37–48; idem, 'Les soldats français', in: Jean-Jacques Becker and Stéphane Audoin-Rouzeau (eds), *Les Sociétés européennes et la guerre de 1914–1918* (Paris: Publications de l'Université de Nanterre, 1990), pp. 357–366.
35. On British working class soldiers, see David Englander and James Osborne, 'Jack, Tommy and Henry Dubb, The Armed Forces and the Working Class', *Historical Journal* 21 (1978), 593–621. See also Reimann, *Der Große Krieg*, who points to the many similarities in the semantics of British and German soldiers.

36. See the seminal formulation of this thesis by Mosse, *Fallen Soldiers*, pp. 159–181.

37. Patrick Krassnitzer, 'Die Geburt des Nationalsozialismus im Schützengraben. Formen der Brutalisierung in den Autobiographien von nationalsozialistischen Frontsoldaten', in: Jost Dülffer and Gerd Krumeich (eds), *Der verlorene Frieden. Politik und Kriegskultur nach 1918* (Essen: Klartext, 2002), pp. 119–148.

38. For a critique of the brutalization thesis see Benjamin Ziemann, 'Germany after the First World War – A Violent Society? Results and Implications of Recent Research on Weimar Germany', *Journal of Modern European History* 1 (2003), 80–95 (online at: http://eprints.whiterose.ac.uk/4748/ (accessed on 20 October 2009)).

39. Richard Bessel, 'The Great War in German Memory: The Soldiers of the First World War, Demobilization and Weimar Poltical Culture', *German History* 6 (1988), 20–34, here pp. 32f.; compare idem, 'The "Front Generation" and the Politics of Weimar Germany', in: Mark Roseman (ed.), *Generations in Conflict. Youth Revolt and Generation Formation in Germany 1770–1968* (Cambridge: Cambridge University Press, 1995), pp. 121–136; Benjamin Ziemann, 'Die Erinnerung an den Ersten Weltkrieg in den Milieukulturen der Weimarer Republik', in: Thomas F. Schneider (ed.), *Kriegserlebnis und Legendenbildung. Das Bild des 'modernen' Krieges in Literatur, Theater, Photographie und Film* (Osnabrück: Universitätsverlag Rasch, 1999), vol. I, pp. 249–270.

40. Ute Frevert, *A Nation in Barracks. Modern Germany, Military Conscription and Civil Society* (Oxford/New York: Berg, 2004), p. 182. See ibid., pp. 149–235, for a comprehensive analysis of conscription in Imperial Germany.

41. Cited ibid., p. 182.

42. See Ziemann, *War Experiences*, pp. 15–27; Verhey, *Spirit of 1914*, pp. 58–114.

43. Verhey, *Spirit of 1914*, pp. 97–103; for a slightly different argument, based on a different sample, see Alexander Watson, '"For Kaiser and Reich". The Identity and Fate of the German Volunteers, 1914–1918', *War in History* 12 (2005), 44–74.

44. Bessel, *Germany after the First World War*, p. 5.

45. See Frevert, *Nation in Barracks*, quotes p. 5.

46. Ibid., pp. 157–159.

47. Ibid., pp. 160–170.

48. Ziemann, *War Experiences*, pp. 74, 79f.

49. For these figures see Bessel, *Germany after the First World War*, pp. 5–7; Ziemann, *War Experiences*, pp. 30f.

50. On postal censorship, see Ulrich, *Augenzeugen*, pp. 78–105.

51. For some reflections on these issues see Benjamin Ziemann, 'Feldpostbriefe der beiden Weltkriege – eine ‚authentische' Quellengattung?', in: Peter Eigner, Christa Hämmerle and Günter Müller (eds), *Briefe, Tagebücher, Auto-*

biographien. Studien und Quellen für den Unterricht (Vienna: Studienverlag, 2006), pp. 63–75.

52. As examples for studies in this fashion see Ziemann, *War Experiences*; Christa Hämmerle, '"You Let a Weeping Woman Call You Home"? Private Correspondences during the First World War in Austria and Germany', in: Rebecca Earle (ed.), *Epistolary Selves. Letters and Letter-Writers, 1600–1945* (Aldershot: Ashgate, 1999), pp. 152–182.

53. On the study of historical semantics see Benjamin Ziemann and Miriam Dobson, 'Introduction', in: Miriam Dobson and Benjamin Ziemann (eds), *Reading Primary Sources. The Interpretation of Texts from Nineteenth- and Twentieth-Century History* (London: Routledge, 2008), pp. 1–18, here pp. 6–8; compare also Miriam Dobson, 'Letters', in: ibid., pp. 57–73.

54. Watson, *Enduring the Great War*, p. 10, wrongly asserts that postal censorship reports were only produced from mid-1917.

55. See Helmut Otto, 'Der Bestand Kriegsgeschichtliche Forschungsanstalt des Heeres im Bundesarchiv-, Militärisches Zwischenarchiv Potsdam', *Militärgeschichtliche Mitteilungen* 51 (1992), 429–441.

56. See Christhard Hoffmann, 'Between Integration and Rejection: The Jewish Community in Germany, 1914–1918', in: John Horne (ed.), *State, Society and Mobilization in Europe during the First World War* (Cambridge: Cambridge University Press, 1997), pp. 89–104; on the 'Jew count', see Werner T. Angress, 'The German "Judenzählung" of 1916. Genesis – Consequences – Significance', *Leo Baeck Institute Year Book* 23 (1978), 117–137; the German version of this article contains an extended appendix with primary documents: idem, 'Das deutsche Militär und die Juden im Ersten Weltkrieg', *Militärgeschichtliche Mitteilungen* 19 (1976), pp. 77–146.

57. For perceptions and experiences of Jewish front-line soldiers, see the war letters in: Sabine Hank and Hermann Simon (eds), *Feldpostbriefe jüdischer Soldaten 1914–1918. Briefe ehemaliger Zöglinge an Sigmund Feist, Direktor des Reichenheimschen Waisenhauses in Berlin*, 2 vols (Teetz: Hentrich & Hentrich, 2002).

58. See David Schoenbaum, *Zabern 1913. Consensus Politics in Imperial Germany* (London: Allen & Unwin, 1982).

59. Cf. Benjamin Ziemann, 'Fahnenflucht im deutschen Heer 1914–1918', *Militärgeschichtliche Mitteilungen* 55 (1996), no. 1, 93–130, here 108, 122. More generally, see Alan Kramer, 'Wackes at War: Alsace-Lorraine and the Failure of German National Mobilization, 1914–1918', in: Horne (ed.), *State, Society and Mobilization*, pp. 105–121.

60. See the memoirs by the Alsatian farmer Dominik Richert, *Beste Gelegenheit zum Sterben. Meine Erlebnisse im Kriege 1914–1918*, ed. Angelika Tramitz and Bernd Ulrich (Munich: Knesebeck & Schuler, 1989).

Document Sources

1. Alexander M. Frey, *Die Pflasterkästen. Ein Feldsanitätsroman* (Frankfurt/Main: Fischer Taschenbuch Verlag, 1989), pp. 213f.

2. Wilhelm Lamszus, *Das Irrenhaus. Visionen vom Krieg. II. Teil* (Hamburg: Janssen, 1919) (first edn 1912), foreword by Carl von Ossietzky, pp. 8f.

3. *BZ am Mittag*, no. 186, 9 August 1914, 'Ein schwäbischer Dienstbefehl'.
   Robert Gaupp, *Wahn und Irrtum im Leben der Völker. Rede des Rektors am Geburtstag des Königs* (Tübingen: Mohr, 1916), p. 20.
   Rheinisch-Westfälische Zeitung, 2 September 1914, 'Kriegsbilder aus der Weltstadt'.
   Heinrich Resch, 'Geisteskrankheit und Krieg' (lecture given 19 February 1915), *Allgemeine Zeitschrift für Psychiatrie und Psychisch-forensische Medizin* 72 (1916), 121–133, here 121.
   Walter Fuchs, 'Mobilmachungspsychosen', *Ärztliche Sachverständigen-Zeitung* no. 3 (1915), 25–29, 26.
   BArch, R 9350, no. 266, fol. 13: war diary of pastor Franck from the Melanchthon church in Berlin-Treptow, 22 August 1914.

4. *Münchener Neueste Nachrichten* no. 395, 4 August 1914, morning issue, p. 3, 'Der zweite Mobilmachungstag'.
   Konrad Dürr, *Erinnerungen und Gedanken aus meinem Leben*, ed. P. Högler (Öllingen: n.p. 1987) , p. 83.
   Siegfried Jacobsohn, *Die ersten Tage* (Konstanz: Reuß & Itta, 1916), pp. 13, 29, 30, 48, 72.
   BHStA/IV, HS 3410, war diary Georg Schenk.

5. Carl Zuckmayer, *Als wär's ein Stück von mir. Horen der Freundschaft* (Frankfurt/Main: Fischer Taschenbuch Verlag, 1969, first edn 1966), p. 168.
   W. Blankenburg, 'Schlachtenmut und Prüfungsangst', *Nationalliberale Blätter* 27 (1915), 462–464, here 462, 464.

6. BA/MA Freiburg MSg2/2640, 'Kriegserinnerungen' by Paul Wittenburg (typewritten), 3, 5, 6, 13.
   Oskar Maria Graf, *Wir sind Gefangene. Ein Bekenntnis aus diesem Jahrzehnt* (Berlin: Verlag der Büchergilde Gutenberg, 1928), p. 82.
   Siegfried Kracauer, *Ginster – von ihm selbst geschrieben* (Berlin: Fischer, 1928), p. 69.
   Berliner Lokal Anzeiger no. 404, 11 August 1914, 'Berliner Landsturm'.

Helene Hurwitz-Stranz (ed.), *Kriegerwitwen gestalten ihr Schicksal. Lebenskämpfe deutscher Kriegerwitwen nach eigenen Darstellungen* (Berlin: Heymann, 1931), p. 22.

W. Suckan, 'Psychosen bei Frauen im Zusammenhang mit dem Kriege', *Allgemeine Zeitschrift für Psychiatrie und psychisch-gerichtliche Medizin* 72 (1916), 328–355, 336.

Paul Plaut, 'Psychographie des Kriegers', Beihefte zur Zeitschrift für angewandte Psychologie no. 21: *Beiträge zur Psychologie des Krieges*, ed. William Stern and Otto Lipmann (Leipzig: J.A. Barth, 1920), pp. 1–123, here pp. 11f.

7. Otto Binswanger, *Die seelischen Wirkungen des Krieges* (Stuttgart/Berlin: Deutsche Verlags-Anstalt, 1914), p. 21.

8. Valentin Strohschnitter, *Der deutsche Soldat 1913–1919* (Frankfurt/Main: Henzel & Doland, 1930), p. 44.

   E. Redlich, 'Über Encephalitis pontis et cerebelli', *Zeitschrift für die gesamte Neurologie und Psychiatrie* 37 (1917), 1–36, 23.

9. BHStA/IV, Stellv. Gen.Kdo. I. A.K. 537: decree by the Bavarian War Ministry No. 29774, 2 September 1914, 'Betr.: Behandlung der Kriegsfreiwilligen und Ersatzmannschaften'.

   Karl Löwith, *Mein Leben in Deutschland vor und nach 1933. Ein Bericht* (Frankfurt/Main: Fischer Taschenbuch Verlag, 1989), pp. 1f.

   BArch, R 9350, no. 271, 'Feldpostbriefe an den Verband der Bergarbeiter Deutschlands 1914–18', letter by Franz Tholl, 29 November 1914, fol. 243.

   BA/MA Freiburg, MSg2/2317, war diary by David Pfaff (born 1890), Füsilier-Regiment 80, 2 August–4 November 1914 at the Western Front.

   BHStA/IV, MKr 2822, war letter by a soldier from the 1. bayer. Fußartillerie-Rgt, received from the anonymous sender by the Bavarian War Ministry on 30 September 1914.

10. BHStA/IV, Amtsbibliothek 9584, war letters by the peasant farmer and Landwehr soldier Stefan Schimmer from Öllingen (Franconia), who first served with 1. Komp./Ersatzbataillon bayer. 4. Ldw.-Inf.-Rgt, then was sent to the front with bayer. Ersatzbataillon 7, 30. Res.-Div. (typewritten).

11. Karl Bonhoeffer, 'Über die Bedeutung der Kriegserfahrungen für die allgemeine Psychopathologie und Ätiologie der Geisteskrankheiten', in: Otto von Schjerning (ed.), *Handbuch der ärztlichen Erfahrungen im Weltkriege 1914/18, vol. 4, Geistes- und Nervenkrankheiten*, ed. Karl Bonhoeffer (Leipzig: Barth, 1922/1934), pp. 3–44, here p. 5.

    H. Günther, 'Sind die Kriege gefährlicher geworden?', *Die Umschau*, vol. 18 (1914), II, 808–813, here 808, 809, 810.

    Max Weber, 'Zwischenbetrachtung. Stufen und Richtungen der religiösen Weltablehnung', *Archiv für Sozialwissenschaft und Sozialpolitik* 41 (1916), 387–421, 398.

BHStA/IV, Stellv. Gen.Kdo. I. A. K. no. 1678, postcard by the soldier Ernst Block, 17 September 1915.

12. BHStA/IV, Militärgerichte no. 6382, letter by Johann Preisinger, 7. Komp. bayer. 12. Inf.-Rgt, 31 October 1914.
'Lebenserinnerungen' by the typesetter Felix Fonrobert, written in 1979, private possession.
BHStA/IV, HS 3410, war diary by Georg Schenk, lance-corporal, 6. Komp./bayer. 21. Inf.-Rgt, entry from 20 August 1914.

13. War letter (copy) of a war volunteer, 18 November 1914, private possession.
StAH, Senat Kriegsakten A IIIz 17a, Bd. 3, letter by Carl Puvogel, 14 December 1915.

14. BArch, R 8034 II, no. 7599, fol. 73: Norddeutsche Allgemeine Zeitung no. 282, 14 November 1914, 'Unsere Kriegsfreiwilligen'.
Private possession, war letter by C. Krull, 28 June 1915 from the Western Front.
BArch, R 9350, no. 271, 'Feldpostbriefe an den Verband der Bergarbeiter Deutschlands 1914–18', Wilhelm Platta, fol. 196.
BArch, R 9350, no. 271, 'Feldpostbriefe an den Verband der Bergarbeiter Deutschlands 1914–18', Heinrich Klöpfel, fol. 141f.
BArch, R 9350, no. 271, 'Feldpostbriefe an den Verband der Bergarbeiter Deutschlands 1914–18', Gustav Pröpper, fol. 203f.
BArch, R 9350, no. 271, 'Feldpostbriefe an den Verband der Bergarbeiter Deutschlands 1914–18', B. Meier, fol. 159.
BArch, R 9350, no. 271, 'Feldpostbriefe an den Verband der Bergarbeiter Deutschlands 1914–18', Nikolaus Osterroth, fol. 192.
BArch, R 9350, no. 271, 'Feldpostbriefe an den Verband der Bergarbeiter Deutschlands 1914–18', Karl Otten, fol. 183f.

15. BHStA/IV, MKr 13346, war letter, presented to the Bavarian War Ministry by the Reichstag deputy Trendel from Regensburg on 2 November 1914, letter written on 17 October 1914.

16. Letter by the farmer and lance-corporal Jakob Eberhard (Landsturm-Bataillon Dillingen) to his wife Anna in Bruck (Bezirksamt Neuburg a.D.), 26 May 1915, private possession.
BHStA/IV, Militärgerichte no. 6409, letter by the bricklayer Georg Saarn, gunner in the Munitions-Kolonne 3., Fußartillerie-Munitions-Kolonnen-Abt. 10, 22 October 1915 to his wife in Heroldsbach (Franconia).
Letter by Alois Wagner, 12. Komp.bayer. 17.R.I.R., 15 November 1915 to the *Gütlerin* (smallholder) Maria Wagner in Baigertsham, Post Bad Höhenstadt (private possession of Benjamin Ziemann).
Letter by G.T., 4. Kompanie 3. Ers.-Inf.-Reg., bayer. 9. Res.-Div., 25 February 1917 to his wife in Gollhofen (Franconia). Private possession.
BArch, R 9350, no. 271, 'Feldpostbriefe an den Verband der Bergarbeiter Deutschlands 1914–18', fol. 228f., Richard Schiller.

BArch, R 43, no. 2398/7–8, fol. 49, 50f.

Letters written by Joseph Reininger from Gammersham (Upper Bavaria), born in 1889. Reininger was killed on 12 December 1917. Private possession. BHStA/IV, Militär-Gericht 6. Ldw.-Div. F 7, letter by Johann Friedrich, 3. Komp. Landsturm-Btl. Bamberg, to his wife, 23 September 1917.

17. BArch, R 9350, 271, 'Feldpostbriefe an den Verband der Bergarbeiter Deutschlands 1914–18', fol. 212f., Otto Rümmler 2. Komp. Ers.-Btl. R.I.R. 36, 7 October 1914.

BArch, R 9350, 271, 'Feldpostbriefe an den Verband der Bergarbeiter Deutschlands 1914–18', fol. 287–289, Fr. Langhorst, 2 January 1915.

BArch, R 9350, 271, 'Feldpostbriefe an den Verband der Bergarbeiter Deutschlands 1914–18', fol. 98f., August Balke, 75. Res.-Div., 8 August 1915.
BArch, R 9350, 262, fol. 25–26, 28.

BArch R 9350, 271, 'Feldpostbriefe an den Verband der Bergarbeiter Deutschlands 1914–18', fol. 233f., August Schmidt, 28 October 1914.

Staatsbibliothek Berlin – Preußischer Kulturbesitz, Handschriftenabteilung, Ms. Germ. fol. 1651, p. 91, entry from 7 April 1917.

Staatsbibliothek Berlin – Preußischer Kulturbesitz, Handschriftenabteilung, Ms. Boruss. fol. 1084, pp. 124f., entry from 6 May 1917.

18. BHStA/IV, MKr 2345, letter Helene Wendtlandt to the Prussian War Ministry, 9 August 1918.

BHStA/IV, MKr 11484, report by Zentralpolizeistelle Bayern to Bavarian War Ministry, 10 August 1917.

BHStA/IV, Stellv. Gen.Kdo. I. A.K. no. 1980, Vertrauensmann Ersatz-Btl. 20. Inf.-Regt to Ersatz-Btl., 24 April 1918.

BHStA/IV, MKr 2335, 'Bericht eines höheren Feldpolizei-Beamten', send to the Bavarian War Minister Kreß by the deputy Prussian War Minister Franz Gustav v. Wandel, 31 August 1916.

BHStA/IV, Stellv. Gen.Kdo. I. A.K. no. 592, Stellv. Gen.Kdo. I. Bayer. AK, 9 June 1916.

19. Georg Wunderle, *Das Seelenleben unter dem Einfluß des Krieges. Eine psychologische Skizze* (Eichstätt: Bromer, 1914), pp. 25f.

HStA/MA Stuttgart, M 750, letters by Lieutenant Eberbach as a French PoW, 25 October 1915, 29 October 1915.

Walter Ludwig, 'Beiträge zur Psychologie der Furcht im Kriege', *Beihefte zur Zeitschrift für angewandte Psychologie no. 21: Beiträge zur Psychologie des Krieges*, ed. William Stern and Otto Lipmann (Leipzig: J.A. Barth, 1920), pp. 125–172, pp. 165f.

Paul Plaut, 'Psychographie des Kriegers', *Beihefte zur Zeitschrift für angewandte Psychologie no. 21: Beiträge zur Psychologie des Krieges*, ed. William Stern and Otto Lipmann (Leipzig: J.A. Barth, 1920), pp. 1–123, here pp. 26f.

Der Arbeitsnachweis. Zeitschrift für Arbeitslosigkeit, Arbeitsvermittlung, Auswanderung und innere Kolonisation, Vienna 1915, pp. 272–279.

BHStA/IV, MKr 13815, Zentralpolizeistelle Bayern 31 August 1917 to Bavarian War Ministry with enclosed *Bruderbriefe*.

Bibliothek für Zeitgeschichte Stuttgart, Sammlung Schüling, vol. 5, 1, Feldpostkarte Hermann Droege, 7 September 1914.

Berliner Tageblatt no. 175, 4 April 1916.

BArch, R 9350, no. 272, fol. 4f.

Private possession, war letter E. Reubke, 14 May 1918.

Paul Plaut, 'Psychographie des Kriegers', *Beihefte zur Zeitschrift für angewandte Psychologie no. 21: Beiträge zur Psychologie des Krieges*, ed. William Stern and Otto Lipmann (Leipzig: J.A. Barth, 1920), pp. 1–123, p. 69.

20. Johann Knief, war letter, 29 September 1914 to an editor of the *Vorwärts*, in: *Der erste Weltkrieg. Dokumente*, ed. Helmut Otto and Karl Schmiedel (Berlin: Militärverlag der DDR, 1983), pp. 93–97, pp. 95f.

BA/MA Freiburg, W-10/50627, Ernst Otto, 'Die Kriegstagebücher im Weltkriege' (manuscript), pp. 1–18, p. 16; also published in: *Archiv für Politik und Geschichte*, December 1925, issue 12.

Dominik Richert, *Beste Gelegenheit zum Sterben. Meine Erlebnisse im Kriege 1914–1918*, ed. Angelika Tramitz and Bernd Ulrich (Munich: Knesebeck & Schuler, 1989), pp. 28f.

Bergarbeiterzeitung, no. 42, 17 October 1914, war letter from October 1914, Western Front.

BHStA/IV, Militärgerichte no. 6205, testimony given on 14 December 1914 and 5 January 1915. The court-martial proceedings were suspended.

BArch, R 9350, no. 271, 'Feldpostbriefe an den Verband der Bergarbeiter Deutschlands 1914–18', fols 287–289, letter by Fr Langhorst from the Western Front, 2 January 1915.

Paul Plaut, 'Psychographie des Kriegers', *Beihefte zur Zeitschrift für angewandte Psychologie no. 21: Beiträge zur Psychologie des Krieges*, ed. William Stern and Otto Lipmann (Leipzig: J.A. Barth, 1920), pp. 1–123, pp. 33f.

Private possession, war letter C. Krull, 29 July 1916.

BHStA/V, Slg. Varia 1697/58, war letter from 2 July 1916 (copy).

Erich Kuttner, 'Vergessen! Die Kriegszermalmten in Berliner Lazaretten', *Vorwärts*, 8 September 1920.

BArch, R 9350, no. 271, 'Feldpostbriefe an den Verband der Bergarbeiter Deutschlands 1914–18', Franz Tholl, 10 May 1916, fol. 248.

BHStA/lV, bayer. 6.Inf.-Div. Bund 81, war letter by the 'Infanterist' Birzer, 11.Komp./bayer. 6. Inf.-Rgt., 20 August 1917.

BHStA/IV, MKr 11106, report by the Bavarian 6th Infantry Division to Bavarian War Ministry, 14 September 1917.

BHStA/IV, bayer. 6. Inf.-Div., Bund 81, report by the 'Postüberwachungssteile 40, Deutsche Feldpost 402' (copy), 25 August 1917.

BArch, R 9350, no. 271, 'Feldpostbriefe an den Verband der Bergarbeiter Deutschlands 1914–18', fol. 93f., letter by Heinrich Aufderstrasse, 14 April 1918.

BHStA/V, Slg. Varia 1697/2a, 'Erinnerungen' by Alois Hengl (written in 1982).

Hellmuth Gruss, 'Aufbau und Verwendung deutscher Sturmbataillone im Weltkrieg', Diss. phil. (Berlin: 1939), pp. 73f.

21. Robert Gaupp, *Die Nervenkranken des Krieges, ihre Beurteilung und Behandlung. Ein Wort zur Aufklärung und Mahnung an weite Kreise unseres Volkes* (Stuttgart: Verlag des evangelischen Preßverbands, 1917), pp. 4f., 9.

Private possesion, war letter by Franz Müller, 21 January 1915.

Private possession, war letter Wilhelm Pfuhl, 17 November 1916.

Professor Friedländer, 'Grundlinien der psychischen Behandlung. Eine Kritik der psychotherapeutischen Methoden', *Zeitschrift für die gesamte Neurologie und Psychiatrie* 42 (1918), 99–139, 116, 124.

W. Schmidt, 'Die psychischen und nervösen Folgezustände nach Granatexplosionen und Minenverschüttungen', *Zeitschrift für die gesamte Neurologie und Psychiatrie* 29 (1915), 514–542, 522f.

H. Christoffel, 'Depression im Zusammenhang mit nervöser Erschöpfung bei Kriegsteilnehmern', *Zeitschrift für die gesamte Neurologie und Psychiatrie* 45 (1919), 262–268, 264f.

Ernst Simmel, 'Zur Psychoanalyse der Kriegsneurosen (1919)', in: idem, *Psychoanalyse und ihre Anwendung. Ausgewählte Schriften*, ed. by L.M. Hermanns and U. Schultz-Venrath (Frankfurt: Fischer Taschenbuch Verlag, 1993), pp. 21–35, p. 23.

Dr Kehrer, 'Zur Frage der Behandlung der Kriegsneurosen', *Zeitschrift für die gesamte Neurologie und Psychiatrie* 36 (1917), 1–22, here 12.

BHStA/IV, Stellv. Gen.Kdo. I. A.K. no. 727, KM/Medizinalabteilung, decree 27 March 1918.

BHStA/IV, MKr 18389, 'Antworten der Medizinalabteilung auf Beschwerden von Landtagsabgeordneten 1914–18, Fall Heidenreich', n.d.

BHStA/IV, Stellv. Gen.Kdo. I. A.K. no. 727, Bavarian War Ministry/Medical Department, 14 September 1918.

22. A. Messer, 'Zur Psychologie des Krieges', *Preußische Jahrbücher* 159 (1915), 216–232, 230.

Hermann Cron (ed.), *Das Archiv des Deutschen Studentendienstes von 1914* (Potsdam: Reichsarchiv, 1926) (typewritten manuscript), pp. 18f.

Archiv des Bistums Passau, Dekanats-Akten II, Fürstenzell 12/1, 'Seelsorgsberichte der Pfarrämter Hohenstadt und Holzkirchen an das Bischöfliche Ordinariat Passau', 13 June 1916 and 16 July 1916.

Hanns Bächtold, *Deutscher Soldatenbrauch und Soldatenaberglaube* (Straßburg: Trübner, 1917), pp. 1f., 22f.

23. BHStA/IV, Militärgerichte no. 3344, letter by Georg Stempfle to his son, the mechanic August Stempfle, 19 April 1917.
Hermann Cron (ed.), *Das Archiv des Deutschen Studentendienstes von 1914* (Potsdam: Reichsarchiv, 1926) (typewritten manuscript), p. 32.
Vertraulich! Nachrichtenblatt der Ausschüsse für volkstümliche Belehrung und Unterhaltung (3–6, für Kriegsaufklärung im Bereich des IL Armeekorps), ed. Stellv. Gen.Kdo. 2 A. K., Nr. 1–6, Stettin 1917–18, n.p.
Bayerische Staatsbibliothek, Munich, Handschriftenabteilung, Schinnereriana, letter by a woman from Straßdorf to her husband, 28 August 1917.
Bayerische Staatsbibliothek, Munich, Handschriftenabteilung, Schinnereriana, letter from 9 April 1917.

24. BHStA/IV, MKr 13346, letter by priest and deacon Benedikt Hebel, Member of the Reichstag, 14 April 1915 to the Bavarian War Ministry, with a war letter dated 8 April 1915 enclosed (copy).

25 BA/MA Freiburg, W-10/50794, fol. 77, 'Briefauszüge zum Überwachungsbericht vom 31.8.1918'.
BArch, R 9350, no. 271, 'Feldpostbriefe an den Verband der Bergarbeiter Deutschlands 1914–18', letter by Karl Otten, 27 August 1916, fol. 186.
BHStA/IV, Militärgerichte no. 6241, Josef Pfaffinger, son of smallholders, 25 June 1917 to his parents in Oberham (Lower Bavaria).

26. HStA/MA Stuttgart, M 1/4 1696, 'Zusammenstellung über besondere Vorkommnisse, Wünsche. Klagen und Beschwerden', fol. 19 (15 May 1917).
Dominik Richert, *Beste Gelegenheit zum Sterben. Meine Erlebnisse im Kriege 1914–1918*, ed. Angelika Tramitz and Bernd Ulrich (Munich: Knesebeck & Schuler, 1989), pp. 112f.
BHStA/IV, Militärgericht 6. Landwehr-Division, H 5, fol. 19, letter by Peter Hammerer, 3 November 1916 to his wife Rosina Hammerer in Haslach (Allgäu), Post Wertach.
BHStA/IV, Militärgericht 6. Landwehr-Division, H 5a, fol. 12f., 'Ärztliches Gutachten des Oberarztes und Bataillons-Arztes Dr. Kaindl, 1. Bataillon 12. Landwehr-Infanterie-Regiment, über den Landwehrmann Peter Hammerer', 21 May 1916.

27. BA/MA Freiburg, MSg2/3461, war letters by Lance-corporal Adolf Benedict to his parents, letter written 26–27 June 1915.
BA/MA Freiburg, MSg2/2640, 'Kriegserinnerungen' by Paul Wittenburg (typewritten), p. 24.

28. BArch, R 9350, no. 271, 'Feldpostbriefe an den Verband der Bergarbeiter Deutschlands 1914–18', letter by A. Reddigond, 28 April 1915 from the camp Beverloo in Belgium, shortly before leaving for the front, fol. 206f.
BArch, R 9350, no. 271, 'Feldpostbriefe an den Verband der Bergarbeiter Deutschlands 1914–18', letter Richard Schiller, 13 October 1915, fol. 229.

Hermann Cron (ed.), *Das Archiv des deutschen Studentendienstes von 1914* (Potsdam: Reichsarchiv, 1926) (typewritten manuscript), p. 47.
'Lebenserinnerungen', Felix Fonrobert, private possession.

29. BHStA/IV, Stellv. Gen.Kdo. I. A. K. no. 423, decree by Bavarian War Ministry, 16 October 1916.

30. *Der Dolchstoß-Prozeß in München Oktober–November 1925. Eine Ehrenrettung des deutschen Volkes. Zeugen- und Sachverständigen-Aussagen* (Munich: Birk, 1925), p. 108 (statement Erich Kuttner).
Staatsbibliothek Berlin – Preußischer Kulturbesitz, Handschriftenabteilung, Ms. Boruss. Fol. 1084, pp. 98f., entry from 17 January 1917.

31. BA/MA Freiburg, RM 121/345, 'Geheimbefehl an alle Befehlshaber (inkl. Komp.-Führer) pp., Marinekorps/General-Kommando, B.-Nr. 83 IIa', 6 January 1917.
War letter dated April 1916 from the Western Front, in: Walther Lambach, *Ursachen des Zusammenbruchs* (Hamburg: Deutschnationale Verlagsanstalt, n.d. [1919]), pp. 59f.

32. BArch, R 9350, no. 271, 'Feldpostbriefe an den Verband der Bergarbeiter Deutschlands 1914–18', letter B. Meier from Russia, 5 November 1915, fol. 158.
WUA, Gutachten Hobohm, 'Auszüge aus Mannschaftsbriefen der 8. Armee', pp. 31–34.
BA/MA Freiburg, W-10/50794, 'Briefauszüge zum Überwachungsbericht' 12 July 1917, fol. 14f.
Cited in Hermann Kantorowicz, *Der Offiziershaß im deutschen Heer* (Freiburg i.Br.: Bielefeld, 1919) (written in 1916), p. 12.
BHStA/IV, Militär-Gericht 6. Ldw.-Div. B22, letter by Johann Brandl, 6 May 1917.
BArch, R 9350, no. 271, 'Feldpostbriefe an den Verband der Bergarbeiter Deutschlands 1914–18', Theodor Wagner, 14 March 1917, fol. 261.
BA/MA Freiburg, W-10/50794, 'Briefauszüge zum Überwachungsbericht', 23 June 1918, fol. 69–74, fol. 74.
BArch, R 9350, no. 271, 'Feldpostbriefe an den Verband der Bergarbeiter Deutschlands 1914–18', Franz Lauterbach, 2 August 1917, fol. 156.

33. BArch, R 9350, no. 305, fol. 31: 'Aus Sundgau und Wasgenwald. Feldzeitung der Armeeabteilung B', 19 December 1917.

34. HStA/MA Stuttgart, M 1/4 1695, decree by Prussian War Ministry no. 1164, 23 October 1915.
Private possession, war letter C. Krull 31 August 1917.
BArch, R 9350, no. 271, 'Feldpostbriefe an den Verband der Bergarbeiter Deutschlands 1914–18', Wilhelm Rütjerodt, 18 July 1916, fol. 281.
BHStA/IV, MKr 2338, bayer. Ldw.-Inf.-Rgt. 6 to 5. Ldw.-Brigade, 11 October 1917.

HStA/MA Stuttgart, M 1/4 1696, 'Zusammenstellung über besondere Vorkommnisse, Wünsche, Klagen und Beschwerden', fol. 17 (15 May 1917).
BHStA/IV, MKr 13350, letter by *Landtag* deputy Auer (SPD) to Bavarian War Ministry, 30 September 1916.
Ärztliche Sachverständigen-Zeitung 21 (1915), 156.

35. Cited in Heinrich Wandt, *Etappe Gent* (Vienna and Berlin: Agis-Verlag, 1926), p. 88.
BArch, R 9350, no. 271, 'Feldpostbriefe an den Verband der Bergarbeiter Deutschlands 1914–18', Franz Lauterbach, 2 August 1917, fol. 155.
Wilhelm Appens, Charleville, *Dunkle Punkte aus dem Etappenleben* (Dortmund: Gerisch, n.d. [1920]), pp. 15, 16, 17.
BArch, R 9350, no. 276, letters to pastor H. Falck in Berlin, letter by Herrmann, 7 June 1915, fol. 8.
Heinrich Wandt, *Etappe Gent* (Vienna and Berlin: Agis-Verlag, 1926), p. 153.
BArch, R 9350, no. 271, 'Feldpostbriefe an den Verband der Bergarbeiter Deutschlands 1914–18', Willy Hauffe, 15 May 1916, fols 32, 34.
Heinrich Wandt, *Etappe Gent* (Vienna and Berlin: Agis-Verlag, 1926), pp. 155f.

36. WUA, Gutachten Hobohm, p. 208.
HStA/MA Stuttgart, M 33/2, vol. 14, excerpt from the 'Württembergisches Militärverordnungsblatt', no. 6, 3 February 1917, p. 87.
HStA/MA Stuttgart, M 750, war letter by Willi (surname unknown), 25 February 1915.
Verhandlungen Reichstag, vol. 307, Berlin 1916, p. 905, citation from a war letter, mentioned in a speech by the member of parliament Davidsohn (Social Democratic Party), 7 April 1916.
Verhandlungen Bayerischer Landtag, vol. 13, p. 855, speech by the *Landtag* deputy Dr Max Süßheim (Social Democratic Party), 9 May 1916.
BHStA/IV, Stellv. Gen.Kdo. I. A.K. no. 597, 'Verfügung Kriegsministerium no. 1723 Ia', 19 February 1916.
Generalquartiermeister Ia no. 4242, 4 March 1917, printed in: WUA, Gutachten Hobohm, p. 378.
BA/MA Freiburg, W-10/50794, fol. 6f.
HStA/MA Stuttgart, M 33/2, Bd. 14, Armeeoberkommando 4. Armee no. 947, 29 January 1916, 'Armeetagebuch no. 13 (Jan. 1916), Betr.: Verbot der Briefbeförderung durch Urlauber'.
Verhandlungen Bayerischer Landtag, vol. 13, p. 857, speech by the *Landtag* deputy Dr Max Süßheim.
BHStA/IV, Militärgerichte no. 6313, letter Michael Kappelmeier, reserve-NCO, 10. Komp. bayer. 12. Inf.Rgt, 11 October 1914, sent in by master joiner Möggenried.
BHStA/IV, Militärgericht 6. Ldw.-Div. E 13, letter Johann Wilhelm Entz, NCO, 8. Komp. bayer. 1. Ldw.-Inf.-Rgt, to his wife, 20 July 1917 (typewritten copy).

37. BArch, R 43, no. 2402, anonymous letter to the Reich chancellor, 19 November 1915.
BHStA/IV, MKr 2822, anonymous complaint from Nuremburg to Bavarian War Ministry, 22 November 1915.

38. BHStA/IV, Stellv. Gen.Kdo. I. A. K. no. 592, decree Prussian War Ministry no. 4002/8. 15.C1, 6 September 1915.
Münchener Medizinische Wochenschrift/Feldärztliche Beilage 61 (1914), 2052.

39. BHStA/IV, Stellv. Gen.Kdo. I. A.K. no. 592, decree Bavarian War Ministry no. 7581, 29 January 1915.
'Lebenserinnerungen', Felix Fonrobert, private possession.
HStA/MA Stuttgart, M 77/1, no. 119/48, Königl. Oberkriegsgericht XIII. Königlich Württembergisches Armeekorps/Abschrift, court-martial sentence F. Sautter, 12 November 1915.

40. Franz Töns, 7. Reserve-Jäger-Bataillon, 13. Division, 13 December 1914 to his mother in Hopsten (Westphalia), private possession.
Carl Zuckmayer, *Als wär's ein Stück von mir. Horen der Freundschaft* (Frankfurt/ Main: Fischer Taschenbuch Verlag, 1969, first edn 1966), pp. 195f.
Liller Kriegszeitung – Eine Auslese aus Nr. 1–40, ed. Hauptmann der Landwehr Hoecker, Rittmeister a.D. Freiherr v. Ompteda, Berlin, 1915, pp. 141f.
BA/MA Freiburg, MSg2/198, war letters by Lieutenant Fischer, letter dated 7 December 1915.
BHStA/IV, HS 1984, 'Eine Verbrüderung mit den Franzosen bei Givenchy', written in 1928 by Otto Weber, member of the Veteran's and Warrior Association Buchloe, served with 8. Komp./bayer. 1. Inf.-Rgt during the war.

41. BA/MA Freiburg, RM 120/345, Marinekorps, G-Anlage zum K.T.B. no. 221/16, 6 October 1916.
BHStA/IV, MKr 2330, Bavarian State Ministry of the Interior to Bavarian War Ministry, 15 March 1916.
BHStA/IV, Stellv. Gen.Kdo. I. A.K. no. 916, Bavarian State Ministry of the Interior to Bavarian War Ministry, 24 August 1916.
HStA/MA Stuttgart, M 77/1, vol. 63 (8), *Württemberger Zeitung*, 20 September 1917; postcard by Georg Weile, 20 September 1917.

42. BHStA/IV, Militärgerichte no. 6201, letter by Adolf Armbrust, 11. Komp. bayer. 15. Inf.-Rgt, 15 January 1918.
BHStA/IV, Stellv. Gen.Kdo. I. A. K. no. 641, 'Bericht an Vertreter des Kriegsministeriums in Gefangenenangelegenheiten bei der Kaiserl. Dt. Gesandtschaft Bern', 8 September 1917.
Staatsbibliothek Berlin – Preußischer Kulturbesitz, Handschriftenabteilung, Ms. Germ. Fol. 1651, pp. 92f., entry from 25 April 1917.
Archiv des Bistums Augsburg, personal papers Karl Lang, Kriegschronik Pfarrer Karl Lang (written in 1934), pp. 52–54.

BHStA/IV, Militärgerichte no. 3524, letter by building locksmith Otto Biegner from Munich, 8. Komp. bayer. 1. Inf.-Rgt, 12 August 1917 to his sister.

BHStA/IV, Militärgerichte no. 6232, statement by farmhand Karl Böck, 7. Komp./bayer. 15. Inf.-Rgt, 28 August 1918.

BHStA/IV, Militärgerichte no. 6580, letter by farmhand Jakob Wirth, 1. Komp./bayer. 23. Inf.-Rgt, 9 December 1915 to his brother Ludwig.

BHStA/IV, Militärgerichte no. 6299, letter by farm labourer Georg Heinle, Feldrekrutenkomp. 6/bayer. 2.Inf.-Div., 28 July 1917 to Fanny.

43. BHStA/IV, I. A. K. Bund 96, decree Chef des Generalstabes des Feldheeres, 28 November 1914.

BHStA/lV, I. A.K. Bund 173, decree Chef des Generalstabes des Feldheeres Ia 39 904 op., 20 November 1916.

HStA/MA Stuttgart, M 750, sapper K. Betsch, 24 February 1916 (war letters by employees of the life insurance company 'Alte Stuttgarter').

BA/MA Freiburg, MSg2/3461, war letters by Lance-corporal A. Benedict to his parents in Nuremberg, letters written 16/17 June 1915.

Dominik Richert, *Beste Gelegenheit zum Sterben. Meine Erlebnisse im Kriege 1914–1918*, ed. Angelika Tramitz and Bernd Ulrich (Munich: Knesebeck & Schuler, 1989), pp. 319f.

HStA/MA Stuttgart, M 33/2, Bd. 31, decree Prussian War Ministry, 29 December 1916.

44. BHStA/IV, MKr 2332, 'Aktennotiz des Pressereferates des bayer. Kriegsministeriums, gez. v. Sonnenburg (Pressereferent)', 15 June 1917, and excerpts from letters.

45. BHStA/IV, Stellv. Gen.Kdo. I. A. K. no. 1539, letter by Josef Sigl from Nevers to family Angerbauer in Ascholshausen (copy), sent by 'Militärische Überwachungsstelle I. bayer. A. K. beim Bahnpostamt München I' to Chef des stv. Generalstabes der Armee Abt.IIIb, 12 May 1917.

BA/MA Freiburg, W-10/50794, 'Briefauszüge zum Überwachungsbericht', 31 August 1918, fol. 82.

46. Dominik Richert, *Beste Gelegenheit zum Sterben. Meine Erlebnisse im Kriege 1914–1918*, ed. Angelika Tramitz and Bernd Ulrich (Munich: Knesebeck & Schuler, 1989), pp. 311f.

'Lebenserinnerungen', Felix Fonrobert, private possession, n.p.

GLA, 456 FS/106, Stellv. Gen.Kdo. XIV. AK/Abt. Ia, Nr. 1298/17, 2 May 1917, fol. 67f.

47. BHStA/IV, bayer. 2.Inf.-Div. Bund 24, bayer. 4. Inf.-Brig. to 2.Inf.-Div., 28 July 1916.

HStA/MA Stuttgart, M 33/2, Bd. 31, 'Armee-Befehl General v. Watter', 24 November 1916 to XIII. Army Corps.

HStA/MA Stuttgart. M 77/1, Bd. 63, Chef des Generalstabes des Feldheeres la Nr. 8915 geh. Op., 25 June 1918, 'Betr.: Überläufer'.

BHStA/IV, MKr 11232, decree by Prussian War Ministry, 5 November 1918.

48. F. Mörchen, 'Das Versagen und die seelisch-nervösen Abwehrreaktionen der minderwertig Veranlagten im Kriege', *Zeitschrift für die gesamte Neurologie und Psychiatrie* 44 (1919), 340–384, 361.
F. Mörchen, 'Das Versagen und die seelisch-nervösen Abwehrreaktionen der minderwertig Veranlagten im Kriege', *Zeitschrift für die gesamte Neurologie und Psychiatrie* 44 (1919), 340–384, 366f.

49. BHStA/IV, Kriegsbriefe 340, war letters by Hans Spieß.

50. BHStA/IV, Militärgericht bayer. 6.Ldw.-Div. B 11, letter Josef Beigel, 2. Komp./Ldw.-Inf.Rgt 40, to his wife, 20 March 1917.
BHStA/IV, Militärgericht 6. Ldw.-Div. D 9, Alois Deuringer, 3. Komp./bayer. Ldw.-Inf.-Rgt 1, to his wife, 25 March 1917.

51. BHStA/IV, Stellv. Gen.Kdo. I. A.K. no. 2403, 'Bericht Vertrauensmann für Aufklärungstätigkeit Reservelazarett München H über häufig wiederkehrende Fragen der Mannschaften an die Vertrauensmänner', 30 November 1917.
BHStA/IV, Stellv. Gen.Kdo. I. A.K. no. 451, Bavarian War Minister no. 228373 A/17, 8 January 1918 to deputy commanding generals in Bavaria.
BHStA/IV, Stellv. Gen.Kdo. I. A.K. no. 2404, report by 'Vertrauensmann' I. Ersatz-Btl./bayer. 12. Inf.-Rgt to Ersatz-Btl., 27 December 1917.
Hermann Cron (ed.), *Kriegsbrief-Sammlung des Deutschen Transportarbeiter-Verbandes* (Potsdam: Reichsarchiv, 1926) (typewritten manuscript), pp. 5f., p. 4.
Stadtarchiv Regensburg, NL Heim 1316, Michael Kitzelmann, bayer. Ldst. Fußartl. Batl., 3. Batterie, 21 April 1918 to Georg Heim.
BHStA/ IV, MKr 2339, letter by Otto Meßmer from 12 February 1918, relayed by Dr Albert Meßmer in a letter to the chief of press department in the Bavarian War Ministry, 18 February 1918.

52. BHStA/IV, MKr 2324, Ludwig Frhr. v. Gebsattel, deputy commanding general II. bayer. A.K., 27 June 1917 to Bavarian War Minister (strictly confidential).
Die Schuld am Zusammenbruch. Eine Vortragsdisposition über die deutsche Innen- und Außenpolitik vor und während des Krieges, die militärische, wirtschaftliche und finanzielle Führung im Kriege (Berlin: Zentralverlag, 1920), p. 44.

53. BA/MA Freiburg W-10/50794, 'Briefauszüge zum Überwachungsbericht', 24 February 1918, fols 54, 60, 48, 49, 52, 54, 59, 55, 64, 64.

54. Ludwig Bergsträsser, supplement II, in: WUA, 4. Reihe, 11. Abt., vol. 5, pp. 262–335, p. 279 (letter by Lance-corporal Gettmann, 2 January 1918).
Private possession, letter 21 March 1918 from the rear area in the West.
BHStA/IV, Stellv. Gen.Kdo. I. A. K. no. 2407, 'Monatsbericht des Vertrauensmannes Ldst. Btl. IB 18', 23 March 1918.
HStA/MA Stuttgart, M 750, Letter NCO Fiessmann, 5 May 1918.
Franz X. Bergler, '"Es sieht ja mit Frieden werden gar nichts gleich". Briefe von der Front', *Allmende* 18/19 (1987), 1–17, 16.

55. BArch, R 9350, no. 271, 'Feldpostbriefe an den Verband der Bergarbeiter Deutschlands 1914–18', letter by Heinrich Aufderstrasse, 1 May 1918, fols 88–91.

56. Private possession, letter 13 October 1918 from the rear area in the West; BA/MA Freiburg, W-10/50794, 'Briefauszüge zum Überwachungsbericht', 17 October 1918, fol. 112.
 BA/MA Freiburg, W-10/50794, 'Briefauszüge zum Überwachungsbericht', 31 August 1918, fol. 76.
 BHStA/IV, Stellv. Gen.Kdo. I. A.K. no. 593, Bavarian War Ministry to stellv. Gen.Kdo. bayer. I. II. III. A.K, 29 May 1918.
 GLA Karlsruhe, 465 F8/106, 'Ergänzender Bericht, Stimmung der Truppe betr.', 11 September 1918, fol. 444.

57. BA/MA Freiburg, MSg2/998, leaflet, dropped by French aeroplane, September 1918.
 BArch, R 9350, no. 271, 'Feldpostbriefe an den Verband der Bergarbeiter Deutschlands 1914–18', Heinrich Aufderstrasse, 27 August 1918, fol. 101.
 BArch, R 8034 II, no. 7615, fol. 32, *BZ am Mittag* no. 144, 18 October 1918.

58. Hans Thimme, *Weltkrieg ohne Waffen. Die Propaganda der Westmächte gegen Deutschland, ihre Wirkung und ihre Abwehr* (Stuttgart: Cotta, 1932), pp. 264–271, pp. 268f.
 Hans Thimme, *Weltkrieg ohne Waffen. Die Propaganda der Westmächte gegen Deutschland, ihre Wirkung und ihre Abwehr* (Stuttgart: Cotta, 1932), p. 169; ellipsis by Thimme.
 Hans Thimme, *Weltkrieg ohne Waffen. Die Propaganda der Westmächte gegen Deutschland, ihre Wirkung und ihre Abwehr* (Stuttgart: Cotta, 1932), p. 279.
 BArch, R 43, no. 2398/12, anonymous letter to Chancellor Hertling, 11 August 1918, fol. 19.
 Der Zusammenbruch der Kriegspolitik und die Novemberrevolution. Beobachtungen und Betrachtungen eines ehemaligen Frontsoldaten (Berlin: Verlagsgenossenschaft „Freiheit", 1919), S. 15.
 Der "Dolchstoß". Warum das deutsche Heer zusammenbrach (Berlin: Zentralverlag, 1920), p. 9.

59. BHStA/IV, Stellv. Gen.Kdo. I. A. K. no. 593, 'Bericht Rentier Schütz' 27 January 1918 to Stellv. Gen.Kdo. II in Stettin.
 Decree by the Chef des Generalstabes des Feldheeres, 12 March 1918, printed in: Albrecht Kästner (ed.), *Revolution und Heer. Auswirkungen der Großen Sozialistischen Oktoberrevolution auf das Heer des imperialistischen deutschen Kaiserreichs 1917/18. Dokumente* (Berlin: Militärverlag der DDR, 1987), p. 49.

60. HStA/MA Stuttgart, M 77/1, Bd. 27, letter by Maria Geiger, 12 May 1918.

Further Reading

Bibliographical Information

Jahresberichte für deutsche Geschichte, online at: http://jdgdb.bbaw.de/cgi-bin/jdg/cgi-bin/jdg (accessed on 20 October 2009)

Krieg und Literatur/War and Literature. International Yearbook on War and Anti-War Literature, from vol. 1, Osnabrück: 1989

German History, 1914–1918

Bessel, Richard: 'Mobilizing German Society for War', in: Roger Chickering and Stig Förster (eds), *Great War, Total War: Combat and Mobilization on the Western Front, 1914–1918*, Cambridge: 2000, pp. 437–451

Chickering, Roger: *The Great War and Urban Life in Germany: Freiburg, 1914–1918*, Cambridge: 2007

Chickering, Roger: *Imperial Germany and the Great War, 1914–1918*, Cambridge: 1998

Daniel, Ute: *The War from Within. German Working Class Women in the First World War*, Oxford: 1997

Davis, Belinda J.: *Home fires burning: food, politics, and everyday life in World War I Berlin*, Chapel Hill and London: 2000

Stibbe, Matthew: *British Civilian Internees in Germany. The Ruhleben Camp, 1914–1918*, Manchester: 2008

Stibbe, Matthew: *German Anglophobia and the Great War 1914–1918*, Cambridge: 2001

1914: The Beginning of the War

Chickering, Roger: '"War enthusiasms?" Public opinion and the outbreak of war in 1914', in: Holger Afflerbach and David Stevenson (eds), *An Improbable War. The Outbreak of World War I and European Political Culture Before 1914*, New York and Oxford: 2007, pp. 200–229

Horne, John and Alan Kramer: *German Atrocities, 1914. A History of Denial*, New Haven and London: 2001

Verhey, Jeffrey: *The Spirit of 1914: Militarism, Myth and Mobilization in Germany*, Cambridge: 2000

Watson, Alexander: '"For Kaiser and Reich". The Identity and Fate of the German Volunteers, 1914–1918', *War in History* 12 (2005), 44–74

Ziemann, Benjamin: 'German Soldiers in Victory, 1914', in: Peter Liddle, John Bourne and Ian Whitehead (eds), *The Great World War 1914–45. Vol. 1: Lightning Strikes Twice*, London: 2000, pp. 253–264

Front-line Experiences

Kramer, Alan: *Dynamic of Destruction: Culture and Mass Killing in the First World War*, Oxford: 2007

Ulrich, Bernd: *Die Augenzeugen. Deutsche Feldpostbriefe in Kriegs–und Nachkriegszeit 1914–1933*, Essen: 1997

Ulrich, Bernd and Benjamin Ziemann: 'Das soldatische Kriegserlebnis', in: Wolfgang Kruse (ed.), *Eine Welt von Feinden. Der Große Krieg 1914–1918*, Frankfurt: 1997, pp. 127–158

Ziemann, Benjamin: *War Experiences in Rural Germany, 1914–1923*, Oxford and New York: 2007

Ziemann, Benjamin: 'Geschlechterbeziehungen in deutschen Feldpostbriefen des Ersten Weltkrieges', in: Christa Hämmerle and Edith Saurer (eds), *Briefkulturen und ihr Geschlecht. Zur Geschichte der privaten Korrespondenz vom 16. Jahrhundert bis heute*, Vienna: 2003, pp. 261–282

German Military History, 1914–1918

Deist, Wilhelm: 'The Military Collapse of the German Empire', *War in History* 3 (1996), 186–207

Geyer, Michael: 'How the Germans learned to Wage War. On the Question of Killing in the First and Second World War', in: Paul Betts, Alan Confino and Dirk Schumann (eds), *Between Mass Death and Individual Loss: The Place of the Dead in Twentieth-Century Germany*, New York: 2008, pp. 25–50

Geyer, Michael: 'Insurrectionary Warfare: The German Debate about a Levée en Masse in October 1918', *Journal of Modern History* 73 (2001), 459–527

Hull, Isabel V.: *Absolute Destruction. Military Culture and the Practices of War in Imperial Germany*, Ithaca: 2005

Jones, Heather: 'The German Spring Reprisals of 1917: Prisoners of War and the Violence of the Western Front', *German History* 26 (2008), 335–356

Liulevicius, Vejas G.: *War Land on the Eastern Front. Culture, National Identity, and German Occupation in World War I*, Cambridge: 2000

Meteling, Wencke: 'German and French Regiments on the Western Front, 1914–1918', in: Heather Jones, Jennifer O'Brien and Christoph Schmidt-Supprian (eds), *Untold War. New Perspectives in First World War Studies*, Leiden and Boston: 2008, pp. 23–61

Stephenson, Scott: *The Final Battle. Soldiers of the Western Front in the German Revolution of 1918*, Cambridge: 2009

Ulrich, Bernd: 'Militärgeschichte von unten, Anmerkungen zu ihren Ursprüngen, Quellen und Perspektiven im 20. Jahrhundert', *Geschichte und Gesellschaft* 22 (1996), 473–503

Watson, Alexander: *Enduring the Great War: Combat, Morale and Collapse in the German and British Armies, 1914–1918*, Cambridge: 2008

Ziemann, Benjamin: 'Fahnenflucht im deutschen Heer 1914–1918', *Militärgeschichtliche Mitteilungen* 55 (1996), 93–130

'War Neuroses'

Kaufmann, Doris: 'Science as Cultural Practice: Psychiatry in the First World War and Weimar Germany', *Journal of Contemporary History* 34 (1999), 125–144

Lerner, Paul: *Hysterical Men: War, Psychiatry and the Politics of Trauma in Germany, 1890–1939*, Ithaca: 2003

Lerner, Paul: 'Psychiatry and Casualties of War in Germany, 1914–1918', *Journal of Contemporary History* 35 (2000), 13–28

Ulrich, Bernd: 'Nerven und Krieg. Skizzierung einer Beziehung', in: Bedrich Loewenstein (ed.), *Geschichte und Psychologie*, Annäherungsversuche and Pfaffenweiler: 1992, pp. 163–192

Interpretations and Commemorations of the War Experience

Bessel, Richard: *Germany after the First World War*, Oxford: 1993

Brocks, Christine: *Die bunte Welt der Krieges. Bildpostkarten aus dem Ersten Weltkrieg 1914–1918*, Essen: 2008

Cohen, Deborah: *The War Come Home. Disabled Veterans in Britain and Germany, 1914–1939*, Berkeley: 2001

Forner, Sean A.: 'War Commemoration and the Republic in Crisis: Weimar Germany and the Neue Wache', *Central European History* 25 (2002), 513–549

Kester, Bernadette: *Film Front Weimar. Representations of the First World War in German Films of the Weimar Period* (1919–1933), Amsterdam: 2003

Kühne, Thomas: 'Comradeship, Gender Confusion and Gender Order in the German Military, 1918–1945', in: Karen Hagemann and Stefanie Schüler-Springorum (eds), *Home Front. The Military, War and Gender in Twentieth-Century Germany*, Oxford and New York: 2002, pp. 233–254

Kundrus, Birthe: 'Gender Wars. The First World War and the Construction of Gender Relations in the Weimar Republic', in: Karen Hagemann and Stefanie Schüler-Springorum (eds), *Home Front: The Military, War and Gender in Twentieth-Century Germany*, Oxford and New York: 2002, pp. 159–179

Mosse, George L.: *Fallen Soldiers: Reshaping the Memory of the World Wars*, New York and Oxford: 1990

Schneider, Thomas F. (ed.): *Kriegserlebnis und Legendenbildung. Das Bild des 'modernen' Krieges in Literatur, Theater, Photographie und Film*, 3 vols, Osnabrück: 1999

Ulrich, Bernd: 'Die umkämpfte Erinnerung. Überlegungen zur Wahrnehmung des Ersten Weltkrieges in der Weimarer Republik', in: Jörg Duppler and

Gerhard P. Groß (eds), *Kriegsende 1918. Ereignis – Wirkung – Nachwirkung*, Munich: 1999, pp. 367–375

Winter, Jay: *Remembering War. The Great War between memory and history in the twentieth century*, London: 2006

Winter, Jay: *Sites of Memory, Sites of Mourning. The Great War in European Cultural History*, Cambridge: 1996

Ziemann, Benjamin: 'Germany after the First World War – A Violent Society? Results and Implications of Recent Research on Weimar Germany', *Journal of Modern European History* 1 (2003), 80–95 (online at: http://eprints.whiterose. ac.uk/4748/ (accessed on 20 October 2009))